MANUFACTURED SCHEMA

Thatcher, the Miners and the Culture Industry

D. V. KHABAZ

Manufactured Schema

Thatcher, the Miners and the Culture Industry

Copyright © 2006 D. V. Khabaz

The moral right of the author has been asserted.

Apart from any fair dealing for the purposes of research or private study, or criticism or review, as permitted under the Copyright, Designs and Patents Act 1988, this publication may only be reproduced, stored or transmitted, in any form or by any means, with the prior permission in writing of the publishers, or in the case of reprographic reproduction in accordance with the terms of licences issued by the Copyright Licensing Agency. Enquiries concerning reproduction outside those terms should be sent to the publishers.

Matador
9 De Montfort Mews
Leicester LE1 7FW, UK
Tel: (+44) 116 255 9311 / 9312
Email: books@troubador.co.uk
Web: www.troubador.co.uk/matador

ISBN 1 905237 61 8

Typeset in 11pt Stempel Garamond by Troubador Publishing Ltd, Leicester, UK
Printed in the UK by The Cromwell Press Ltd, Trowbridge, Wilts, UK

Matador is an imprint of Troubador Publishing Ltd

*To my friend and companion, Asia
and to my Sadek family*

CONTENTS

Preface   *xi*
Introduction   *xiii*

ONE
THE THEORY OF CULTURE INDUSTRY
Contemporary Relevance or a Theoretical Impasse?

Introduction	1
The genesis of the theory of culture industry	3
Culture, technology and the rise of instrumental rationality	3
Lukacs' theory of reification	8
Authoritarianism and state capitalism	11
Other influential ideas in the genesis of culture industry	18
The definition of culture industry	24
Mass culture and ideology	32
The material basis of culture industry	33
The characteristic features of the culture industry	39
Standardization	40
Pseudo-individuality	42
Schematization	43
Stereotypes	44
The nature of domination in modern societies	47
A critique of Adorno's theory of culture industry	59
Is the thesis of culture industry still relevant?	61
Agency and social actors: a definition and brief analysis	66
Conclusion	68

TWO
THATCHERISM: FROM THEORY TO RESEARCH
The Concepts – Indicators Model

Introduction	71
The meaning of Thatcherism	72
The origins of Thatcherism: a historical perspective	75
Phase one: Initial inception	76
Phase two: The road to power	80
Phase three: Thatcher in power	82
Theorizing Thatcherism	89
Economic oriented theories of Thatcherism	89
Alan O'Shea's cultural theory of Thatcherism	93
Raymond Williams' mobile privatization	94
Hall's authoritarian populism	95
Jessop's two nations	97
Thatcherism as a multi-faceted populism	104
Thatcherism and the media: the underlying traits	107
Thatcherism and the national press	107
Thatcher and media pressure	111
Thatcherism and publicity strategy	112
The Prime Minister's press secretary	116
The indicators: methodological approach	122
Conclusion	129

THREE
THE PRESS IN THE THATCHER YEARS:
A model for British Culture Industry?

Introduction	131
The 'Murdoch' factor in the British Press industry:	
Macro Agency in the Internal Sphere	133

CONTENTS

Thatcher–Murdoch reciprocity: The path to the ownership of *Times* Newspapers	135
Murdoch–Thatcher reciprocity: Content analysis of the *Sun*, the *News of the World* and *The Times*	137
The sample	138
The categories	138
The 1979 General Election	140
The 1983 General Election	142
The 1987 General Election	144
Murdoch's Proprietorial Style	146
Other Press Barons in the 1980s	149
The Pattern of Press Ownership in Post-War Britain	152
The Function of Capital: Macro Agency in the External and Internal Spheres	154
The Function of the Mass Market: Collective Agency in the External Sphere	157
Technological Reformation in the British Press Industry: Macro Agency in the Internal Sphere	161
The Wapping Dispute: Collective Agency in the Internal and External Spheres	165
The Impact of Wapping	180
Conclusion	193

FOUR
THE MINERS' STRIKES AND THE PRESS INDUSTRY:
A Comparative Study

Introduction	197
The Methodological Principle: Overcoming Problems of Reliability	199
The Sampling Procedure	202
Procedure for Assessing Editorial 'Attitude'	204

Analysis of the Empirical Data:
The Quantitative Dimension   205
The Degrees of 'Editorial Hostility'   206
Analyses of the Categories in Each Newspaper:
The Frequency of the Selected Concepts and Phrases   208
The Qualitative Dimension   213
The Miners and the Press: From 'Special Cases to
the Enemy Within'   214
The Miners as 'Special Cases'   215
The Miners as 'The Enemy Within':
'The Standardization Process'   226
Public Opinion   232
The Miners' Disputes, Law and Order, and the
Press Industry: The Standardization Process   237
The Miners, the Labour Movement and the Press:
The 'Stereotype Process'   242
The Miners' Dispute, the Press and the Defeatist
Culture: The Schematization Process   253
The Trade Unionists' Opinion   267
Conclusion   269

Epilogue   272

Appendix 1: Content analysis of the categories
            for the 1984–85 sample   279
Appendix 2: Content analysis of the categories
            for the 1972–74 miners' strikes   287

Bibliography   301

PREFACE

This book assesses the utility of the Frankfurt School's theory of 'culture industry' as an analytical model for a better understanding of the function and organisation of the modern mass circulating press media in Britain.

The theory of 'culture industry' first introduced in the 1930s at a time of authoritarian irrationalism, can illuminate contemporary developments in culture, polity and society. This claim is not a mere justification for 'Adornoism', but an attempt to identify core themes in the School's cultural analyses which continue to merit attention. The theory of culture industry poses questions against a conventional political-economic approach to culture. Consequently it is not the question of economic determinism which matters but rather the 'commodification ofcultural outputs'.

In this re-assessment it will be argued that despite numerous critical appraisals the culture industry thesis remains a valuable analytical tool in a sociological assessment of the modern media industry. This book will examine these critiques of the theory and will offer proposals to defend its conceptual capabilities. Accordingly, it will be argued that late capitalist culture has acquired a certain degree of autonomy as well as becoming increasingly crucial to the survival of the whole world system.

In an attempt to justify the relevance of the theory, several proposals will be offered to enhance the scope of its paradigm to accommodate socio-politically advanced societies such as Britain. It will be argued, and empirically systematized, that as the original theory of culture industry enabled Adorno to derive certain analytical concepts in the earlier part of this century, it may be utilized to derive new conceptual tools with the help of which modern and complex politico-cultural phenomenon, such as Thatcherism, can be sociologically analysed. The empirical dimension of this book, therefore, attempts to utilize concepts generated by the theory of culture industry and assess the impact of media upon the recent developments in British popular culture.

INTRODUCTION

The last two decades have seen major developments in the British media industry such as the introduction of pay TV, digital and electronic innovations and new printing technology at Wapping. Undoubtedly, the impact of these exciting developments upon the social and economic sectors of British society has been profound. There are hardly any sections of modern British society which has not been affected by the technological developments in media and communication.

The importance of these advancements has prompted an extensive debate in the academic circles on the social, economic and cultural effects of these transformations. However, this debate has been largely characterized by a concentration on ideological appraisals of different institutions of the British media industry and a hasty rejection of the theory of culture industry as a useful analytical tool for the study of socio-cultural impact of modern media.

The marginalization of the culture industry thesis in the tradition of British media studies could be attributed to the publication of several influential books and articles such as Perry Anderson's *Considerations on Western Marxism* (1976), Goran Therborn's *The Frankfurt School* (1977) and Tom Bottomore's declaration: 'the Frankfurt School in its original form, and as a school of Marxism or sociology, is dead.'[1]

Fundamentally, in their view, the problem with the Frankfurt School is its idealistic and elitist approach, detaching them from the material struggle of the working class in Europe. Accordingly, for a long period British media studies were mostly influenced by Althusserian orthodoxy and the rejection of the base-superstructure model and an emphasis upon relatively autonomous ideological forms. The direct links between ideology

---

[1] Bottomore *The Frankfurt School* (Chichester: Harwood), 1984, p.2

and the mode of production were largely ignored for a general concentration upon manipulation by ideological state apparatuses. In recent years, however, media studies in Britain seem to be placing new emphasis upon the crucial questions of class-based social psychology and political economy which thus far had been ignored. This emphasis was always available in Theodor Adorno and Max Horkheimer's theory of culture industry. As we shall see later, in his analysis of contemporary capitalism, the culture industry and commodity consumption Adorno goes further than Marx when he argues that the commodity form had permeated and transformed areas of life outside of the economic sphere.

The ubiquity of the exchange principle has become one of the major features of modern capitalism. The cultural sphere has not escaped this invasion. It too suffers from the effects of commodification and reification. This is most notable in the culture industry. The penetration of the exchange principle into new areas of life and the production of culture for commodified consumption, Adorno argued, prevents people of knowing themselves as 'subjects'.

The original theory of culture industry remains a novel approach which examines the ways in which the structure and processes of the public sphere are determined by capitalist commodity production in general.

Moreover, for Adorno, within the larger socio-economic context individual psyche had been weakened by reification and the loss of economic autonomy. The culture industry is nurtured by the profit-making nature of the modern system. In this respect both the culture industry and individual psychology have become 'social facts'. The culture industry continues to mass produce standardized materials for distribution and exchange on the market. The present study will strive to provide a detailed assessment of this aspect of the theory.

Indeed, in an attempt to reassert the utility of the Frankfurt School's theory of culture industry the problem of 'structure and agency' remains a pressing issue in modern social theory. However, this book aims to explore an equally crucial area of social theory; the problem of 'culture and agency'. In doing so there are two fundamental themes which have an important impact upon this endeavour.

Firstly, the cultural and structural spheres are perceived as substantively different. This is to argue that the concepts used aim to capture and respect the differences between the two spheres. Secondly, although different spheres of social life have their own logic and inherent specificity, we have to recognize the necessity of viewing social life as an interplay between interests and ideas.

In modern advanced capitalist societies the links between the political, economic and cultural spheres are increasingly strengthened. Within this context, the primary task of this work is to offer an alternative sociological analysis for the problem of culture in contemporary Britain. Accordingly, it was decided to focus upon an institution of modern popular culture, the press industry, for a detailed examination of the role and impact of the cultural spheres in contemporary societies.

In a critical re-assessment it will be argued that the Frankfurt School's theory of culture industry, at its most useful approach, provides a rather sophisticated model of analysis on the contributions of modern popular culture to the processes whereby 'consent is manufactured' in modern, socio-politically advanced societies.

It also illuminates the wider consequences of the full integration of an institution of contemporary mass culture into core sectors of capital. In this context, the following points will be highlighted.

Firstly, the concept, it will be argued, cannot be applied to socio-politically advanced societies such as modern Britain without reconsidering its theoretical scope over and beyond the *Dialectic of Enlightenment*. The theory of culture industry, I will argue, was part of an on going conceptual development shaped by Adorno over many years and in different works which appeared after the original analysis presented in the *Dialectic* and first published in 1947.

In this context, it will be argued that the theory of culture industry must be viewed in relation to other important works by Adorno.[2]

---

[2] *Dialektik der Aufklarung* was first published in Amsterdam in 1947

Initially, the concept developed from the School's experience of a totalitarian era in the 1930s. The phenomenon of fascism in Germany, and later the 'Stalin factor' in Russia, had a profound impact upon the fundamental premises of the critical theory. The concept was then used to theorize how societies were increasingly resembling one another. In this respect, the critical theorists were influenced by the Weberian theory of 'formal rationality' which was used inadequately to expand an analysis of the link between political, cultural and economic spheres in society.

After the Second World War Adorno, in particular, began a reconstruction of the concept and reconsidered some of its original premises. At its core, the theory was used by Adorno to show the role and function of increasing capital concentration in the organization of modern media.

Today, it seems, the functions and purposes of disparate social institutions are increasingly overlapping and the bond between the political, economic and cultural spheres are becoming stronger. Indeed, in terms of 'ownership and control', many modern social institutions are intertwined with each other. In this sense the culture industry has much more to do with the modern phenomenon of monopolistic power, particularly in the British press industry.

This book will empirically demonstrate that in modern Britain press proprietors continue to expand their economic interests in other spheres of the leisure industry. The essential feature of the modern culture industry is, it will consequently be claimed, to strive for decentralization.

Fundamentally, working within the tradition of critical theory, this work aims to view the British press industry as a component of the culture industry, which is connected both to corporate capitalism and the political system. Accordingly, in an empirical analysis I will asses the role, and impact, of the national press in the age of 'Thatcherism'. The media has been defined by Adorno as an integral aspect of the culture industry and, therefore, an important institution of it, the press, will be used as an independent unit of analysis. There are several reasons for the inclusion of the press in this study.

Firstly, by the 1980s the average Briton read more newspapers than any comparable Western nation. In terms of newspaper consumption, United Kingdom occupied second position after Sweden with 479 for every one thousand inhabitants.[3]

Secondly, as noted by Francis William 'Newspapers are unique barometers of their age. They indicate more plainly than anything else the climate of the societies to which they belong'.[4] At the height of the miners' strike in 1985 three press proprietors dominated the British national dailies and Sunday papers with 80 per cent of the market: Rupert Murdoch owned 33.1%, Robert Maxwell owned 29.8% and Lord Mathews owned 18% share of the market.[5]

Working within such framework of analysis, this study will assess the wider consequences of the full integration of the modern British press into core sector of capital with a particular reference to the miners' strike of the 1984-85.

Thirdly, the inclusion of the press as an independent variable has practical significance. The research axiom of this book involves retrospective analysis of media output. A comparative content analysis of the national press is, therefore, more yielding to historical research than other media outputs such as television. In this methodological context, it will be argued that the theory of culture industry remains proficient to generate conceptual tools to study the complex relationship between the political, economic and the cultural spheres in modern societies. In doing so, the concept of 'multi-faceted populism' will be proposed and

[3] The newspaper reading habit: an international table; circulation per 1,000 inhabitants:

SWEDEN	526
UNITED KINGDOM	479
NORWAY	459
DENMARK	367
NETHERLANDS	325
WEST GERMANY	324
UNITED STATES	282
ITALY	238

(Source: United Nations Yearbook – 1985)

[4] T. Baistow, *Fourth-Rate Estate: An Anatomy of Fleet Street* (London: Comedia), 1985, p.1

[5] Source: The archives at the Audit Bureau of Circulation Limited, 207 High Street, Berkhamsted, Herts.

explored to offer an alternative analysis for the link between Thatcherism, the success of the 'New Right' and the press industry in recent decades.

This book is comprised of four substantive chapters. The first chapter, entitled 'THE THEORY OF CULTURE INDUSTRY: Contemporary Relevance or a Theoretical Impasse?', will outline and discuss the theoretical aspects of the book. The principal aim of this chapter is to provide a critical analysis of the Frankfurt School's theory of culture industry. In order to control the scope of Adorno and Horkheimer's highly voluminous analyses of modern mass culture, the book will concentrate on selected themes which directly relate to the forthcoming discussion on the link between Thatcherism and modern British press.

Firstly, it will deal with the School's analysis of 'authoritarian state capitalism', then the chapter will discuss School's critique of 'formal rationality' and its relevance to our discussion of the modern press and polity. It will then present a general discussion of the School's theory of mass culture before presenting a critical analysis of the School's theory of culture industry with particular reference to Adorno's interesting debate on the role of astrology and sport in modern mass culture.

The first chapter will conclude with a section on the merits and utility of the theory of culture industry whereby a new theoretical definition will be presented and discussed.

The next three chapters present and discuss various the methodological aspects of the book. In an attempt to empirically corroborate the theoretical propositions offered in the first chapter, the book will focus upon the recent cultural and political developments in Britain.

Chapter Two, 'THATCHERISM: FROM THEORY TO RESEARCH: The Concepts- indicators Model', is an assessment of the origins of Thatcherism in which the nature, and consequences, of Thatcherite popularity and the role of the press in the 1980s will be examined.

Chapter Three, THE PRESS INDUSRTY IN THATCHER YEARS: A model for British Culture Industry?' is an assessment of the modern press and will discuss its role, and position, in the development of culture industry in contemporary Britain. The focal point of this chapter is to empirically analyze the reciprocal relationship between Murdoch and Thatcher in the 1980s, and to analyze the impact, and consequences of this cooperation for individuals, society and culture.

Chapter Four, 'THE MINERS' STRIKES AND THE PRESS INDUSTRY: A Comparative Study', is the empirical assessment of the role, and the impact, of the national press during the miners' strikes of the 1970s and the 1980s. This chapter will demonstrate the differential approach by the national press to the miners and their strikes in two different time spans. Ultimately, this chapter intends to argue that there seem to be a 'correlation' between the editorial contents of the press and public opinion in relation to these important events.

This book will conclude with a summary statement to evaluate the main issues raised in these chapters and briefly discuss the overall consequences of the present research for the study of media, culture and society.

ONE

THE THEORY OF CULTURE INDUSTRY
Contemporary Relevance or a Theoretical Impasse?

Introduction

This chapter will critically assess the theory of culture industry in order to demonstrate its contemporary relevance for the study of modern mass circulating and technologically advanced media. Primarily, this chapter will argue that the theory of culture industry still merits attention precisely because it continues to present promising theoretical and empirical prospects not only in the field of sociology but also cultural studies, communication, political economy and psychology.

Furthermore, some of the boldest, and yet most impressive, claims of culture industry thesis have not been empirically explored in the field of the modern British mass circulating media industry.

British sociological research on the function and structure of modern media seem to be reluctant in utilizing the relevant components of the culture industry thesis despite Adorno's influence on important media commentators such as Paul Lazarsfeld, Elihu Katz, Herbert Schiller and Dallas Smythe. Indeed, very rarely are there accounts of modern British media without a reference to Adorno's theory of culture industry and yet there is little empirical analysis to assess some of its valuable theoretical insight which remains as relevant today.

Compiled over a period of four decades, Adorno's theory of mass culture includes an impressive theme utilizing philosophy, psychology, sociology and economic critique. The culture industry, far from being a culture by and for the masses, aims for profits, and is controlled by fewer and fewer interwoven multinational corporations. It utilizes marketing, financial and managerial expertise along with talented technicians, musicians, reporters, writers and actors. The modern mass produced culture reaches out to a vast audience across the globe watching the same television outputs, movies and reading similarly formatted newspapers and journals. The Western culture industry, it is argued, occupies a powerful position in the lives of an immense majority.

In a novel approach to the problem of modern culture Adorno's combination of Marxian critique of political economy and Freudian instinct theory attempts to capture the standardization and homogenization of the modern culture promoting the ideology of capitalism through its function and praxis.

Fundamentally, working within the tradition of critical theory, this study views the British press as part of the culture industry, which is connected both to corporate capitalism and the political system. In this context, it will be argued that the press industry, far from being a monolithic force, is a highly conflictual mass medium in which competing economic, political, social and cultural forces intersect.

Furthermore, by attempting to assess the continued relevance of Adorno's theory of culture industry this revision will outline some of the theoretical and methodological concepts directly related to the purposes and scope of this book.

The first part of this chapter will locate the 'essential' elements in the genesis of the theory, before outlining four of its major and distinct features, derived from Adorno's analysis which focused upon the dominant characteristics of commodified culture. Although these features are diverse and have their own logic, Adorno repeatedly stressed these concepts which accompany the commodification of cultural goods. These are 'standardization', 'pseudo-individualism', 'schematization' and 'stereotypes'. The latter parts of this chapter will analyse each one of these four dominant features of the commodified culture individually and will show how these concepts could be utilized methodologically to provide an empirical examination of the contents of the national press in relation to the miners' strike of 1984–85.

This chapter, however, begins with a detailed analysis of some of the most important ideas in the genesis of the theory of culture industry which at times may seem like a defense of Adorno's position. This study does not intend to propose a mere justification for neo-Adornoism, but to reconsider some of the valuable points of the Adorno's influential insight into the purposes, and functions, of modern mass culture.

The Genesis of the Theory of Culture Industry

There are numerous influential ideas which lie at the core of the Frankfurt School's theory of culture industry. The latter parts of this section will assess some of these ideas in more detail.

Firstly, however, this section will focus upon three major themes which lie at the core of the theory: Max Weber's theory of rationality, Georg Lukacs' theory of reification and, finally, the critique of state capitalism by Franz Neumann and Friedrich Pollock. This chapter will examine each one of these elementary ideas before embarking upon a more general discussion of other important conceptual components in the formation of the theory.

Culture, Technology and the Rise of Instrumental Rationality

'Whoever speaks of culture speaks about administrations as well'
Adorno

In the *Dialectic of Enlightenment* the failure of the proletarian revolution in advanced capitalist societies was seen as the result of a conformist mass culture and control over social consciousness through the culture industry.

Following Weber, Adorno and Horkheimer stressed that western culture was dominated by 'instrumental or formal' rationality, its goal the control over human action and society through a dehumanised science and technology. Adorno and Horkheimer ask how had the ideals of the Enlightenment, of freedom, justice, autonomy of self, led to a social world structured in conformism, the dictatorship of fascism and the 'totally administered world' of modern capitalism? The answer was located in the inner tension of Enlightenment rationalism, between the universal ideals of science which freed individuals from the constraints of mythology and unreason, and the positivist, quantitative and pragmatic goals of science empirically realised in the culture of utilitarianism. This conflict is shown in the development of bourgeois society itself, because the principles of calculation and systematization have the effect of rationalizing culture, transforming science and reason into modes of technological domination which marks the beginning of the fall of the autonomous individual.

This section examines the origins and implications of the expansion of formal rationality, as analysed by the Frankfurt School, in order to reinforce the theoretical basis of this study as it is connected to our discussion of the implementation, and consequences, of new technology in the press industry.

This section begins with Weber's discussion of rationality for its major impact upon the subsequent analyses by the critical theorists, and then proceeds to discuss some major points raised by Adorno, Horkheimer and Herbert Marcuse.

For Weber, formal rationality meant calculability, efficiency and impersonality, that is, reduction of rationality to its formal, instrumental side. Weber defined formal rationality with regard to economic action as 'a system of economic activity will be called 'formally rational' according to the degree in which provision for needs ... is capable of being expressed in numerical, calculable terms, and is so expressed.'[1]

Weber's concept of rationality embodied a whole range of tendencies connected to scientific and technological progress and

---

[1] See Max Weber, *'Economy and Society'*, Roth & Wittich (Eds.) Vol. I (New York, 1968), p.85

their impact upon the cultural and institutional manifestations of traditional society. These include the expansion of bureaucracy alongside the expansion of industrialization, the erosion of traditional forms of life, the development of rational decision making in private law and economic activities and above all the rise of cultural secularization.

Weber believed that on the one hand the capitalist mode of production was substantively successful in efficiency, but traditional values were being lost. This form of progress in rationality, Weber argued, was irreversible and this consequently meant a loss of freedom and meaning. With growing social rationalization – the rise of formal and calculable reasoning in the state and economy – the modern individual is incapable of replacing the meaning content of devalued culture with an autonomous one. Collective social life is nothing but a rationalized hierarchical apparatus of managers and experts. This is what Weber called an 'iron cage' with individuals of limited skills and aspirations living inside it.

Socialism, Weber believed, was not only unable to resolve this problem, but would indeed accelerate it through the extension of a central and bureaucratic control of the economy. Weber, unlike Marx, was therefore pessimistic as he envisaged no means of escaping from the 'iron cage' of modernity.

Overall, Weber's detailed analysis of formal and substantive rationality stresses the tension between them, as obviously there is a need for both forms in any organization but that the formal begins dominating in the modern world.

The Frankfurt School analysis of rationality centres around the concept of 'instrumental rationality' and is essentially an assessment of the ways in which its expansion undermines the process of critical or substantive reasoning. Subjective or instrumental reason is determined by the operational value for the domination of men and nature. In cultural terms the subjectivization and formalization of reason is manifested as reification, which results in the transformation of all products of human activity into commodities. The mechanism for achieving that transformation is the anonymous economic apparatus.

Critical or substantive reason, in contrast, emphasizes ends and harmony as a principle inherent in reality. 'The degree of reasonableness of man's life could be determined according to its harmony with...totality'. *(Dialectic*, p.13)

The critique of instrumental rationality by the Frankfurt School was not to condemn it for the expansion of technological civilization. The principal target was to produce a critique of rationalization process which contributes to its 'irrationality'. In modern advanced societies the cyclical economic crises are closely coupled with the technological rationality. Therefore, it is the capitalist process of production which is the source of threat to humanity's spirit, not the technological progress.

Following Weber, Marcuse sees the distinguishing feature of modern society in its high level of technical rationality. The total control exercised by this rationality is seen as a historical process from the practice of capitalist appropriation, but in its present stage it is no longer possible to recognize the capitalist origins which are behind the rationalization process. According to this form of analysis rationality is seen as a process whereby bureaucracy and technology are themselves becoming agencies of control.

Marcuse equated instrumental reason with technological rationality and stressed that the long historical process of capital accretion has created a set of values which nurture and encourage subordination and incorporation. These set of values, part of the essential characteristic of technological rationality, include, amongst others, the rationalization and standardization of production and consumption and the development of mass communication.

Individuals living in modern capitalist societies are increasingly required to act 'rationally' to sustain their livelihood. Since this rational behaviour is nothing but an enforcement of the established order, it is an adaptive and passive response suitable only for the functioning of the system.

With the expansion of the capitalist mode of production and the division of labour, which are controlled from some central location, the bureaucratic organizations are increasingly responsible for the development of a rational order within society. These contribute to blocking out a developing pattern of 'critical thinking'.[2]

Similarly, Adorno saw the rational disenchantment of the world beneath the banner of Taylorism as a 'standardization' of every day life, part of the self-destruction of the Enlightenment which was responsible for the emergence of fascism. Culture industry, for Adorno, is nothing more than one aspect of that dialectic of enlightenment in which technical rationality has become the rationality of domination per se, and, unlike Walter Benjamin, he does not differentiate technical rationality in a capitalist system from that in a socialist society.[3]

Horkheimer distinguished between 'subjective and objective reasons' which is essentially the same as Weber's formal and substantive rationality. Fascism, for Horkheimer, is the culmination of the technical rationality of bourgeois-capitalist society, in which enlightenment is reversed into barbarism by a dialectical twist.

Fascism encourages the revolt of the nature of the individual and suppresses that revolt at the same time. A qualitatively new perfection of instrumentation and formalization of reason had been achieved in fascism:

> *'in modern fascism, rationality has reached a point which it is no longer satisfied with simply repressing nature; rationality now exploits nature by incorporating into its own system the rebellious potentialities of nature. The Nazis manipulated the suppressed desires of the German people.'*[4]

In the *Dialectic of Enlightenment* Adorno and Horkheimer see modern societies as dominated by formal rationality where the thinking process has been 'objectified' in order to 'become an automatic, self-activating process; an impersonation of the

[2] See H. Marcuse, *'Some Modern Implication of Modern Technology'*. Also see D. Held, *'Introduction to Critical Theory'* (L.A: UCL Press), 1980, pp 67-8
[3] For an interesting discussion on this topic see A.Huyssen, 'Introduction to Adorno', *New German Critique*, 6, Fall, 1976
[4] M. Horkheimer, *'Eclipse of Reason'* (New York: Oxford University Press), 1947, p21

machine that it produces itself so that the ultimately the machine can replace it'.[5]

The essential problem with the Frankfurt School's analysis of technological rationality, as Paul Connorton sees it, is that it primarily rests upon a set of 'over-simplified' categories of fascism, monopoly capitalism, totalitarianism and technology, a set of categories which was formed before the World War Two.

Moreover, Marcuse seems to be in a position of analytical incoherence when he is discussing the problem of instrumental rationality:

'...is it possible to define a boundary... between technology and the political use of technology? This situation is complicated by the fact that technology has become both an instrument and a competitor of politics. On the one hand, science and technology have become important instruments of political action; on the other hand, they have developed a life of their own and so become a new source of authority and power in society, one with which those directly involved in political action have to reckon.'[6]

Closely related to Weber's theory of rationality, Lukacs' analysis of reification forms another major theme in the genesis of 'culture industry'.

Lukacs' theory of reification

The early works of Georg Lukacs and Karl Korsch challenged the Marxian deterministic and positivistic interpretations of historical materialism and the suitability of the methodological model of the natural sciences for understanding history.

The publication of Lukacs' *History and Class Consciousness* and Korsch's *Marxism and Philosophy* constituted a fundamental

[5]*'The Dialectic of Enlightenment'*, p.25. Quoted by D.Held, 'Introduction to Critical Theory', op.cit. p.69
[6]P. Connerton, *'The Tragedy of Enlightenment'* (Cambridge: Cambridge University Press), 1980, p.90

reappraisal of Marxism and provided a new challenge to radical orthodoxy. They provided a basis for a re-examination of Marxian theory and praxis in relation to contemporary events.

Lukacs argued that Marx, later in his life, understood the importance of human subjectivity and that orthodox Marxists failed to grasp the significance of examining both the objective conditions of action and the ways in which these conditions are understood. Marxists missed the essential elements in preventing the emergence of a revolutionary agent.

For Lukacs historical materialism must be seen in the context of the proletariat's struggle. Moreover, the class conflict also involves the theorists 'explicating objective possibilities imminent in the dynamic of class relations'.[7]

Marxism, therefore, cannot be separated from the practices of a particular social class.

Lukacs, following his mentor Hegel, maintained that the standpoint of the proletariat is society's subject-object, and it is the basis from which the totality can be understood. The position of the proletariat, for Lukacs, is unique because of its capacity to understand and transform society. Even if the mass revolutionary working class praxis does not come about, one is still able to talk of its objective possibility because this is embodied in the historical process. The role of theory is to develop radical consciousness and the elevation of political involvement.[8]

The radical revolutionary consciousness may be distorted, Lukacs argued, because of the process of reification the productive activities of the worker appearing as strange and alien to them.

Following Marx's analysis of alienation, Simmel's account of the commodification of culture, and Weber's theory of

---

[7] G. Lukacs, *History and Class Consciousness*, Tran: R. Livingstone (London: Merlin Press), 1971, p.3
[8] Both Lukacs and Marx regarded the separation of fact and value as an expression of capitalist society and ny no means ultimate. Lukacs, therefore, went on to identify the proletariat as a potential universal class around which the truth of society can be revealed. As Lukacs saw the proletariat as the identical subject-object of history, he contrasted Weber's account of rationalization with the relative irrationality of the whole.

rationalization, Lukacs aims to show how reification penetrates all aspects of social life.

'... *the problem of reification was the central structural problem of capitalist society in all its aspects.*'[9]

For Lukacs reification was not a subjective phenomenon. Its origins lie in the productive processes which reduce the workers and their products to commodities.[10]

Lukacs' concept of reification was used by the Frankfurt School to show how the increased rationality of capitalist society became the basis for totalitarianism. Within the School's analyses of 'authority', reification is not injected ideologically into people's minds, but rather in a practical and perceptual disposition. This is not then a 'culture and personality' approach, but culture is located in the structure of society and its practices.

Adorno's explicit reference to Lukacs shows that the concept of reification was the initial breakthrough for the School's study of modern capitalist culture.[11]

It is important to mention that this was the School's initial approach to the problem of culture and that later this stance was somewhat modified as the critical theorists began to move away from Lukacs.[12]

Some aspects of Lukacs's legacy, therefore, were retained by the School, such as the attack on the Marxist orthodoxy, the relationship between production and culture, the interplay of history and theory, and the effects of reification and the way each sphere of society contains within itself the possibility of unraveling the totality. These were all praised by the School, and the School's critique of modern forms of authoritarianism and mass culture is rooted in Lukacs's cultural approach to the form of objectivity of the capitalist society.

Other aspects of Lukacs's ideas, however, were treated with

[9]G. Lukacs, Op.cit. P.83
[10]For an interesting discussion see Feenberg (1986), Chp.3
[11]Adorno, 'Erpresste Versohung', '*Noten Zur Literatur II*' (Frankfurt: Suhrkamp), p.152
[12]The School, as a whole, later distanced itself from Lukacs's early Marxism, rejecting the notion of subject-object identity as mistaken and misleading in principle.

caution by the School. Primarily, they seriously questioned the role of the proletariat as the subject-object of history and later treated the concept of proletariat as an agent of social change with extreme pessimism. This stance is more explicit in Marcuse's writings than in any of the other members.

Generally, for the Frankfurt School, the prevention of critical thinking is closely related to the growth and survival of capitalism together with the rise of formal rationality. This state of affairs is, in turn, accountable for the growth of authoritarianism and coercion in 'totally administered society'.

The next section will present a detailed examination of the School's assessment of authoritarianism and state capitalism for a better understanding of its research project .

Authoritarianism and State Capitalism

The Frankfurt School's analysis of the authoritarian state is one of the most important aspect of the critical theory which opens the way to a deeper understanding of the dynamics of modern social movements in the context of the psycho-social bases of authority.

The critique of mass society and of technology was an essential part of the Frankfurt School's analysis of the authoritarian state. The culture industry was one aspect of the ability of modern capitalism to neutralize conflict and instability. Another was the mobilization of authoritarian mass movements.

The fascist phenomenon had a major impact upon the critical theorists and consequently they all agreed that fascism was closely connected to the inner dynamics of capitalism. Accordingly, the School began to focus upon the changing relationship between technology, the economy and the state in Western capitalist societies. Most of the theorists believed that the breakdown of liberal capitalism gave way to an authoritarian state. The causes for such an outcome were related to the progress of capitalism.

This connection became the subject of some heated debate amongst the members. On the one hand Franz Neumann,

Herbert Marcuse and Otto Kirchheimer argued that the rise of fascism in the political sphere is closely connected to the development of monopolization and 'cartelization' in the economic sphere. In Behemoth Neumann argued that the survival of monopolistic capitalism depends upon the labour market being controlled by authoritarian means because 'democracy would endanger the fully monopolized system'. (p. 290)

On the other hand, Adorno and Horkheimer, who supported Friedrich Pollock's views on state capitalism argued that the authoritarian state represented the appearance of a new social formation. This was a 'post-market' society, characterized by the substitution of the market by state planning, wherein the individual capitalist is turned into a rentier and bureaucratic management becomes a substitution for market-based investment decisions. Adorno, in particular, believed that state capitalism could take either 'democratic' or 'totalitarian' forms, but, in either form: 'today the forces of production and the relations of production are one... material production, distribution, and consumption are ruled together.' (Adorno: *Minima Moralia*, p.165)

This section will examine the differences between Neumann and Pollock each separately for a better comprehension of the Frankfurt School's approach to the problem of authoritarianism and state capitalism. Neumann's views, which will feature here first, was supported by Marcuse and Kirchheimer.

One of the central theories of Neumann's *Behemoth* is that National Socialism is or is tending to become a non-state. 'we are confronted with a form of society in which the ruling groups control the rest of the population directly, without the mediation of that rational though coercive apparatus hitherto known as the state.' (*Behemoth*: p. xii)

The large corporations were seemingly the only sector of society to benefit from this development. Fascism swiftly moved to protect the interests of these cartels with a policy which clearly sided with them at the expense of smaller and medium sized businesses.

Neumann, following Marx's assertion that accumulation of

capital is unstable and generates concentration and centralization, argued that monopoly and centralization is responsible for an ever-expanding and interdependent economic formation. Since this form of economic system was vulnerable and had a fragile equilibrium, an interventionist state is developed to provide political and economic stability. The state involves itself in finance capital. With the expansion of industrialization, invested money becomes increasingly fixed capital. The risks involved in massive investments requires the state to safeguard their production and their markets.

Both Neumann and Marcuse were in agreement that an authoritarian state is the product of monopolistic capitalism. When National Socialism and monopoly capital merge the product is a new political compromise which ensured the interdependence of Nazis and capital. The Nazis and monopolies found a common interest to attain maximum efficiency and production for a continuous supply and, hence, domination and control. Capitalist accumulation depends upon efficiency which in turn affects technology and rationality. Greater productivity and concentration of ownership is dependent upon increased efficiency assisted by the application of technology.

The Nazis were also excessively concerned with the stability of monopoly capital because they were fearful of the consequences of the fall in profit margins of the big corporations.

They were also concerned with the possibility of a dissatisfied population. In an attempt to reduce these fears the Nazi Party decided to protect the monopolistic system and assist the structural development of all business conducts.

The fascist phenomenon was seen by Neumann as the outcome of a relationship between the Party, big monopolies, the armed forces and the bureaucracy. In this situation the only guarantee for survival was a rapid economic expansion. The cartels and the Party found an 'identical aim' in military expansion, which rapidly assisted the stability of the Nazi economy.

For Neumann there was no inevitability in the collapse of

monopoly capitalism even if Germany were to be defeated in the war. Only a conscious political movement supported by the oppressed masses would provide an alternative to the established order. Initially there will be an antagonism between 'the magical aspect of propaganda' staged by the system and the concrete experience of the working classes who are, in reality, regarded by the authoritarian order as a mere extension of the means of production. This conflict is exacerbated by the pain caused by the confrontations between those elements within the armed forces and the owners of monopoly cartels. Moreover, as the skilled workers see their industrial products are used as tools of mass destruction their critical consciousness increasingly develops, paving the path to a mass support for the overthrow of the National Socialiste régime.

Neumann's analysis of the relations between the Party, the state, the army and the economy is a clear indication that the differences with Pollock were basically about choice of words.

Pollock, on the other hand, shared Neumann's view that a monopolistic situation cannot eradicate the crisis of liberal capitalism. Instead the ever-present economic problems such as unemployment produce severe political unrest. State interventionism, therefore, becomes the only method of dealing with such symptoms. The development of the interventionist state, for Pollock, involves changes of far-reaching economic, social and political consequences, as it increases the capacity of large businesses to resist pressures for price decreases and make profits with price increases.

In two essays written in 1941 *'State Capitalism'* and *'Is National Socialism a New Order?'* Pollock explores the newly emergent social order: state capitalism. Here state capitalism is described as the successor of private capitalism in which the state acquires important new functions which previously were those of individual capitalists, but the basic features of classic capitalism remains the same: profit and selling of labour power. Pollock distinguishes between two forms of state capitalism, totalitarian and democratic. Within the totalitarian form the state is the means of power of a new ruling group, a combination of leading bureaucrats in business, state, and party: 'Everybody who does not belong to this group is a mere object of domination.'[13]

In the democratic form the state is controlled by the people, yet profit maintains its traditional importance as an incentive. General planning, however, assumes priority over the individual's interest. A widespread technical rationality attempts to assess the needs, and the fluctuations, of the market through statistics, systematic training of labour, and rationalization of administrative aspects of economy. The democratic form of state capitalism is, therefore, governed by a detailed bureaucracy and managerial control of big businesses.

Crucially though, Pollock argued that in both forms of state capitalism, the state has the same function. It has replaced the market as the institution with the function of balancing production and distribution. Pollock, however, concentrated on the totalitarian form of state capitalism which later became the basis for a general critical theory of state capitalism, one which was more fully developed by Adorno and Horkheimer. They shared Pollock's view that state capitalism, in either form, could regulate class conflict, and therefore prolong its survival for a foreseeable future.

For Pollock the central characteristic of the state capitalist new order was, as argued above, the replacement of the market by the state. Although a market, a price system and wages still persist, they no longer serve the general function of regulating the economic process. The state formulates a general plan and executes its fulfillment. As a result, neither the law of the market nor other 'economic laws' such as the tendency of the rate of profit to fall or to be equalized, no longer retain their previously important function. Under such conditions the hierarchy of bureaucratic political structures occupies the centre of social existence. Market relations are replaced by those of a command hierarchy in which a one-sided technical rationality is above the place of law. The majority of people, therefore, become paid employees of the political apparatus, lacking political rights,

---

[13]See Pollock, 'State Capitalism: Its Possibilities and Limitations', *'Studies in Philosophy and Social Sciences'*, Vol IX, 1941, p.201

powers of self-organization and the right to strike. People are subordinate to the whole, as the impetus to work is given either by political terror or psychic manipulation. Individuals are mobilized as means, because of their productivity, rather than as ends in themselves.[14]

It seems that, for Pollock, the primacy of the political meant that the economy becomes totally manageable as he repeatedly emphasized that there are no economic laws or functions which could hinder the functioning of state capitalism. However, state capitalism can be overcome through 'crises in political legitimation'. The primacy of the political is a historical process for resolving the economic ills of liberal capitalism. In the light of the Great Depression, Pollock argued that the primary tasks of the new social organization would be to maintain full employment and basic social order. The replacement of the market by the state means that mass unemployment would immediately involve a political crisis, one which would challenge the authority of the system. The state capitalist form necessarily requires full employment for its fundamental legitimacy.

The totalitarian capitalist state is confronted with additional problems. It is an expression of an antagonistic society in its worst shape. This is because the interests of the ruling class prevent the people from using the forces of production by using full control of the organization of society. Due to the acuteness of this conflict the totalitarian state cannot allow for a substantial rise in the general standard of living. For Pollock a rise in the living standard would enable people to reflect upon their condition and develop critical consciousness out of which a revolutionary spirit could emerge.

Totalitarian state capitalism is therefore faced with the problem of how to maintain full employment and promote further technical progress without allowing a substantial rise in living standard. Pollock's simple solution may be applicable to all late capitalist societies. Only a permanent war could provide these tasks simultaneously. The greatest threat to the totalitarian

---

[14]See Pollock, 'Is National Socialism a New Order?, *'Studies in Philosophy and Social Sciences'*, Vol IX, 1941, pp. 440-55

form is peace. A high standard of living could only be maintained by democratic state capitalism, which Pollock seemed to view as an unstable form because either class differences would assert themselves in which case a totalitarian state would eventually emerge, or democratic control of the state would abolish the last remains of class society, thereby leading to socialism. State capitalism, ultimately, in either form, contained contradiction and conflict.

Pollock's analysis was heavily criticized by Neumann for two reasons. Firstly, Pollock neither developed a theory for the transition from monopoly capitalism to state capitalism nor offered any evidence that Germany was state capitalist in any of its essential characteristics. Secondly, Neumann questioned the existence of state capitalism:

> 'The concept of state capitalism cannot bear analysis from the economic point of view. Once the state has become the sole owner of the means of production it makes it impossible for a capitalist economy to function, it destroys that mechanism which keeps the very processes of economic circulation in active existence. Such a state is therefore no longer capitalistic. (Neumann: Behemoth, p.183)

Ultimately, these theoretical differences between Pollock and Neumann were never resolved. Adorno and Horkheimer, however, favoured Pollock's conceptualization of 'state capitalism', and viewed Neumann's analysis as too orthodox and mechanistic.

A closer examination of Adorno and Horkheimer's views reveals that they, too, were unclear about the future development of capitalism. There was no doubt for Adorno that the problems of class antagonism and cyclical crises would persist under capitalism. However, he stressed that capitalism would find a way to deal with these problems, despite the possibility that this might not be managed successfully. By the 1960s when Adorno published Culture Industry Reconsidered, he viewed culture industry as symptomatic of an authoritarian state. In contrast to his earlier analysis, the catchwords are no longer barbarism and fascism, but rather 'status quo' and 'conformity', reflecting the economic and political stabilization of the advanced capitalist societies.[15] Adorno, nevertheless, saw the very essence of advanced capitalist societies as a major threat to a subjectivity which belongs to the aesthetic existence.

Horkheimer's position is rather more uncertain as there are signs in his early writings of a tension between believing in the conclusive collapse of capitalism on the one hand, and a pessimistic vision on the other. This uncertainty is clearly exemplified in *The Authoritarian State*. Horkheimer sees state capitalism as a 'transient phenomenon' on its way for an inevitable collapse, yet later he shifts his views to argue that with state capitalism future forms of oppression are possible.[16]

David Held, amongst other commentators, argue that the Frankfurt School, as a whole, shared some common grounds on this particular issue. They all agreed that in both totalitarian and democratic societies the polity has increasingly become important. Furthermore, they believed that there has been an increasing tendency in technical rationality in the following areas: for general efficiency as opposed to traditional desire for individual profitability, the method of state intervention from a market complementing to a market-replacing method, bureaucratic planning, and the centralization of decision making procedures.[17]

Having briefly discussed the problem of the authoritarian capitalism the chapter will now address other influential ideas in the formation of the theory of culture industry.

Other Influential Ideas in the Genesis of Culture Industry

The Frankfurt School's theory of mass culture was never completed and remains a fractured theory from its inception to later developments. This section intends to focus on the School's

---

[15]In the *Dialectic of Enlightenment* the terms 'barbarism' and 'barbarity appears 26 times.
[16]See Horkheimer, 'The Authoritarian State', Telos, 15, Spring 1976, pp 12-15
[17]D. Held, *'Introduction to Critical Theory'*, op.cit. p.64

views on the changing patterns of culture and will locate the Frankfurt School's studies within their general approach on culture. The works examined in this chapter are the School's massive and impressive materials on more general studies of the development of cultural forms in the 19th and 20th centuries. The analysis of the culture industry carried out by the School is diverse in approach and methodology. By utilizing the method of content analysis Adorno's work seems more sharply focused and immensely intertwined with the Marxian theory of value. His theory of culture often concentrates on production, reproduction, exchange, distribution and the consumption of cultural activities.

Horkheimer and Marcuse, in contrast, tended to be more philosophical and theoretical.

A brief discussion on these approaches is appropriate here to demonstrate the differences between these thinkers.

A careful consideration of the School's early work suggests that most of its members believed that in a world where capital is highly concentrated, and where the economy and political processes are increasingly intertwined, people are caught up in a 'world of total administration'. As a result of such developments, most members of the School argued, the importance of political economy diminished as it could no longer understand the penetration of market and bureaucratic organizations into other areas of life. Concepts and ideas and new paradigms, therefore, had to be developed to make these changes theoretically understandable. Gradually, the School turned its attention to the assessment of the way in which ideas and beliefs are transmitted by popular culture, the way in which the personal, private realm is undermined by the external (extra-familial) socialization of the ego and the management and control of leisure time.[18]

The School stressed the urgency of developing a sociology of mass culture, as it perceived individual consciousness was being increasingly shaped by the agencies which organize free time such as the radio, television, film and the press.

Marcuse, Adorno and Horkheimer, more than others, stress

---

[18]See: H. Marcuse, *'Five Lectures'* (Boston: Shapiro & Webber), 1970, Introduction

the inseparability of critique and sociology. When one is confronted with a cultural phenomenon, one must be able to analyse and assess its origins, formation and reception. It is through this form of analysis that one can understand given works in terms of the social origins, content and function or, as Adorno argued, in terms of the social totality of that work. Consequently, as the totality expresses itself through its cultural activity, which in turn contains within itself a socio-economic reference of the whole, the conditions of production and distribution must be examined in order to provide a well-informed analysis of these cultural products and activities.

Horkheimer and Adorno emphasized the impact of the organization of society on cultural phenomena. Accordingly, a sociology of culture or a theory of culture should contain in itself a reference to the complex processes of production, distribution, exchange and consumption.

Adorno and Horkheimer's attention to the studies of mass culture began to form in the late 1930s and early 1940s. This was due to the emergence and the phenomenal growth of the mass leisure, entertainment and media industries, specifically the way in which the Nazis successfully manipulated radio and advertising agencies. The urgency for a critical analysis of the changing patterns of mass culture became more imperative as the historic immigration to the U.S.A became inevitable.

In previous sections it was argued that the School's style of thought was distinct from the Marxist orthodoxy of the time. It was pointed out that culture was not perceived as part of the superstructure of society, but instead they insisted on the inadmissibility of treating culture in the manner of conventional cultural criticism away from its position in the social totality. Adorno made this point explicit when he argued that culture could not be understood in terms of itself.[19]

Culture is, therefore, seen as emerging from the organizational basis of society and inseparable from the social totality. Marcuse too, while discussing bourgeois culture,

---

[19] Adorno, 'Cultural Criticism and Society', in *Prism* (London: N. Spearman Ltd), 1967, p29

distinguishes between the spheres of material culture and intellectual culture:

> *Material culture is the actual patterns of behaviour in earning a living, the system of operational values, and includes the social, psychological and moral dimensions of family life, leisure time, education and work. Intellectual culture refers to the higher values, science and the humanities, art, religion.*[20]

In *Negations*, Marcuse sees the bourgeois cultural norm as serving both to project unrealized possibilities and to harmonize illusions. Bourgeois dreams stay at the level of relegated ideals to the inner world of humanity. Of course this relegation is due, Marcuse argues, to the nature of material production. At this relegated level, human liberation, ethics and duties are mere spiritual qualities. In the *Affirmative Character of Culture* Marcuse says culture speaks of the dignity of humans and preserves beauty for the soul. (p.95)

In his study of mass culture Marcuse introduces a series of original categories of his own. The most important being that of 'repressive desublimation' which means the systematic limitation on the scope of desublimation, the reduction of the sensual, pleasurable and erotic to specific sexual experiences.[21]

In *One Dimensional Man*, the development of mass culture is seen by Marcuse as increasingly establishing a false harmony between public and private interests, thus reinforcing privatization and consumption orientations. Above all, this development undermines the genuine working class culture and increases the domination of instrumental reason.

Amongst all members of the School, Walter Benjamin tends to use a rather different notion of mass culture. The notion of 'autonomy' separates Benjamin's view from the rest of the School's members. The authenticity of a thing is the essence of all that is transmissible from its beginning, ranging from its

[20] H.Marcuse, *Counterrevolution and Revolt* (Boston: Beacon Press), 1972, p.83
[21] H. Marcuse, *Eros and Civilization* (Boston: Beacon Press), 1955, chp10

substantive duration to its testimony to the history which it had experienced.²²

Benjamin (and Kracauer) occupy a unique position amongst the Frankfurt School's members for being 'optimistic' about the effects of new techniques and cultural media. Not only did Benjamin argue that the film industry, through its technical structure, could produce shock effects and burst everyday perceptions of the world, leading to a heightened presence of mind but also:

> *Mechanical reproduction of art changes the reaction of masses toward art. The reactionary attitude toward Picasso painting changes into progressive reaction toward a Chaplin movie. The progressive reaction is characterized by the direct, intimate fusion of visual and emotional enjoyment with the orientation of the expert. With regard to the screen the critical and the receptive attitudes of the public coincide.* (Benjamin: *Illuminations, p.234*)

The new techniques used by mechanical reproduction could be of assistance to the revolutionary struggle. The tasks which have faced the human apparatus of perception at the turning points of history cannot be solved by contemplation alone. They are mastered gradually by habit. The ability to master certain tasks in a state of distraction proves that their solution has become a matter of habit. Consistent and reliable revolutionary habits could be learned through a radical politicization of art. (Benjamin: *Illuminations*, p.240)

Benjamin stressed the possibility of the functioning transformation of aspects of mass culture because of the transformation of forms and instruments of production by a progressive intelligentsia, an intelligentsia interested in liberating the means of production.²³

---

²²See W.Benjamin, 'The Work of Art in the Age of Mechanical Reproduction', in '*Illuminations*, edited with an introduction by Hannah Arendt, Translated by H.Zohn, (London: Fontana), pp 224-5

²³Benjamin, 'The Author as Producer', 1934, in *Understanding Brecht* (London: New Left Books), 1973, p.95

Against the views of Adorno, Horkheimer, Marcuse and Leo Lowenthal, Benjamin argued that the 'writer himself from a supplier of the production apparatus turns into an engineer who sees his task in adapting that apparatus to the ends of the proletarian revolution.'[24]

Adorno criticized Benjamin's optimism on two fronts. The collective experience in the cinema, Adorno stressed, was anything but good and revolutionary. The worst aspect of bourgeois sadism, for Adorno, was in the audience's laughter. Furthermore, Adorno, in a letter to Benjamin, criticized him for his overriding confidence in the spontaneous power of the proletariat. It was far too simple, Adorno argued, to believe that mechanical reproduction would bring about radical transformations in perception and consciousness.[25]

The School's general approach to culture was centered around the notion that the new technique of cultural production and reception had to be understood in the context of the decline of autonomous art and the rise of the culture industry. The modern production of mass culture is to enhance political control and to attach mass audiences to the status quo. On Adorno's account, normative culture in the twentieth century has become functional for a world of commodity production. It is made for entertainment and its consumability. The kind of cultural artifacts which submit to the rules of the market are no longer an autonomous culture. In the age of technological progress and immense capital accumulation, artistic alienation and other forms of negation tend to disappear.

By proposing the notion of culture industry, Adorno, Horkheimer and Marcuse set out to provide some responses to such problems as why and how cultural form, content, style and aura have been transformed by the developments of mass culture and to what extent these changes transformed the meaning and function of culture. In the following section, the concept of culture industry will be assessed in more depth.

[24]*ibid*, p.142
[25]Adorno sent this letter to Benjamin's London residence, dated 18 March 1936

The Definition of Culture Industry

This section begins with the School's definition of the concept followed by a critical analysis of two aspects of the culture industry astrology and sport. Adorno and Horkheimer defined the concept as:

> *The industry appeals to, develops from and reinforces a state of dependence, anxiety and ego weakness. The message it conveys is most often one of adjustment and obedience. It impedes the development of autonomous, independent individuals who judge and decide consciously for themselves. Its essential content can be reduced to one axiom: since things cannot be other than they become that which thou art. Through displaced wish fulfillment, substitute gratification, the industry seeks to meet individual needs for diversion and distraction. It provides vitamin tablets for another working day. It provides ways to keep people going. It demands from its masses passivity, susceptibility and a sense of smugness about the individual, actual and potential achievements.*
>
> *Identification with dominant norms and values is inculcated. More importantly, its suppression of reason, sensuality and spontaneity promotes only pseudo-activity i.e. marginally differentiated types of social practice. The individual is tolerated only so long as his identification with the generality (social totality) is unquestioned. Above all the Culture Industry is anti-enlightenment.*[26]

The critical theorists seemed to be unified over certain fundamental issues as far as the notion of mass culture was concerned. Primarily, the nature and the mode of distribution of power in contemporary societies requires a general tendency to perpetuate and defend the status quo via economic, political and cultural control. Consequently, major sectors of artistic and

---

[26] Adorno & Horkheimer, *Dialectic of Enlightenment* (New York: The Seabury Press), 1972, p137

cultural activities are absorbed and transformed into destructive methods of consciousness control. Meanwhile art and culture become factories or industries. 'Artistic products are turned into a species of commodity ... marketable and interchangeable like an industrial product.' (*Dialectic of Enlightenment*: p.158)

Secondly, all members agreed that the pursuit of profit has been transferred onto cultural spheres. This process is highlighted by the increased interchangeability between different spheres of economic activities and the dependence of culture upon industrial and finance capital. The advertising agencies lay down new standards of cultural activities. Such pressures as big box office hits demand the production of attractive packages designed to sell directly for either want or need. Even where the culture industry does not directly produce for profit, its products are determined by such pressures and guidelines.

The term culture industry, however, was used rather ambiguously and unevenly in the *Dialectic of Enlightenment*. In 'Culture Industry Reconsidered' Adorno attempts to be more clear on the subject. Here, Adorno argues that the concept of culture industry should be used metaphorically as, generally speaking, cultural media does not resemble ordinary patterns of industrial output. Individual kinds of productions such as artistic creations and musical compositions are maintained. There are, of course, exceptions to this general pattern of which cinema is one example. 'The term industry replaced the notion of mass because we wished to exclude from the outset the interpretation agreeable to its advocates: i.e. it is a matter of something like a culture that arises spontaneously from the masses themselves.' [27]

Horkheimer also believed that the notion of mass culture tended to be misleading because 'culture today is not the product of genuine demands; rather it is the result of demands which are evoked and manipulated.'[28] Nonetheless, both Adorno and Horkheimer continued to use the term mass culture, but always

---

[27]See Adorno, 'Culture Industry Revisited', *New German Critique*, no.6, 1975, p.12 (Trans: Anson Rabinach)
[28]Horkheimer, 'Art and Mass Culture', *Studies in Philosophical and Social Science*, Vol. IX, no.2, 1941, pp302-3

with the connotation of culture industry. Culture industry, Adorno emphasized, does not and should not refer to production in itself, but rather to the standardization of cultural activities as well as to the rationalization of production, promotion and distribution techniques. 'The expression of industry is not to be taken literally. It refers to the standardization of the thing itself...and to the rationalization of distribution techniques, but not strictly to the production itself.'[29]

The prime target of culture industry is mass consumption, which ultimately has a great impact upon the determination of that consumption. The producer, just like the consumer, has no sovereignty because the culture industry is now well integrated into the mode of monopoly capital. Profitability and consumable outputs are culture industry's fundamental operational targets. Its survival depends upon its reproduction and it operates to ensure its sustainability. With the exception of the Nazis' use of the mass media, radio in particular, Adorno and Horkheimer pointed out that the ideological effects of the culture industry need not be the result of conscious manipulation, but that they are a result of the exchange of cultural artifacts through which fetishism is reinforced as ideology.[30]

Generally speaking, for most members of the School the cultural spheres of contemporary societies reflect the contradiction between the forces and relations of production. Under such conditions the culture industry is committed almost entirely to the development of cultural activities which are compatible with the preservation of the status quo. Thus, Adorno and Horkheimer argued, the effects of capitalist contradiction on consciousness can be controlled. What seemingly preoccupied Adorno and Horkheimer was to show how the outputs of the culture industry fall short of claims made on their behalf, even by the industry itself that is, culture industry leads to the prominence of the effect.

[29] Adorno, 'Culture Industry Revisited', *op.cit*, p.3
[30] D. Held, 'Introduction to Critical Theory, *op.cit*. Held is more elaborate than my analysis here

Thriving on techniques of mechanical reproduction and instrumental reason, the culture industry creates diversions, distractions and entertainment. Through the process of the institutionalization of needs and desires, culture is a mere symptom of such societal arrangements. The purposelessness of everyday life for many individuals requires a distraction and means of escape. In the age of mechanized labour processes people are not masters of their own destiny. Adorno, in an interesting analysis 'The Stars Down to Earth' , showed his conviction that capitalism creates conditions of dependence on the powerful, who can give or not give things popularly demanded.[31]

The culture industry creates dependency needs. In a society ridden with problems such as career prospects, crises and booms, earning anxieties and family problems one can take refuge, temporary as it may be, in the world of entertainment. It provides fun, relaxation and relief from the demands and the relentless efforts of daily life. This kind of cultural activity is provided without labour or concentration, both of which are crucial components of the autonomous culture. Mass media capitalizes and exploits those irrational susceptibilities and neurotic symptoms ever-present within most people. To seek a way out of these pressures through media is indeed paradoxical, as it is the media that reinforces those conditions of boredom:

> *The modern mass media tend particularly to fortify reaction formation i.e. utilizing the energy of a repressed wish to constitute a habit and/or set of attitudes in reaction against it and defense concomitant with actual social dependence.*[32]

The culture industry aims to provide entertainment and fun for the masses, whereas in actual fact this image is nothing but the portrayal of a reified world which is not only passive and

---

[31] *Los Angeles Times*. This article is also published in *Telos*, no19, Spring 1947. This article will be discussed elsewhere in this chapter
[32] *ibid*, p32

uncritical but tends to be merely reproductive of the established order. The culture industry stands for adjustments to existing social organisations. Through its entertainment business, the capacity for wage labour is perpetuated. The culture industry achieves its effects, Adorno argued, through targeting the attentive but passive, relaxed and uncritical reception which it induces through the production of patterned and predigested cultural entities.

Adorno and Horkheimer characterized these cultural entities in terms of their negation of style, for culture industry's style kills style. The artistic production is less and less divorced from reality.

It is what Marcuse called art's second alienation from alienation that is disappearing today. In the *Dialectic of Enlightenment* the industry's products are portrayed as having no content or style and they are essentially mimetic. The industry becomes an extension of the outside world. Dominant interpretations of reality are reproduced and reinforced by the industry's outputs. The scripts, the plots, the editorials, the characters and the endings tend to identify with the dominant social relations.

Structural similarities arise in cultural forms as a result of the technique of the industry, such as distribution and mechanical reproduction. Successful and popular works are imitated and reproduced to cash in on their appeal. However, the new releases must maintain some originality which may be defined as *pseudo – individualization:*

> Not only are the hit songs, stars, and soaps cyclically recurrent and rigid invariable types, but the specific content of the entertainment itself only appears to change. The details are interchangeable, actors become ready made clichés to be slotted in anywhere, doing nothing more than fulfilling the purpose allotted to them in the overall plan (Dialectic of Enlightenment: p.125).

Magazines usually present little real news content and certainly no intellectual surprises. Anything is suitable for popular consumption as long as it meets certain minimum requirements. Standardization, Adorno believes, aims at eliciting standard responses as cultural products, commodities, embodying a system of response mechanisms which tend to atomize reactions and weaken the forces of individual resistance.[33]

Models and frameworks of interpretation are offered by the culture industry which in turn eliminate any genuine attempt by the individuals to form an answer for themselves. The industry recognizes the fact that individuals have several layers of personality, so it too has a structure which is multi-layered. This is to engulf the consumer as completely as possible. Adorno attempts

to show this effect through several examples. In an attempt to analyse a comedy show Adorno says 'the script is a shrewd method of promoting adjustment to humiliating conditions by presenting them as objectively comical and by giving a picture of a person who experiences even her own inadequate position as an object of fun apparently free of any resentment.'[34]

With greater detail and clarity, Adorno attempts to show the response formation and presuppositions of culture industry by concentrating on 'astrology' in mass media. Conventional astrology is, for Adorno, institutionalized superstition, an utterly ridiculous strategy to ease the pressures of daily life by promising better things in the future. In a study over three months, Adorno comes to the conclusion that although fate is projected by the industry to be set by the stars, a pragmatic and conformist attitude to everyday living is recommended by astrologers, for it can ensure satisfaction and the prospect of high rewards. The fictitious reasonableness of the advice offered by the astrologer masks the arbitrary and entirely opaque nature of their words. Your survival and happiness according to astrologers, depends on coming to terms with your inner and outer life. They recommend accepting all that is thrown at you,

---

[33] Adorno, 'On Popular Music', *Studies in Philosophical and Social Science*, Vol. IX, 1941, p.22
[34] See Adorno, 'Television and the Patterns of Mass Culture', in: B. Rosenberg & D. White (eds), *Mass Culture* (Ill: Free Press), 1957, pp 480-1

such as your family situation, your job and your social hierarchy. To be rational is to adjust your needs and wants to a given set of social arrangements. Astrology, Adorno believed, apparently emphasizes individualism and independent thinking, while simultaneously strengthening and reinforcing dependencies, adjustments to the status quo and the work ethic.[35]

Like other products of mass culture, sport and astrology offer an instant short cut both to an understanding of the social order and to a fictitious escape into a supposedly different world, which in actual fact is nothing but a reified social world. Sport, for Adorno, occupied a more important position in the development of mass culture because: 'if one were to summarize the most important trends of present-day culture, one could hardly find a more pregnant category than that of sports.'[36]

Adorno analyzed sport as an institution of social domination and yet another element, as part of cultural formation, for the apparent failure of the working class to fulfill their revolutionary destiny. For Adorno, sports was an integral aspect of social domination. This process is achieved because: 'sports serves the purpose of habituating people to the demands of material life by translating the physical discomfort of the few into the secondary pleasure of the many ... nobody takes notice of the fact that praxis is being smuggled in with sport.'[37]

Here Adorno simply implies that sport functions as an after-image of work and incorporates most of the basic elements of the modern capitalist mode of production. The institution of sport is therefore regarded as the embodiment of the rationality, norms and values of work. Hence, Adorno rejects the notion that sport provides a form of escapism from social reality arguing that it is only a dreary imitation of it. In this sense sport is seen as utterly connected to a capitalist ethos combining 'aggressiveness with an authoritarian disposition.' Adorno goes on to stress that 'sport ... in a more explicit political vein serves as a model for totalitarian

---

[35]See Adorno, 'The Stars Down to Earth', pp. 41-7
[36]See Adorno, *Prisms*, Trans: S. Weber (Cambridge, Mass: MIT Press), 1981, p.56
[37]See Adorno, *Aesthetic Theory*, Trans: Len Hardt, (London: Routledge & Keegan), 1984, p439

mass rallies.'[38]

The formal rationality which operates behind the facade of sport separates it from the realm of emancipation. It is regressed to the status of a *pseudo-activity* stripped of any significant meaning. Just as there is no fulfillment in work, no serious reflection is allowed in what comes after, leisure and sport. Consequently sport, for Adorno, becomes 'the apparent antithesis of serious activity, it both exemplifies infantility and legitimates, through the sheer force of its own conspicuous example, the pursuit of mindless activity for its own sake'. It is this very example which accounts for the spread of its vacuous mentality into such spheres as art and politics, a development that Adorno calls 'the sportification of politics.'[39]

It is not surprising, therefore, that Adorno links the institution of sport to the corruptive phenomenon of mass culture and instrumental reason. 'The mass collectivization of its [sport]life is to get in training for it by using the hours apparently left to freedom to coach oneself as a member of the mass.'[40]

Yet despite his sharp critical analysis of the institution and function of sport, Adorno insists that sport may acquire a critical capacity in social life. There is, Adorno points out, a double-consciousness apparent in sport and leisure in which the standardized output of the culture industry is combined with a visible 'doubt about its blessings':

> *People certainly consume and accept what the culture industry presents them in their leisure. But with some reservation they indeed don't take as real... Obviously, the integration of consciousness and leisure has still not completely succeeded. The real interests of the individuals are still strong enough in limits to withstand total integration.*[41]

---

[38]Quoted by W. Morgan, Adorno on Sport: The Case of Fractured Dialectic', *Theory and Society*, 17, 1988, p. 818
[39]W. Morgan, *op.cit*, p.819
[40]See Adorno, 'Minima Moralia', *op.cit*, 1974, p.139
[41]Adorno, 'Freizeit', in: *Stichwort: Kritische Modelle*, 2, p.655

The element which sharpens the critical capacity in sport is its playful dimension and its ability to intermingle illusion with the sense of 'not being real.' What normally follows in sporting situations is the underlying notion that 'its only a game' which reminds partakers that there is more here than meets the eye. The essential problem with Adorno's analysis of sport is related to his theory of society as a whole. For Adorno, society reproduces itself with ideologies whose basic principles are indistinguishable from the social reality they portray. Because these ideologies merely duplicate existing reality they cannot be divorced from a critical theory of society. Therefore, critical principles themselves are ideologically deformed.

The next section briefly expands upon the connection between mass culture and ideology as analyzed by the critical theorists.

Mass Culture and Ideology

In their analysis of mass culture, the Frankfurt School saw the transition from autonomous cultural forms to standardized/pseudo-individualized ones as simultaneously marking a transformation in the nature of ideology.

The critique of ideology is possible only in so far as ideology contains a rational element with which the critique can deal. Capitalism can be claimed as just, but when people are nothing but objects of calculation, consumers and dominated by the culture industry, ideology represents nothing other than manipulative contrivance.[42]

For the School these are the typical conditions when we deal with television, film, radio or mass media:

> *The socially conditioned false consciousness of today is no longer objective spirit; it is not crystallized blindly and anonymously out of the social process, but rather is tailored scientifically to fit the society.*[43]

---
[42] See Frankfurt Institute: 'Ideology', in *Aspects of Sociology* (London: Heinemann),. 1973, p.190
[43] *ibid*, p.200- amended translation

Ideology is therefore no longer seen as just a socially necessary illusion, but rather it is in the process of becoming a planned construct which reproduces and consolidates the dominant order. Before embarking upon the critique of the Frankfurt School's cultural analyses, it is appropriate to sum up the previous sections.

This chapter, thus far, aimed to demonstrate the pattern of cultural development as viewed by the members of the School, mostly concentrating on Adorno's work, because his analyses in this area are detailed and highly focused. Also, an attempt was made to illustrate the School's primary preoccupation with production and consumption of cultural forms. This portrayal may seem negative and pessimistic. However, these are the essential characteristics of the Critical Theory. Despite the negative assessment of many aspects of mass culture, Adorno did not completely reject the validity of new techniques of production and reproduction. Furthermore in the late 1960s Adorno added significant reservations to any thesis that maintained the total commercialization and reification of culture:

Society remains class struggle, today as in the period when that concept originated. The fundamental contradictions of society remain undiminished and as a necessary result, consciousness is not, nor can it be, totally integrated. (Adorno: *Freizeit*, p.65)

Having discussed the underlying issues inherent in the theory of culture industry the remainder of this chapter will focus on some very specific notions involved within the culture industry debate.

The Material Basis of Culture Industry

Apart from Freud's theory of instincts, Marx's critique of political economy of capitalism provided Adorno with the basic theoretical paradigm. Marx's analysis of the capitalist modes and relations of production, his theory of class relations and alienation enabled Adorno to go beyond the 'extra-psychic' connection between the individual and society.

Despite his belief that capitalism had arrived at a new phase, for Adorno the 'totally administered society' retained some of its fundamental features. Within the larger socio-economic context individual psyche had been weakened by reification and the loss of economic autonomy and the culture industry is nurtured by the profit making nature of the modern system. In this respect both culture industry and individual psychology have become social facts. The culture industry continues to mass produce standardized materials for distribution and exchange on the market. With the penetration of the exchange principle into the new areas of life, the production of culture for commodified consumption, argued Adorno, prevents people of knowing themselves as 'subjects.'

In an attempt to extend Marx's analysis of class society, Adorno argues that a different form of socio-economic division has emerged. A new ruling group or elite, combining the interests of industrial and business monopolies with those of the state, emerged over and against the mass of individuals which now includes both the bourgeoisie and the proletariat. In this new social order domination manifests itself in a more polarized dichotomy. The new state of affairs 'vindicates the theory of class struggle with monopolization and centralization, directly placing in complete opposition to each other the most extreme power against the most extreme powerlessness.'[44]

However, Adorno differs from Marx by locating his analysis of domination within a new format. What has changed in the late capitalist societies is that those who are exploited are no longer able to consider themselves as a class. This is due to the immense growth of monopoly capital which now appears as an institution which engulfs individuals. The resulting reification enhances the problem of class relations. Furthermore, Adorno argues, it is no longer possible to distinguish between the classes. The ruling class has 'disappeared behind the concentration of capital', and given the merger between the proletariat and bourgeoisie and

---

[44] Adorno, 'Reflexionen zur Klassentheroie', *Sociologiche Schriften I* (Frankfurt: Suhrkamp), 1972, pp.373-91. Translated by D. Cook

more generalized lack of class consciousness, those who benefit most from the new order are left to pursue their interest.[45]

Adorno's analysis of class complements that of Marx. Mass society for Adorno was the latest manifestation, and a historical outgrowth, of class society, and as the old classes merge into one another the new mass class face a new political elite which 'oppresses those who support it and the worker with the same police threat, imposes on them the same function and the same need.' This merger between the classes into a 'mass' is by no means to imply that a new homogeneous group has been formed.

It is still possible to speak of classes because of the persistence of economic exploitation 'screened from objectivity, the difference between the classes grows objectively with the increasing concentration of capital'.[46]

The new mass are now confronting anonymous political and economic power, living in a society where exploitation and domination is exercised by an abstract political and economic power whose hold on society is more powerful than they possessed in Marx's time.

Adorno has been accused, by an American commentator, Helmut Dubiel, of excessively relying upon the 'super structural' realm and not sharing Marx's views on the primacy of economic spheres. There is no doubt that this aspect of Adorno's theory is underdeveloped, but there is evidence that Adorno was very much aware of the importance of economic factors. As early as 1951, Adorno argued in '*Minima Moralia*' that the primacy of the economy in decision-making could be demonstrated everywhere' (*Minima Moralia*: pp.112-13) In his last essay, Late Capitalism or Industrial Society, Adorno writes:

> *The dynamics of the system as a whole reveal that the control of economic processes is increasingly becoming a function of political power...There are compelling facts which cannot, in their turn, be adequately interpreted*

---

[45] Adorno, 'Reflexionen zur Klassentheroie', pp.377-380
[46] See Adorno, *Society*, Translated by F. Jameson, Salmagundi, Ill, no.10-11 (1969-70), p.150

without invoking the key concept of capitalism. Human beings are as much as ever, ruled and dominated by the economic process.[47]

In borrowing Marx's concepts of use and exchange value, Adorno was able to provide a new account of modern culture dominated by the exchange principle. In fact Adorno is amongst the first thinkers who attempted to provide a critique of the commodity character of the culture industry's outputs. The products, Adorno argued, obey the laws of exchange. Therefore, its cultural outputs increasingly play an important role within the general scheme of the capitalist economic system. Modern cultural products show their utility primarily as exchange value:

Pure use-value, whose illusion the cultural goods must preserve in completely capitalist society, must be replaced by pure exchange-value, which precisely in its capacity as exchange-value deceptively takes over the function of use-value.[48]

Cultural commodities such as media outputs, therefore, have acquired a fetish character and virtually become illusory in appearance. In the *Dialectic of Enlightenment* Adorno and Horkheimer argue:

What might be called use value in the reception of cultural commodities is replaced by exchange value; in place of enjoyment, there are gallery visiting and factual knowledge; the prestige seeker replaces the connoisseur. The consumer becomes the ideology of pleasure industry, whose institution he cannot escape... Everything is looked at from only one aspect: that it can be used for something else, however vague the notion of this use may be. No

---

[47] Adorno, 'Late Capitalism or Industrial Society', in V. Meja, N. Stehr (ed), *Modern German Sociology* (New York: Columbia University Press), 1987, p.237
[48] Adorno, 'On the Fetish Character in Music and the Regression of Listening', Trans: M. Goldbloom, in Areto and Gebhardt (eds), *The Essential Frankfurt Reader* (NY: Urizen Books), 1978, p.279

object has an inherent value; it is valuable only to the extent that it can be exchanged. (p. 158)

In his attempt to apply Marx's concepts of use-value to cultural commodities Adorno seems to have overlooked a major problem:

The major problem stems ultimately from the lack of intrinsic connection between the usefulness to the consumer of a particular type of cultural artifacts, and the physical form of commodity under which it is sold.[49]

Some recent studies on the reception of cultural commodities have confirmed that although exchange-value of cultural commodities has undermined their use-value, yet, such commodities do retain a use-value. John Fiske and Bill Ryan, amongst others, attempt to show that the use-value of cultural outputs may take as many forms as there are individuals who are exposed to them.[50]

However, an analysis of the nature, and the character, of the commodified culture is a highly complex debate which reveals the essential feature and the problems of modern capitalism. Adorno's proposals in the field of cultural commodities deserves a more systematic theoretical and empirical attention. Particularly since the products of the culture industry can be reproduced or used repeatedly, by many different individuals, their use-value may be different in each instance.

Despite the Frankfurt School's minimal contribution to the debate on the economic base of the culture industry in monopoly capital Adorno has been influential in some of the contemporary studies of the political economy of the mass media. Even if only implicitly, Adorno remains a pioneer in identifying the more important economically motivated tendencies and traits of both the culture industry and its outputs.

[49]See T. Lovell, *Pictures of Reality: Aesthetics, Politics, Pleasure* (London: BFI), 1980, p.18
[50]See B. Ryan, *Making Capital from Culture: The Corporate Form of Cpitalist Cultural Production* (NY: W. de Gruyter), 1991. And also J. Fisk, *Understanding Popular Culture* (NY: Unwin Hyman),1989

Most contemporary commentators in the field of media, culture and society have found some aspects of Adorno's theory useful (Abercrombie and Longhurst: 1998, pp. 19-20).

With regard to American dominance of the international communications and cultural markets, Herbert Schiller insists that this was now better understood as 'transnational corporate cultural domination', with more players from Europe and Asia, although the USA was by far still the leader.[51]

Although Armand and Michele Mattelart acknowledge that the new research trends in media studies, such as ethnography, represent a 'greater open-mindedness' in comparison to past paradigms, they warn that 'this new epistemological approach can be led astray into a new ideology of assent.' On this issue the Mattelarts are very close to Schiller's position that these new paradigms come dangerously close to serving the established order:

> *This rising wave that at present is carrying forward certain conceptions of ordinary pleasure is far from being an innocent, unpolitical development. For, beyond the theme of pleasure itself, what should be observed is its function in the mode of legitimating of a system of communication.*[52]

Graham Murdock and Peter Golding, have shown that the concentrated ownership and the dependence of the culture industries on other economic sectors is established 'primarily through reciprocal investments and shareholdings and interlocking directorship, and also through advertising.'[53]

Murdock and Golding, however, are critical of Adorno's inability to demonstrate how the American culture industry actually works. What is needed for them is a concrete and Marxian analysis of material production.

---

[51]See H. Schiller, 'Not Yet the Post-Imperialist Era', pp.97-116 in C. Roach (ed), *Communication and Culture in War and Peace* (Newbury Park, CA), 1993
[52]Mattelart & Mattelart, *Rethinking Media Theory*(Minneapolis: University of Minnesota Press) 1992, p.106
[53]See Murdoch and Golding, 'For a Political Economy of Mass Communication', *Socialist Register*, 1973, Miliband and Saville (eds), (London: Merlin Press), 1974

Nicholas Garnham goes one step further by attempting to construct a political economy of mass communication with reference to the works of Adorno. Garnham, despite acknowledging the importance of the Frankfurt School's account of the economic base, is critical of their '...failure to insufficiently take into account the economically contradictory nature of the process they observed and thus to see the industrialization of culture as unproblematic and irresistible.'[54]

In the American context, Bill Ryan attempts to provide empirical confirmation for Adorno's view on the 'standardization' process in culture industry. In order to encourage the creation of 'original' products, the owners of the means of cultural production grant a certain degree of autonomy to those involved in the process. Nonetheless, despite the relative autonomy of the production team there is a tendency towards formula and cliche in creation and it flows from the formatting of the creative stage of production. By formatting the process of production, Ryan argues, a further step has been taken to control production in some sectors of the industry.[55]

Before going into more detail on the major aspects of the culture industry thesis, this section concludes by arguing that although Adorno was aware of the material basis of the production of the commodified culture, his treatment of the political economy of the culture industry is fragmentary, cursory and underdeveloped. A number of contemporary commentators have attempted to take up where Adorno left off. Some of these studies have been mentioned above. However, this chapter will further assess upon the areas of culture industry theory where Adorno outlined the crucial points of his theoretical approach.

The Characteristic Features of the Culture Industry

The section above argued that despite Adorno's occasional

---

[54] N. Garnham, 'Contribution to a Political Economy of Mass Communication', *Media, Culture and Society*, I, 1971, pp 123-46
[55] B. Ryan, *Op.cit*, p.146

reference to the political economy of the commodified cultural output, a more in-depth analysis of the reproductive techniques used in these production, marketing and advertising was never fully developed. This section, however, aims to explore those areas of the culture industry thesis which received a more systematic attention by Adorno.

In his lengthy discussion of the commodified culture, Adorno concentrated on four distinctive, and dominant, features of the culture industry. These are *'standardization'*, *'pseudo-individualism'*, *'schematization'* and *'stereotypes'*. These concepts enabled Adorno to argue that the culture industry's reified products reflect the more widespread damage that modern capitalism inflicts upon individuals. These aspects of the culture industry aim to conceal whatever conflicts may still exist between particular individuals and the general socio-economic order.

In the following section each one of these features of the culture industry will be explored in detail in order to assess the continued relevance of the 'basic assumptions' of the culture industry theory.

Standardization

All industrial mass production necessarily eventuates in standardization... Under centralized conditions such as exist today [these] standards have become frozen .... and they are rigidly enforced upon material to be promoted....[56]

Adorno's concept of 'standardization' of cultural commodities is an intricate discussion of three essential points. The 'sameness of cultural outputs, the economic of market concentration and regressive reception.' (*Dialectic of Enlightenment*: p. 134)

When Adorno, in the passage above, refers to 'these standards' he aims to refer to a particular section of production. The process of standardization occurs, partly because of the 'imitation' and not the mass production techniques. As different

[56] Adorno, 'On Popular Music', *Op.cit*

corporations compete in the same cultural sphere, they begin to imitate those products proven to be successful. This results in a gradual 'freeze' in standards. Adorno correctly points out that it is industrial mass production and reproduction which is ultimately responsible for the standardization of the cultural output.

Secondly, the increasing standardization of cultural products is related to the growing concentration in ownership of the means of cultural production, claiming that 'the economics of market concentration' accounts for standardization:

Films, radio and magazines make up a system which is uniform as a whole and in every part; Under monopoly capitalism all mass culture is identical .... the achievement of standardization and mass production...[57]

Thirdly, the regressive tendencies in the reception of cultural artifacts is another contributing factor in the process of standardization. Although most of Adorno's analysis in the regressive tendencies of the consumers is related to music, yet there are some remarks which may be applicable to other sections of the culture industry. For Adorno modern consumers, due to the monotonous nature of their jobs, demand products which are 'familiar' to them and are made easier for consumption. These demands are indicative of 'deconcentration of perception.'

The mass demand for 'familiarity' of the cultural products is part of psychological dispositions which encourages their standardization and themselves are a result of a socialization process which tends to erode consumers' autonomy, spontaneity and individuality. The standardization of cultural commodities, therefore, serves the ideals of the capital, in its most concentrated form, and the owners of the cultural means of production. Related to the standardization process is the second dominant feature of the 'culture industry', the concept of pseudo-individuality.

[57]*Dialectic of Enlightenment*, quoted by B. Ryan, *Op.cit*

Pseudo-Individuality

The consumer is unwilling to recognize that he is totally dependent, and he likes to preserve the illusion of private initiative and free choice. Thus standardization... produces the veil of pseudo-individualism.[58]

In this passage Adorno aims to argue that the commercial success of cultural products would be seriously undermined if they are identical to each other. Pseudo-individuality functions in a complementary manner with the standardization process. It creates an illusion that there are real differences between the culture industry's products. This complementary relationship ensures the commercial success of the industry's ultimately imitated materials. Pseudo-individualism allows the consumer to believe that there is a choice, that an editorial, a song, a show or a movie is fundamentally different from the previous ones. It functions like a 'handle' enabling the consumer to remember each product as something unique and different. Pseudo-individuality, however, veils the fact that these materials are virtually the same in most respects. The illusion of originality or novelty is created by using different labels or by promoting superficial differences between them.

What is really new in the products of the culture industry is the managerial directives which very broadly sets the boundaries of the style and the appearance of the product. The choice of a style is very much influenced by the success of other products in the same area of cultural activity.

Adorno, in *Culture Industry Reconsidered*, summarizes the result of the industry's standardization and pseudo-individualization: 'A mixture of streamlining, photographic hardness and precision on the one hand, and individualistic residues, sentimentality and an already disposed romanticism on the other' (p.15).

Adorno has been criticized substantially on the issue of pseudo-individuality. Commentators such as Bernard Gendron

---

[58] Adorno, 'A Social Critique of Radio Music', *Kenyon Review*, Vol II, no2, 1945, p.216

and Salvador Giner accuse Adorno of essentialism and elitism for his adoration for certain traditions in culture.[59]

Although there is no objection in regarding Adorno as essentialist nevertheless, the popular criticism of Adorno as an 'elitist' is unfounded. For Adorno pseudo-culture became the historical successor to what was once 'high' culture. It is 'spirit overcome by fetishism of commodities.'

No one and nothing are immune from commodity fetishism. The commodification and reification of culture has affected even those who belonged to the privileged few: 'Anyone – and by this one always means oneself- might be exempt from the tendency to socialized pseudo-culture is a conceited illusion.'[60]

Closely related to the notions of pseudo-culture and individuality is the concept of 'schematization' of commodified culture.

Schematization

The culture industry's prime service to the consumer is to do his schematizing for him (Dialectic of Enlightenment, p.124)

The concept of 'schematization', originally a Kantian term, was used by Adorno and Horkheimer to argue that the commodified cultural goods undermine the recipients' need to think for themselves. In Adorno's usage of the term it refers to the culture industry's own patterning or pre-forming of the audience's experience. It also refers to what Adorno and Horkheimer call the 'collapse of distinctions between culture and practical life.' They attempted to locate the origins of schematization in advertising, financial markets and, in particular, sporting events. Using the latest advertising techniques, the cultural commodities

---

[59]See B. Gendron, 'Adorno Meets the Cadillacs', in T. Modleski (ed), *Studies in Entertainmnet: Critical Approaches to Mass Culture* (Indianapolis: Indiana University Press), 1986. Also see: S.Giner, *Mass Society* (London: Martin Robertson), 1976
[60]Adorno, 'Theory of Pseudo-Culture', *Telos*, 95, Spring 1993, p.37, Translated by D. Cook

acquire their 'poetic mystery' by taking part 'in the finite nature of production and the reverential awe inspired by objectivity fits smoothly with the schema of advertising.'[61]

Unlike their lack of systematic analysis of advertising and financial markets, Adorno and Horkheimer were more attentive to the institution of sport. 'The sporting events from which the schema of mass culture borrows so many of its features and which represent one its favorite themes have divested themselves of all meaning.'[62]

Just as in sporting events the consumers of the culture industry are encouraged to compete whether by virtue of the way in which goods are offered or through the techniques of advertising.

The main impact of schematization on the audience is to condition or encourage them to understand their own experiences unreflectively in a way similar to that found in the pages of newspapers and television shows. This impact is compounded by the pseudo-realism presented by television patterns since they reproduce life in such realistic detail. Adorno discussed the impact of schema of the cultural commodities upon the recipients in relation to the stereotypes, the fourth feature of the culture industry.

Stereotypes

In spite of all the progress in reproduction techniques, in controls and the specialties, and in spite of all the restless industry, the bread which the culture industry offers man is the stone of the stereotype. (Dialectic of Enlightenment, p.148) "Stereotypes found in products of culture industry ... are cunningly calculated psychological models ... which ... aim to pattern people after mass production"[63]

---

[61] Adorno & Horkheimer, 'The Schema of Mass Culture', in J.M. Bernstein (ed), *The Culture Industry: Selected Essays on Mass Culture* (London: Routledge), 1991
[62] Schema of Mass Culture', *ibid*, p.77
[63] Adorno, 'Prolog Zum Fernsehen', Translated by D.Cook, *Gesammelte Schriften*, 102, (Frankfurt: Suhrkamp), 1977, pp 507-17

In these passages Adorno attempts to expand his analysis of the impact of stereotype upon the recipients. Like schema, stereotypes promotes conformity to prevailing behavioral norms, they facilitate standardized reaction ensuring that recipients do not exceed the limits of what is socially acceptable: 'The repetitiveness, the self-sameness, the ubiquity of mass culture tend to make for atomized reactions and to weaken the forces of individual opposition.'[64]

For Adorno, the culture industry turns stereotypes into rigid and reified clichés and justifies this by its claim for the necessity of 'having to produce an enormous amount of material in the shortest amount of time.'

The utilization of stereotype by the culture industry allows the consumers to feel that they are experts or active participants. This point is aptly explained by Miriam Hansen. 'Identification with the stereotype is advanced by the appeal to a particular type of knowledge or skill predicated on repetition: the identification of a familiar face, gesture or narrative convention takes the place of genuine cognition.'[65]

Adorno, in one of his numerous content analyses of different products of the culture industry, argued that a particular example of stereotype is that of the intellectual as 'an abnormal, and somewhat ridiculous weakling or emotional cripple who does not know how to live. Stereotypes like this curry favour with the international climate of anti-intellectualism.'[66]

Stereotypes and schemata are, therefore, employed by the culture industry to reinforce a largely narcissistic behaviour. Pseudo-individualism attempts to hide the repetitive sameness of stereotypes and schemata as well as the standardization of cultural materials. In addition to allowing the consumers to derive a narcissistic gain from successful recognition of constantly repeated stereotypes, the culture industry may also function as a reinforcement of narcissistic tendencies through

---

[64] Adorno, 'How to Look at Television', in J.M. Bernstein, *The Culture Industry, Op.cit*
[65] H. Hansen, 'Mass Culture as Hieroglyphic Writing: Adorno, Derida and Kracauer', *New German Critique*, 56, Spring-Summer 1992, p.51
[66] Adorno, 'Television as Ideology', *Op.cit.*, p.524

'flattery and making those who belong to the in-group as feeling better, higher and purer than others.'[67]

In short, Adorno analyzed the reified products of the culture industry in the light of four dominant features. In responding to the growing demands of the market, pseudo-individualism mask the increasing standardization of cultural outputs which are accompanied by stereotypes and schematization. Ruled by the exchange value, these outputs can only provide the consumers with regressive perception and social prestige. The culture industry, therefore, always offers the same thoroughly planned, predictable and calculable commodities. With the aid of these concepts Adorno was then able to produce some significant analysis of the use-value of the cultural outputs and the consumers' desire to have them.

Despite the apparent validity of Adorno's analysis, he failed to expand on the important processes involved in the production of cultural commodities.

Garnham is critical of Adorno's failure to see the conflict-ridden nature of the commodification of culture.[68]

In order to finance production costs and increase profit margins, producers use their cultural outputs to capture a stable audience with the highest possible income level which they can then sell to the advertisers. A detailed account of this aspect of cultural commodities, in which they indirectly promote industrial outputs, was not produced by Adorno. Indeed, if distribution and circulation of the cultural products are of crucial importance to the industry's profit, Garnham is critical of Adorno for insufficiently accounting these aspects of his theory.

Furthermore, as shown by Andreas Huyssen, Adorno may have overestimated the limits of reification in the culture industry's products. Even though Adorno recognizes quite frequently that there are limits to the reification of the human subject, he never asks himself whether perhaps there are also

---

[67] Adorno, 'Freudian Theory and the Pattern of Fascist Propaganda', in Arato and Gebhardt (eds): *The Essential Frankfurt School Reader, Op.cit.* pp 118-37
[68] N. Granham, 'Contribution to a Political Economy of Mass Communication', *Op.cit*

limits to the reification of cultural commodities themselves.[69]

Having briefly discussed the main components of the culture industry thesis, the next section will discuss these components in relation to the crucial notion of domination in modern western societies.

The Nature of Domination in Modern Societies

Whenever Adorno's version of the nature of domination in modern advanced societies is discussed, he is mistakenly portrayed as defending a model of domination from 'above.' This section argues that not only did Adorno recognize that domination in modern advanced societies has limits, but also that the culture industry is at its most effective when the consumers are not entirely duped by them. Although there are problems with Adorno's audience analysis, the charge of the 'passive dopes' is an important misinterpretation of Adorno's ideas.[70]

Before trying to defend Adorno, a few words must be said on the notions of 'active audience and resistance' and the authors most clearly associated with these approaches. The most prominent authors associated with the theory of 'active audience' are John Fiske (1986 and 1987) and Larry Grossberg (1984) whose ideas coincided with the increasing validation of cultural studies in the USA.[71]

---

[69]See A. Huyssen, *After the Great Divide: Modernism, Mass Culure, Postmodernism* (Indianapolis: Indiana University Press), 1986, p.24
[70]Adorno, as exemplified in his 'Theses Against Occultism', firmly believed in the influence of 'identity thinking' in the study of culture, a psychodynamic model of 'rhetoric' in which the persuasive force of language lies in its capacity to resonate with the psychological needs of audience. S. Crook develops this analysis further in his introduction to Adorno's 'The Stars Down to Earth'
[71]See: J. Fiske, 'Television: Polysemy and Popularity', *Critical Studies in Mass Communication*, 3 (4), 1986, pp391-408

    J. Fisk,: *Television Culture* (New York: Methuen), 1987
    J. Fiske, *Reading the Popular* (Boston: Unwin Hyman), 1989
    J. Fiske, *Media Matters: Everyday Culture and Political Change* (University of Minnesota Press), 1994
    L.Grossberg, 'Strategies of Marxist Cultural Interpretation', *Critical Studies in Mass Communication*, I, 1984, pp 392-421

In Britain, Willis's work on youth culture (1990) and Buckingham's study of *East Enders*, (1987) can be seen as examples of 'active audience' perspective.[72]

The idea of audience resisting media messages, and the related notion of 'oppositional meanings', has generated a heated discussion between political economy and cultural studies.[73] The idea of 'active audience' is used in the literature to oppose the idea of dominant ideology. Although Fiske in his work (1987) frequently uses the notion of dominant ideology, one understands that individuals who form the audiences are free and able to construct their own meanings from media messages independent of structural influences such as ownership and production patterns. According to this idea there is no longer any one grand, totalizing interpretation of media messages. According to Fiske the notion of resistance is built upon a reading of Gramsci's theory of hegemony. 'Hegemony characterizes social relations as a series of struggle for power. Cultural studies views texts similarly, as the site of a series of struggles for meaning. The dominant ideology, working through the form of text, can be resisted, evaded, or negotiated with, in varying degrees, by differently situated readers.'[74]

The 'active audience' theory has been criticized by many contemporary authors such as Schiller (1993), David Tetzlaff (1991), and Gary Gerbner (1991). Schiller writes:

> *There is much to be said for the idea that people do not mindlessly absorb everything that passes before their eyes. Yet much of the current work on audience reception*

---

[72]See P. Willis, *Common Culture* (OU: Milton Keynes), 1990

D. Buckingham, *Public Secrets: East Enders and its Audience* (London: BFI), 1987

For an excellent review of a variety of recent works in this area, and an alternative analysis, see N. Abercrombie and B. Longhurst, *Audiences* (London: Thousand Oaks), 1988, chp1

[73]See: D. Tetzlaff, 'Divide and Conquer: Popular Culture and Social Control in Late Capitalism', *Media, Culture and Society*, 13 (1), 1991, pp 9-34

W.R Seaman, 'Active Audience Theory: Pointless Populism', *Media, Culture and Society*, 14 (2), 1992, pp 301-11

[74]See J. Fiske, *Television Culture*, p.41

comes uncomfortably close to being apologetic for present day structures of cultural control.[75]

Gerbner, while emphasizing the question of 'public policy', argues:

...the research on resisting audiences' creating their own meanings is meaningless for public policy issues, since this trend does not take into account the commonalities television cultivates... These commonalities are decisive in matters of public policies.[76]

Abercrombie and Longhurst (1998), however, by using the example of contemporary football fans, argue the case for a paradigmatic shift in audience analysis:

This example [football fans] is suggestive of the new complex patterns of interaction which characterize the contemporary audience. Our argument ... has been that this complexity cannot fully be understood from within the BP (Behavioral Paradigm) of the IRP (Incorporation / Resistance Paradigm). The emergent paradigm which we have labeled the 'Spectacle Performance' is more able so to do... This is necessitated by the emergence of the 'diffused audience'. Audience experience can no longer be simply classified as 'simple' or 'mass', for in modern societies, people are members of an audience all the time. Being a member of an audience is constitutive of everyday life. That this is the case is attributable to the fact that our relationship with events and objects in the social world has changed. If the world is increasingly conceived as a spectacle, then so are the people within it, and we become simultaneously performers and audience... This [argument] recognizes much more explicitly the 'media

---
[75] *Op.cit*, p.113
[76] G. Gerbner, *Journey into Media Violence: A Happy Land of Power, Politics and Publicity and Maybe Profits,* mimeograph, 1991, p.8

saturation' of everyday life and the consequent significance of performance, spectacle, narcissisme and imagination. (Audiences: 1998, pp 178- 9, back page*)*

Having briefly discussed the complex debate on the topic of 'audiences', the following section will attempt to defend Adorno from being seen as advocating a 'passive' position for the recipients of media messages.

Firstly, a careful reading of *'The Stars Down to Earth'* suggests that Adorno clearly demonstrates his willingness and expectation for the 'active' participation of the readers of Righter's column, relating its content to their lives or circumstances.

Secondly, Adorno viewed individuals in modern societies as 'deceiving themselves' about the established social order and the culture industry which reproduces and reinforces that order. Adorno explains this notion with an empirical analysis:

A few years ago at the Frankfurt Institute for Social Research we conducted a study ... concerned with the wedding of Princess Beatrix of Holland with the junior German diplomat Claus von Amsberg. The objective was to assess the reactions of the public to the wedding, which was broadcast by all the mass media, dwelt on incessantly by the illustrated weeklies, and so consumed by the public in their free time. Since the way in which the event was presented, like the articles written about it, accorded it an unusual degree of importance, we expected the spectators and readers to treat it just as seriously. In particular we expected to observe the operation of the characteristic contemporary ideology of personalization... The study showed that it was possible to detect symptoms of a split consciousness. On the one hand people enjoyed it as a concrete event in the here and now quite unlike anything else in their everyday life: it was to be a 'unique experience.' To this extent the reaction of audience corresponded to the familiar pattern, according to which even the relevant, possibly political news was transformed into a consumer item by the way in which the information was transmitted. The format of our interview, however, was devised in such a way that the questions concerned with determining the immediate reactions of the viewers, were supplemented by control questions about the political significance that the interviewees ascribed to the grand event. Here it turned out that many of the people interviewed ... suddenly showed themselves to be thoroughly realistic, and proceeded to evaluate critically the political and social importance of the same event, the well publicized once-in-a-lifetime nature of which they had drooled over breathlessly in front of their television sets. (Adorno: 'Free Time', in Bernstein's *The Culture Industry, pp 169-70)*

This deception, however, is not a permanent feature and can be made conscious. The essence of Adorno's assertion here is that since ideology fostered by the culture industry has become threadbare, only a 'thin veil' prevents the individual from recognizing how superficial this ideology has become.

Furthermore, individuals in late capitalist societies were seen by Adorno as the beneficiaries of the Enlightenment. If education were to succeed in exposing the truth about cultural commodities, consumers would be able to see how the culture industry perpetuates conformity to the established order.

In Adorno's work there is a dialectically entwined depiction of domination and resistance. However, in most of his writings Adorno certainly appeared to be far more interested in assessing the nature of domination than assessing the potential for resistance to it. 'The culture industry smirks: becomes what you are, and its lie consists in just this repetitive confirmation and reinforcement of the pure essence of that into which the course of the world has changed people.'[77]

In this passage Adorno aims to show the detailed psychological techniques used by the culture industry in making it difficult for the consumers to transcend the social totality. The

---

[77] Adorno, 'Prolog Zum Fernsehen', *Op cit.* p.514

products of the culture industry, with their relentless reproduction of real, ideologically claim that the way things are is the way they should be. Essentially, therefore, the culture industry 'turn facts into values.'

One of the most common techniques used by the culture industry can be found in its widespread use of stereotypes and schemata. Stereotypical images and schematized themes prevent consumers from thinking beyond the given. They fix and rigidify experience, hence, 'people may not only lose true insight into reality, but ultimately their very capacity for life experience may be dulled by the constant wearing of blue and pink spectacles.'[78]

For Adorno, the culture industry 'assiduously concerns itself with the production of those archetypes in whose survival fascistic psychology perceives the most reliable means of perpetuating the modern conditions of domination.'[79]

By analyzing the psychological techniques used by the Nazis, Adorno sees the employment of stereotypes and clichés by the culture industry as a form of contemporary domination reinforcing the established order. Stereotypes and schematization provide the individual with a egotistic gain by processing the raw material and thereby engaging the audience as 'experts' or as 'active' readers. An example of the stereotypes employed by the culture industry was that popular culture 'glorifies the strong man – its image of the man of action.'

The underlying mechanisms which compels the individual to identify with the stereotypes are 'human need' because 'the manifest or repressed instinctual moment finds expression only in the form of needs, which have today become wholly a function of profit interest.'[80]

Later, in his *Late Capitalism or Industrial Society*, Adorno went on to argue that it may be possible, in principle, to distinguish between true and false human needs. In order to determine which needs are false and which true, one would have

---

[78] Adorno, 'How to Look at Television', *Op cit.* p.147
[79] Adorno & Horkheimer, 'The Schema of Mass Culture', in Bernstein (ed) *The Culture Industry, op cit.* p.80
[80] Adorno, *Sociology and Psychology*, Translated by I. Wohlfarth, *New Left Review*, 46, 1967, p.77

to acquire knowledge of the 'structure of society as a whole... together with all of its mediation.'[81] There is not, however, an easy fit between human needs and their satisfaction by the culture industry. Some needs are simply repressed and others are deflected 'with the help of well-tried psychological techniques... these needs are diverted into a few chosen channels.'[82]

Most other needs which are socially manufactured may be satisfied by the culture industry. This is in effect the focal point of the culture industry's 'indirect domination.' In the *Dialectic of Enlightenment* it was claimed that the use-value of the culture industry was that of social esteem or prestige. Adorno later expanded upon the use-value of culture industry when he argued that the need it gratifies is expressed in the desire to compensate for social powerlessness.[83]

The fact that individuals actually do 'experience' this powerlessness is explained by their conscious or latent recognition of the discrepancy between the normative truth of liberal ideology and its empirical fallacy. In the face of this rupture between their actual state of freedom and autonomy, individuals try to compensate for their inability to bridge the gap by cultivating themselves using the cultural products available to them. Cultivation – or pseudo-cultivation – allows individuals to turn themselves 'either in fact or imagination into aspects of something higher. ' The need to be cultivated manifests egotistic tendencies:

> *The attitude which links pseudo- culture and collective narcissism is that of being in charge, of having a say, of conducting oneself and considering oneself as an expert ... the narcissistic gratification of leading a secret life and belonging to a select group ... This narcissistic gain exempts the individuals from reality testing ... allowing them to live in the delusional systems supplied by the*

---

[81]'Late Capitalism or Industrial Society, Translated by F. Van Gelder, in Misgeld and Stehr (eds), *New German Sociology*, op.cit. p.242
[82]Adorno, 'Sociology and Psychology', *op cit.* p.79
[83]Adorno, 'Theory of Pseudo-Culture', *Telos*, 95, (Spring 1993), pp32-3, Translated by D. Cook

schemata of the culture industry. (*Adorno*: Theory of Pseudo- Culture, *pp33-5*)

People, therefore, derive a sense of empowerment from their pseudo-cultivation, they flatter themselves with the social prestige they believe they gain from it.

The 'indirect domination' by the culture industry is by no means the total obliteration of the consumers' will for resistance.

Radical protests and general dissatisfaction had occurred despite the loss of those qualities which had once facilitated resistance. In his attempt not to integrate sociology and psychology, Adorno sees the possibility for resistance to the established order. However, Adorno does not provide a detailed examination of such resistance, only a few remarks and implicit references to instinctual resistance against the 'totally administered world'. Instead, in a remarkable analysis Adorno argued that there were other bases for resistance other than instinctual. I think it will be appropriate to further examine these issues here.

If the gap between the social totality and individual needs indicates the powerlessness of the individual, it also points to the area in which resistance is possible. The individual's psyche, for Adorno, had not been totally destroyed. Although consumers' consciousness had become increasingly dysfunctional and regressive – owing in part to the culture industry which, in principle, could control 'the beliefs and attitudes of countless people from some central location', Adorno continued to maintain that some, albeit limited, potential for resistance existed on the more conscious level. The preconditions for 'consciousness rising' already exist. The ideology of the culture industry is extremely weak, the consciousness of its consumers is duplicitous and consumers have achieved a degree of 'enlightenment' which cannot be withdrawn randomly. Adorno utterly rejected the idea that individuals in modern societies were 'blind and passive' objects in a formidable system of domination:

> *We cannot content ourselves with merely stating that spontaneity has been replaced by blind acceptance of the*

enforced material. Even the belief that people today react like insects and are degenerating into mere centers of socially conditioned reflexes, still belongs to the facade. Too well does it serve the purpose of those who prate about the new myths and the irrational powers of community.[84]

Despite the charges of being pessimist or elitist, Adorno refused to accept 'inherent contempt of the masses' which underlies the assumption shared by both Nazism and the culture industry that individuals are entirely malleable.[85]
Similarly, Adorno explicitly denies the culture industry's 'complete' control of the consumers and sees:

...the possibility that the messages [of the culture industry] could simply reverberate against the walls of an everyday world skeptical toward the pseudo-reality of the media.[86]

The culture industry overestimates the irrationality of contemporary consciousness. The psychological calculations are not always successful because, at the very least, individuals have an unconscious awareness of the fragility of the industry's ideology.
Adorno repeatedly reminds us that domination has become an open secret. The following remarks are a few examples of Adorno's repeated claim that people are not helpless pawns in an informidable system:

Consumer suspect that the less anything costs, the less it is being given to them... The mistrust of traditional culture as ideology is combined with the mistrust of industrialized culture as swindle. (*Dialectic of Enlightenment*: p. 161)

Elsewhere in the same book the point was reinforced:

---

[84] Adorno, 'On Popular Music', *op cit.* pp47-8
[85] Adorno, 'Freudian Theory and the Pattern of Fascist Propaganda', *op cit.* p.119
[86] Quoted by A. Honneth, *The Critique of Power: Reflective Stages in an Critical Social Theory*, Translated by K. Bayne, (Cambridge, Mass: MIT Press), 1991, p.80

The triumph of advertising in the culture industry is that consumers feel compelled to buy and use its products even though they see through them. (p.167)

In a little know essay written in 1963, Adorno writes:

The millions of people who consume mass culture, which has been tailor made for them and has really turned them into masses for the first time, have no inherently standardized consciousness. Beneath the level of weak ideology, they feel, on the preconscious level, that they are being deceived by the front page of every newspaper, by every cellophane wrapped hit. They probably only approve spasmodically of what they are force fed because they are obliged to evade their consciousness of it as long as they have nothing else.[87]

The idea of 'double consciousness' of the consumers of the culture industry is a subject of more vigorous analysis in *Free Time*:

What the culture industry presents people with in their free time ... is indeed consumed and accepted, but with a kind of reservation ... Perhaps one can go even further and say it is not quite believed in. It is obvious that the integration of consciousness and free time has not yet completely succeeded. The real interests of individuals are still strong enough to resist, within certain limits, total inclusion. ... A Society, whose inherent contradictions persist undiminished, cannot be totally integrated even in consciousness.[88]

Related to this issue, Adorno also spoke of self-deception by the consumers. A great deal of psychic energy is required to

---

[87] Adorno, 'Kann das Publikum Wollen?', *Gesammelte Schriften*, 20.1 (Frankfurt: Suhrkamp), 1986. Translated by D. Cook, p.347
[88] Adorno, 'Free Time', in Bernstein, *Culture Industry, op cit.*, p.169

repress knowledge of the truth. 'People need their will, if only in order to down the all too conscious premonition that something is phony with their pleasure.' Adorno also recognized that making people aware of what they know unconsciously is 'almost insuperably difficult.'[89] People deceive themselves with the rationalization that television 'really entertains them'. Self-deception, therefore, was exercised by the consumers themselves and not by the culture industry. Hence, Adorno distances himself from the idea of passive and blind acceptance of the cultural outputs. This issue of double consciousness, however, was never fully and coherently discussed by Adorno. Indeed, more empirical work needs to be done in the area of self-deception by the audience.

To conclude, the culture industry cannot completely reinforce and control the consciousness and the unconscious of its consumers. It is unable to do so not only because of the contradictions inherent in late capitalism, but also the double –consciousness of the consumers of cultural outputs account entirely for the limits to reinforcement. These limits are also a consequence of the fact that, to a certain extent, people have already been 'enlightened'. Adorno, in *Theory of Pseudo-Culture* argues that the liberal ideology of the Enlightenment does not function solely as an instrument of domination but actually explains why people cannot be dominated completely. Since they have already been 'enlightened' to some degree, individuals are at the very least unconsciously aware of the culture industry's deceptive lies. This enlightenment is described by Adorno as 'not genuine.' Instead he claims that this process had acted as a force on people's consciousness and served as counter – force to the ideology of the culture industry.

A person who 'has grown up under the influence of the culture industry so entirely that it has become his second nature...will often fend off insights which apply to the role of the culture industry's functions and role in the social structure.'[90]

---

[89]'On Popular Music', pp 47-8
[90]Adorno et al., *The Positivist Disputes in German Sociology*, Translated by G. Adey and D. Frisb, (London: Heinemann), 1976, p.43

As an organ of anti-enlightenment, the culture industry constantly disputes the historically achieved state of enlightenment. Ultimately, the solution lies in changes in the structure of the whole – 'that whole which today, in terms of its own law, deforms rather than develops awareness.'[91]

Adorno, once again, never fully developed this idea of structural change in any detail. In short, Adorno acknowledged and briefly examined the dual-consciousness very early in his work. He believed that due to their self-deception, consumers themselves facilitate practices of domination. Making them aware of their cooperation in these practices could have far reaching results.

Despite a lack of systematic analysis in the area of duplicity of consciousness, Adorno's dialectical analysis in the sphere of culture, domination and society remain relevant for contemporary empirical research on media.

Even with consumers' dual consciousness they only partially see through cultural commodities. Whatever needs they may satisfy, these products generally help to reinforce the egotistic tendencies which hinder or prevent freedom. No contemporary account of modern culture and domination can afford to overlook Adorno's analysis of the impact of capitalist form of domination on consciousness. Adorno thought that individuals were losing their capacity to identify and formulate their own needs. The culture industry strives to gratify individual's needs, but consumers no longer know how to wish or what they should wish for. By using this idea, William Leiss has shown that modern advertising has fragmented and isolated consumers' needs, and individuals have become 'confused about the nature and objectives of their wants ... this means that even if some cultural commodities do satisfy unfulfilled needs, the consumer may be unaware that these needs are being met at all.'[92]

The final section of this chapter pulls the strands together and provides a critical reappraisal of the theory of culture

[91]*ibid*, p.43
[92]W. Leiss, *The Limits to Satisfaction: An Essay on the Problems of needs and Commodities* (Montreal: McGill University Press), 1988

industry before proceeding to assess its contemporary relevance in the sphere of mass media research.

A Critique of Adorno's Theory of Culture Industry

This section will assess the limitations of Adorno's analyses from several different points of views. It will be argued that there are several areas in Adorno's work on the essential features and functions of the culture industry which are seriously underdeveloped. In his analyses of commodification of culture, for example, Adorno never fully discussed the rationalization of distribution techniques, marketing and advertising strategies.

When he discussed the reinforcement techniques used by the culture industry, Adorno quite explicitly stated that these techniques are only partially successful. The consumer has a dual consciousness. Therefore, they do not totally accept the industry's products and they are suspicious of them. Moreover, the illusory satisfactions offered by the industry's products result in consumer discontent and may produce resistance.

In *'Free Time'* Adorno argued that individuals' real interests were strong enough to partially resist complete identification with the interests of the totality. This implies that rational self interest which includes freedom, autonomy and spontaneity has not been completely undermined by the culture industry. In some respect the culture industry itself may encourage these tendencies as its ideology probably contains some critical elements. Yet Adorno thought the culture industry's ideology had become fragile and its affirmation of the established order is ludicrously obvious. Indeed, educating the consumers was seen as a way to see through affirmative culture. This section will, briefly, explore these limitations which Adorno himself either implicitly or explicitly ascribed to the commodification of culture.

A number of critics have argued that Adorno seriously overestimated the limits of commodification and reification of the culture industry's outputs. Garnham argues that 'contradictions' are an intrinsic feature to the development of capitalism itself. The conflicts and antagonisms between labour and capital have also made an impact upon the mass media. This displaced contradiction can be seen 'in resistances both actual and ideological to the industrialization of the artisanal modes of cultural production ... and ... in the conflicts between national and international capitals ... or the existence quotas on the importation of foreign film and television material .. and the growing Third World demand for a New World Information Order.'[93]

If the culture industry promises entertainment while promoting business interests, then the cultural commodity may harbour 'an inherent contradiction, a contradiction which, as with the other contradictions within the capitalist mode of production, may be profoundly subversive.'[94] In a similar attempt to show that there may be limits to the commodification and reification of cultural products, Lambert Zuidervaart suggests that reification might not be as pervasive as Adorno asserted or that it might have reversed itself in important respects during recent years. Moreover, Zuidervaart points out it may be more useful that the concept of reification be restricted entirely to the economic dimension of society.[95]

Adorno's uncompromising generalizations about the commodification of cultural products are also open to criticism. Commentators such as Deborah Cook argue that it is not possible to make sweeping comments in advance about all products of the culture industry. Apart from very few attempts at content analysis such as *How to Look at Television* and *The Stars Down to Earth*, *Adorno* rarely judged the culture industry's products on an individual basis. Adorno, therefore, can be criticized for his sweeping assertion that all cultural goods fail to reach aesthetic criteria. Indeed, given his own analysis of the production of the cultural materials, Adorno had to accept that not all of these products are thoroughly commodified. It

---

[93]N. Granham, 'Contribution to a Political Economy of Mass Communication', *op cit*, p.140
[94]Granham, *ibid*, p.136
[95]L. Zuidervaart, *Adorno's Aesthetic Theory: The Redemption of Illusion* (Cambridge, Mass: MIT Press), 1991

would be very difficult to generalize about all such commodities even if some of them are standardized.

Nonetheless, Adorno might argue that the prevailing economic tendencies of late capitalism will prevent all but a few cultural goods from escaping the commodification logic. The use-value of most television and the press outputs has been forged by exchange-value. 'The media have grown increasingly dependent on other industrial and corporate sector for their revenues. As a result, they have also become partners in achieving the social and economic goals of their patrons and owners.'[96]

While the essential premises of Adorno's theory of culture is of crucial importance, one cannot dismiss the idea that some of the culture industry's products already follow the model for cultural practice with political import which Adorno discovered in some cultural products. This idea can only be confirmed by analyzing cultural goods on an individual basis. A thorough reassessment of the culture industry demands empirical accounts of the nature of the cultural practices themselves.

Is the Thesis of Culture Industry Still Relevant?

The Frankfurt School in its original form, and as a school of Marxism or sociology, is dead. (Bottomore: 1984, p 76)

This section will argue that, in spite of the shortcomings in Adorno's study of mass culture, some aspects of the theory of culture industry, far from being dead, continue to prove relevant.

One of these theoretical aspects is Adorno's highly specialized analysis of the culture industry's standardization, egomania, wish-fulfillment, the use of stereotypes and schemata. This would certainly benefit from further empirical research. Indeed, as argued in the course of this chapter, Adorno argued that egomania is a widespread feature of the modern epoch. However, he also agreed that this statement could not be taken

---

[96]B. Bagdikian, *Media Monopoly* (Boston: Beacon Press), 1992

as a universal and necessary condition about all individuals.

Moreover, the theory of culture industry connected with authoritarian irrationalism, we believe, can highlight contemporary developments in culture, polity and society. David Harris, in his analysis of the modern culture, argues:

> ..*the Gramscian tradition lacks an account of the modern culture industry or surveillance apparatuses, and their capacity to fight back by incorporating critics and inverting their work. This account goes missing partly because of the early decision to reject "mass culture theses" and to construct a caricature out of Adorno's and Horkheimer's version.*[97]

In recent decades Adorno has been marginalized in favour of Walter Benjamin's 'materialist' theory of culture. In an attempt to return to Adorno, this thesis aims to argue that the importance of Adorno's cultural analyses poses questions against a conventional political-economic approach to culture. In the critique of the Frankfurt School's theory of culture, outlined earlier, it was argued that late capitalist culture has acquired a certain degree of autonomy as well as having become increasingly important to the survival of the whole world system. Consequently it is not the question of economic determinism which is crucial, but rather the 'commodification of cultural outputs.'

The culture industry thesis, as has been shown, is not based upon an apparent analytical naivety which takes individuals' tastes and pleasures at face value. It is rather an attempt to show how the messages of propaganda and commodified culture operate by resonating with those background factors, so that the 'sense' which is made typically tends towards dependency and conformism. Furthermore, the thesis of 'culture industry' has enough analytical validity to account for the expansion of diversified modern popular culture. As noted by J. Bernstein, the diversity of market segmentation and the cultivation of life style

---

[97]D. Harris, *From Class Struggle to the Politics of Pleasure* (London: Routledge), 1992, p.14

is entirely bogus, a death mask of individuality covering the bland features of the 'consumer clone.' The contemporary importance of the concept of culture industry, Bernstein points out, lies in its relevance to the study of a commodified culture of life styles in which 'a pseudo-aestheticization of social reality, a closing gap between the culture industry and every day life fails to accomplish any true overcoming of the expressions of the work ethic, and thus releases aggression in at least equal measures to its release of desire.'[98]

The glossy 'life style' magazines, newspaper supplements, television productions, travel guides, sports supplements, consumer guides and advertising can be perceived as responses to the panic of dependent personalities faced with choices they are not equipped to make alone. These glossy cultural products are perhaps the contemporary equivalent to Righter's astrological column, but one which recognizes that conformity must be accommodated within diversity. The expansion in the diversity of modern popular culture is perhaps a greater source of dependency and conformism through the process of demand for information.

Indeed to successfully adopt a life-style, one must conform to a greater degree and seek a greater range of information.

Moreover, in terms of the connection between culture and politics, Adorno's analysis of authoritarianism is immensely important. Contemporary authoritarian propaganda such as the 'New Right' movement in the 1980s, might be thought to exhibit two features which Jean Baudrillard identifies in modern culture.

Firstly, authoritarianism has the air of a panic production. Its elements of syncretic pastiche and nostalgia for the family and the nation are a bid for cognitive reassurance in the face of a 'loss of reality.' Secondly, such propaganda simulates a meaningful and shared symbolic order. Baudrillard characterizes 'simulation' in terms very close to those used by Adorno in relation to 'paranoia'; as 'a short-circuit of reality and its reduplication by signs.'[99]

---

[98]J.M. Bernstein, 'Introduction' in Adorno, *The Culture Industry, op cit*
[99]J. Baudrillard, 'Simularca and Simulations', in his *Selected Writings* (Cambridge: Polity Press), 1988, p.182

Adorno's theme of 'bi-phasic ambivalence' is relevant here. Individuals might be conceived of as moving in and out simulations, such as family, work, sport and politics, that projects systems of action and meaning which would be radically incommensurate if translated into propositional form. On this basis a strong case can be made that rhetorical, and Thatcherite, hypostatization of the 'market', the 'family', 'the Nation' as the bedrock reality should be understood as entering a register of paranoia simulation.[100]

In keeping with Adorno's work on culture industry this study aims to focus on a critical approach to the prevailing tendencies which may not as yet have been verified empirically.

In an attempt to study the press industry in contemporary Britain, this study aims to demonstrate that as one of the fundamental contributors to the culture industry, the modern British press has not been the subject of an empirical investigation. In recent decades there has been a large amount of theoretical and speculative analysis of Adorno's theory of culture industry in Britain. Yet, surprisingly, there are no systematic and empirical analyses of the press industry as an important feature of the culture industry. In an attempt to isolate and analyze this feature of the culture industry, some prevailing tendencies of the press in Britain will be examined. These tendencies include the growing monopolization of both industrial and cultural production by ever fewer corporations, the expansion of ever more 'new and improved' cultural and industrial commodities for immediate and unconscious consumption, oppressive police and paramilitary measures assisted by sophisticated surveillance techniques. The disseminating of the ideology of the corporate capital by the media may yet contribute to democratization of political institutions and processes. As the major distributor of marketable entertainment and 'infotainment' supported by monopoly capital, the modern culture industry undermines the potential for more democratically organized and politically

---

[100]For an excellent analysis of 'The Authoritarian Personality', see M. Jay, *Dialectical Imagination: a history of the Frankfurt School* (London: Heineman), 1972

active public spheres. This goal is achieved by colonizing free time and exercising immense influence over the formation of interests and needs, opinions and ideas. Conformity to the established order, abject dependence on the institutions and agencies of the totally administered world, and unprecedented economic and political exploitation by an elite would continue in modern capitalist societies.

The Thatcherite project, it is argued, constitutes an important social setting to research the extent of the validity of the culture industry thesis. Working within the tradition of critical theory the following themes will be examined.

Firstly, British society will be examined in terms of a historically diverse social system, with a relatively strong civil society. Accordingly society is viewed as an outcome of a continuous process of struggle over rules and resources. Thatcherism, it will be argued, was a highly complex and contradictory social and political project that continually modified itself in the face of dilemmas and policy failures. Thatcherism's popularity was based on its ability to serve the interests of different competing groups and mobilizing them around a right wing solution to the post war social and economic problems.

Secondly, the nature of the Thatcherite popularity will be examined within the model of 'domination through consent.' At this point the concept of 'multi-faceted populism' will be offered to demonstrate the complexity and contradictory character of the Thatcherite project, and the nature of 'New Right' popularity in Britain. The concept of 'multi-faceted populism' will also be used to demonstrate the capacity of the theory of culture industry in generating new conceptual tools to analyse complex, popular and authoritarian political projects such as Thatcherism.

Thirdly, the Thatcherite project will be examined in terms of 'culture and agency.' We believe this is a crucial link with what has been argued thus far and the empirical assessment of the press industry in the Thatcher years. Along with any structural analysis presented here, there will be an assessment of the nature of the activity of *'macro actors'*.

Agency and Social Actors: A Definition and Brief Analysis

'Agency', as it is used in this study, emphasizes implicitly the undermined nature of human action as opposed to the alleged determinism of structural theories. Social reality, being a human construction, consists of the meanings and linguistic symbols people use when interacting with each other. Social reality is an ongoing construction of knowledgeable actors whose recurrent interactions create, reproduce and transform the social world.

For a sociological analysis of the extent and differential importance of 'actors' studied, this study proposes a simple distinction of *'micro and macro agency'*, which not only helps to point out the degree to which social systems or consequences of action stretch across time and space, but also makes it possible to appreciate the crucial importance that social hierarchies and the different levels of macro or collective action have towards an understanding of how agents relate to structures and to social systems.

In a more general approach, and since we are dealing with a society which is highly hierarchical in organization and system there are subordinate and super-ordinate systems within which individuals face structural properties to the reproduction of which they directly and significantly contribute. They are also implicated in larger social systems whose structural features are completely unaffected by their participation as single individuals. [See Mouzelis, *'Back to Sociological Theory'*, (London: Macmillan), 1991 particularly chapters 2,3,4 and 5]

Focusing on actors in hierarchical orders it is possible to distinguish, as noted by Mouzelis, between *single, collective and mega actors*. *Single* or *Micro actors* cannot have a very important impact on macro-institutional orders, especially when they occupy social positions at the bottom of the various economic, political and cultural hierarchies, whatever the autonomy they may enjoy vis-à-vis their roles or positions. *Macro actors* on the other hand, are decision-making entities whose strategies entail consequences that extend widely over time and place. This definition of macro actors would include two sets of actors.

Collective actors who generate decisions through interact ional processes based on democratic or non-democratic forms of representation such as business organizations, trade unions, political parties and governmental agencies. *Mega-actors* are single individuals whose economic, political or culturally based social power makes the consequences of their decisions widely felt.

In a more general way, actors occupying positions entailing the control or monopolization of important resources would tend to unite, and establish organizations for defending their monopoly through what Mouzelis calls policies of exclusion or closure (Mouzelis: 1991, p 107).

In terms of the pattern of interaction, strategic conduct and the micro-macro distinction, both Mouzelis and Jonathan Turner, amongst others, emphasize that interactions between concrete social actors can be both micro and macro. To neglect the importance of either would downgrade the specificity of interaction order.

In order to demonstrate our awareness of the crucial importance of 'culture and agency, this study presents an analysis of 'agency' which examines the differential degree of the power enjoyed by various actors in different spheres of society.

Along with any structural analysis presented by this project, there will be an assessment of the nature of the activity of *'macro actors'*. In order to avoid a reductionist approach, this study will be equally attentive to the structural constraints as well as the intention of actors in a social interaction. It will be argued that the structure in which *'Mega actors'*, such as Rupert Murdoch, acted enabled them to propose courses of action.

In this sociological approach to the complex issue of structure and agency, this study will assess the role of *macro (mega and collective)* actors, as opposed to the micro actors who will not feature in our analyses either within the press industry or outside it. In the internal sphere, the role of the proprietors, 'press barons', the journalists, and the editors will be examined. In the external sphere the role of the politicians, economic actors, the public and the decision makers such as trade union leaders and executives will be assessed.

The Thatcherite project, it will be argued, managed to

mobilize the support of 'mega actors' in society and create a new power bloc which went over and beyond class boundaries encompassing the working classes, the 'City' and, more importantly, the middle classes The Thatcherite mission reinforced the ideology of the right, which was to be an acceptance of an individualistic rather than a collectivist view of society. This study, therefore, will assess the ways in which this consent was manufactured with special reference to the national press industry.

Conclusion

Mass culture, for Ivan Illich, is a category of tools and artifacts that shut off dialogue, which are essentially monologic, and create masses of technicized, passive consumers divorced from authority over the means of production. This gigantic machine that we now have must either be converted to convivial uses or thrown onto the junk pile of unplanned obsolescence. Not even television must be ruled out. Illich, in Deschooling Society writes:

> *The choice is between two radically opposed institutional types, one which is "manipulative" and the other "convivial". As society is presently constituted, manipulative institutions- those which make up bureaucratic, rationalized, 'mass society' – dominate, though these are also examples of convivial institutions.*[101]

Schools, for Illich, are the fundamental basis of 'manipulation'. For the world programmed for ever increasing industrial production and consumption, in one way 'massifying' scholastic funnels, Illich contrasts it with a world made transparent by true communication webs. For Illich, it is only through radical political consciousness and practice that convivial institutions can come to out number manipulative ones.

How can we achieve this radical and political consciousness?

[101] I. Illich, *Deschooling Society* (New York: Harper and Row), 1972, p.2

The answer takes us back, once again, to the Critical Theory of the Frankfurt School. A post-industrial utopian vision emerges from the works of Marcuse and Eric Fromm. In *'The Sane Society'* Fromm presents a picture of a 'healthy polity', based on meaningful labour, participatory culture, and communication socialism. For Fromm, the degradation of present mass culture is far removed from the 'collective art', which is ideal. Religious rituals have little importance as secular rituals hardly exist. Fromm goes on to say that there is little in contemporary culture that answers the needs of the total personality because 'The movies, the crime reports, the liquor, the fun are no adequate substitutes for meaningful, shared artistic activities'. (p.349) Cultural transformations, Fromm argues, must not occur violently, but should be achieved through education. Mass media is not simply to be set aside, but will have their 'communitarian uses'.[102]

Marcuse, on the other hand, speculates about the achievement of a 'non-repressive' society. Such a utopian condition would entail regression, an instinctual liberation that in terms of existing institutions, would be a 'relapse into barbarism'. A non-repressive society is to be achieved by the fulfillment rather than by the defeat of progress, by the realization of the utopian promise inherent in technology and mass media. This is summed up in Marcuse's analysis of the 'aesthetic dimension', which in its social development will involve 'the radical changes of labour into play, and of repressive productivity into display'. This is achieved by the conquest of 'want' as the determining factor of civilization.[103]

The utopian similarities between Marcuse and Fromm resemble the post-industrial ideas of Illich who argues for 'the advent of an Age of Leisure as opposed to an economy dominated by service industries.'[104]

---

[102]E. Fromm, *The Sane Society* (New York: Reinhart and Winston), 1976, pp 348-61
[103]H. Marcuse, *Eros and Civilization* (New York: Vintage), 1962, pp 176-181
[104]Here the application of the term 'post-industrial' differs from Daniel Bell's, one of the major proponents of the post-industrial theory. In The End of Ideology Bell argues that in the contemporary capitalist societies conditions have been created (via rising standards of living and education) for more mass consumption of high culture. This so called technically skilled majority, according to Bell, marks the beginning of the end of the

The present levels of scientific and technological advances might just make the concept of leisure on a mass basis possible. By leisure, we do not mean 'free time or idleness', but leisure as a state of being free of everyday necessities or a kind of labour which takes place for its own sake.

Modern, advanced capitalist societies are engaged in a pseudo-leisure of mass mediated distractions. Today the idea of a life of contemplation and cultural enrichment is not being associated with 'leisure', which is indeed what it should be.

Cultural enrichment depends upon the sacred economic motivation. It depends for its very existence on 'leisure' which, in turn, is not possible before the eradication of 'want and/or need'. Raymond Williams, Illich and Marcuse are at times worlds apart in their cultural reflections, but they all unite on the notion of constructing a shared culture of the highest humanistic and creative value on a mass scale.

If we aim for such a utopian value, mass media can no longer be viewed as responsible for decadence or barbarism. This is despite their belief that such a high quality culture will not develop through the mass media as it is today. The modern mass media today carry the blame for the failure of society to realize its 'leisure' potentials; they now produce ideology instead of enlightenment, entertainment instead of contemplation, and pseudo-individuals instead of human beings. To realize a shared culture therefore, a radical transformation of mass media is crucial.

The remainder of this book will empirically explore the conceptual themes raised in this chapter with a particular reference to the role, function and impact of the modern mass circulating print media in Britain

---

Marxian 'proletariat' as a class for and in itself. In defining 'pluralism' as mass society Bell, and the theory of post-industrial society, see society as decentralised and actively participant. The Old ruling classes have now withered away, and new classes of intellectuals, managers and professionals strive to achieve the logic of industrialisation. The old motive of capitalist profit agenda, so crucial to its survival, is now superseded.

TWO

THATCHERISM FROM THEORY TO RESEARCH
The Concepts – Indicators Model

Introduction

In the course of the first chapter, it was argued that a revised theory of culture industry may enable us to present a sociological account of the ways in which dominant ideologies play a significant role in shaping the interpretative schemes of everyday life. It may also provide conceptual tools to research reactions to the 'commodified' modern culture with the actual effects of cultural consumptions.

The second chapter of this study forms the methodological discussion in which the phenomenon of Thatcherism will be empirically analysed. Thatcherism will be regarded as the embodiment of the modern 'authoritarian irrationalism' and it will be argued that Thatcher's success must be attributed to an effective mobilization of popular support for a right wing solution to the economic and political crises. This chapter is divided into two interrelated parts. The first part, the concepts, will examine the intellectual and historical origins of Thatcherism since the 1940s. It will also present and analyse a selection of theoretical approaches to Thatcherism and will demonstrate the utility of a new conceptual tool for a better understanding of this phenomenon. The first part will conclude with an assessment of the relationship between Thatcher and the media in the 1980s.

The second part, the indicators, is a methodological appraisal of various empirical studies of Thatcherism and will discuss, in detail, the methodological approach of this thesis to the relationship between Thatcherism and an organ of culture industry, the press. In this context, the role of the press during the 1980s will be the subject of an empirical examination. However, the expansion and dominance of the New Right, it will be argued, had more to do with the active support of the majority rather than a passive reaction to the ideological messages of the media. This chapter is, therefore, an assessment of the concepts and indicators model in the context of the British social and political climate during the Thatcher era and begins with an analysis of definitions and origins of Thatcherism.

The Meaning of Thatcherism

The focal point of this chapter is the question of Thatcherism. The phenomenal electoral and political success of the Thatcherite project over a decade has been a source of surprise to many, including some Conservatives. Thatcher's success prompted many political commentators to argue that this must be attributed to her successful mobilization of popular support for a right wing solution to economic and political crises. Furthermore, they stress that the inability of the opposition to provide a credible political and social agenda has deepened the crisis of social democracy in Britain. Indeed, for Peter Golding the rejection of Keynesian economic management and praise of the role of the free market was carried on the crest of a populist movement in which a variety of ideological streams intermingled, not all drawn from technical theories about monetarism or the minimal state. In social policy the key themes were the reduction of state services in favour of private provision, an emphasis on individualism and self help, and the apparent retreat of the role of the central state in favour of development management, a structure in fact often masking quite strong central direction.[1]

For Hugo Young, on the other hand, Thatcherism is synonymous with 'market liberalism' of which 'the axiomatic

---

[1]P. Golding, 'Rethinking Common Sense about Social Policy', in D. Bull and P. Wilding (eds), *Thatcherism and the Poor* (London: Child Poverty Action Group), 1983

principle' is that 'state intervention in what markets did to the economy should be held to a minimum.'[2] For a better grasp of these assertions a historical perspective on the inception of Thatcherism will now follow.

The origins and the creation of the term 'Thatcherism' lie at the Institute of Economic Affairs, the free market pressure group started in the 1950s, whose co-founder, Lord Harris of High Cross, was ennobled for his services to her government (Young: 1989 p.87).

The Institute of Economic Affairs together with other research organisations, formed the nucleus in the growth of the 'organic intellectuals' for the Thatcherite project. The Institute was set up as a research and educational trust, and began regular publication in 1957 with specialized studies of markets and pricing systems. As early as 1959, Ralph Harris and Arthur Seldon began to use what later became Thatcherite rhetoric in their joint publications. Other important intellectuals affiliated to the Institute were Alan Walters, Arthur Beals, Enoch Powell, Hamish Gray and Keith Joseph whose early publications formed some of the intellectual agenda for the project of Thatcherism.[3]

The Conservative Philosophy Group was another influential institution which provided intellectual backing for Thatcherism. The Group was formed in 1975 immediately after Thatcher's election as Party leader, and she was a member from the start, along with distinguished academics such as Roger Scruton from London University, John Casey from Cambridge, Anthony Quinton from Oxford and Hugh Thomas (Young: 1989 p.406, Ranelagh: 1991 p.187).

However, despite the usefulness of the term 'Thatcherism', it has been used in very many different, and mistaken, ways. The

---

[2]Hugo Young, *One of Us* (London: Macmillan), 1989, p.536
[3]For some early Thatcherite economic and social discourses see:
 Harris & Seldon, *Advertising in A Free Society* (London: IEA), 1959, specially chp9
 Acton & Seldon, *Agenda for a Free Society* (London: Hutchinson), 1961
 H. Grey, 'The Cost of Council Housing', Research Monograph
 A. Beales, *Education: A Framework for Choice* (London: IEA), 1967
 E. Powell, *Saving in A Free Society* (London: Hutchinson), 1960
 A. Walters, 'Economists and the British Economy', Occasional Papers, IEA, 1978

inappropriate usage of the term includes identifying Thatcherism as a program of policy to Thatcher herself. Clearly her departure did not end the project with which she was connected.

The term Thatcherism, when used uncritically, is an ambiguous concept which depicts the political, economic and social mission of Thatcher as a coherent and unproblematic project. Clearly this was not the case. The Thatcher administrations witnessed bitter divisions, conflicts and rivalries. The policies were determined by specific situations which arose from each policy section. The project was by no means a pre meditated ideological philosophy which deserved the title of Thatcherism.

However, despite reservations about the term, this study will use Thatcherism as a sociological construct or a methodological tool to address a highly contradictory and complex social and political phenomenon which was coherent enough to provoke further academic examination. Thatcher, the only female Prime Minister in the history of British politics whose name has been used to denote a particular political and social project, is important to Thatcherism, but Thatcherism is not to Thatcher. It is rather a style of leadership together with a specific political philosophy.

Thatcherism is also used in this study to denote a particular period in British political history. Thatcherism may capture the complexity of the events after 1975 when Thatcher began to affiliate herself with the doctrine of the New Right. This particular period must be assessed closely with the international events of the 1970s, during which Thatcherism became one particular national response.[4]

Above all, Thatcherism refers to the development of a specific and constantly changing strategy used by Thatcher and her varied groups of political and ideological supporters. This strategy was modified and updated as it gathered momentum, as Thatcher and her supporters adopted it for their self-identity. As part of the strategic development, the impact of Thatcher is also

---

[4]This particular aspect is explored in more detail in A. Gamble, *The Free Economy and The Strong State* (London: Macmillan), 1994

crucial in her attempt to restructure different spheres of society.

This study aims to examine the nature of the Thatcherite project, but will distance this analysis from those approaches whereby Thatcherism is viewed from a perspective of ideologism. The crucial purpose of this study is to assess the impact of the Thatcherite project on British society, focusing upon Thatcherism as a continually modifying political, economic and social mode of action. In doing so, the essential mechanism by which Thatcherism renewed its momentum and vitality may be revealed. For the purpose of a historical analysis of Thatcherism, this study defines Thatcherism as:

> *a highly contradictory and complex political, social and economic program which began its development in the late 1940s. A particularly Conservative and specific project that continually modified itself in the face of dilemmas and policy failures, and with the help of which, new forms of political, social and economic solutions were produced.*

Having provided a working definition of Thatcherism, it is important to locate this phenomenon within a historical context, and examine the events for its rise and expansion.

The Origins of Thatcherism: A Historical Perspective

This section traces the development of Thatcherism since the late 1940s to Thatcher's election as Prime Minister in 1979. It will argue that Thatcherism was the result of a historical process which had its origins in the immediate post-war epoch. Accordingly this section attempts to highlight three themes.

Firstly, Thatcherism represents the erosion of 'old style' Toryism and R.A.Butler's leadership style. It also denotes a gradual breakdown of 'Tory Grandeur' and the 'One Nation' political and social approach. Secondly, the gradual change in the composition of support for the Conservative party, with an increase in middle class support, prompted the arrival of new policies designed to suit their needs. Thirdly, and more importantly, Thatcherism was a response to the crises of the postwar settlement and the Keynesian welfare state.

Phase One: Initial Inception

The 1940s are perceived to be a historical epoch in British politics. The end of the war and the election of the Labour Government are the most significant events. The coalition government during the war included many political figures who were hostile to many aspects of the pre war policy of appeasement. These opponents were also in favour of a major reconstruction of the economy in line with Keynesian economics and social policy.[5]

In spite of the fact that the Conservative Party contained some reformist and progressive figures such as R.A.Butler and Macmillan, the Party suffered an overwhelming defeat in 1945. The results of the election came as a great shock to many Conservatives who assumed that by having Churchill as their leader they were almost certain to enjoy a landslide victory. The defeat strengthened the position of the reformist elements in the Party, encouraging a greater desire for policy review and change.[6]

The most important reforms in the Conservative domestic policies during the 1940s included proposals to change the position of the trade unions, and an expansion of the nationalisation of the public sector, development of education, health and welfare provisions. The late 1940s, therefore, marked the rise of the New Toryism and the prominence of the reformist section of the Party. This process was facilitated through a combination of a limited domestic incorporation of the trade unions and a new bipartisan foreign policy consensus. At this stage, although there were extreme political rhetoric against international communism, there was no Conservative policy for tackling the growing influence of socialism (Gamble: 1988, chp3).

---

[5]See J.D. Hoffman, *The Conservative Party in Opposition* (London: MacGibbon & Kee), 1964
[6]See A. Gamble, *The Conservative Nation* (London: Routledge & Kegan), 1974. Specially chp. 3

The New Toryism, far from being a coherent political movement, provided a period of essential reconstruction of the Party's electoral prospects. In 1951 the Conservatives returned to government following the collapse of the Liberal vote. The Tories' spectacular victory of 1951, followed by two further election victories, proved that the New Toryism managed to adjust its policies to win back the lost voters and present the Party as the best candidate to administer the growing public sector. The Tories' success during the 1950s was partly related to a booming economy that was enjoying the benefits from the growth in the global economy based upon the Fordist industrial production prominent in most advanced capitalist societies. Internally, however, there seemed to be a halt to further state ownership and control, and more emphasis upon monetary rather than fiscal policy. More crucially the new expanded role for the trade unions was generally accepted by the Tories, and there were no new trade unions laws for the entire Conservative term in office. What remained an uneasy issue for the Conservatives at this period was the electoral prospect for the Party amongst a predominantly urban and industrial population. The Party aimed to become a popular Party which could win the working class voters.[7]

The 1950s could also be regarded as the decade when the global power of Britain began to decline. The country's period of long prosperity coincided with the final stages of the British Empire. As the decline of the Empire intensified, the economic foundation of the country began to destabilise.[8]

Attempts were made to prevent any further decline of the economy and sharpen the competitive edge of British businesses. In the late 1950s and early 1960s, Macmillan put forward proposals to modernise the economy and laid the foundation for the extension of links between the state and private capital. Part of this modernisation strategy was devoted to additional public expenditure to improve public services, health and education. At

---
[7]For a detailed historical review see: McKenzie and Silver,*Angels in Marble* (London: Heinemann) 1963
[8]See A. Gamble, *Britain in Decline* (London: Macmillan), 1985

the same time, the Conservatives were committed to developing programs to prevent crises caused by the instability of Sterling.[9]

In order to carry out the new economic strategy, new institutions like the National Economic Development Council and National Income Commissions were set up to encourage cooperation between major producers. The Conservatives, however, failed to produce convincing results for the new economic strategy, and were consequently defeated in the 1964 general election. The most striking aspect of the 1964 election was the commitment of all parties to the modernisation of the British economy.[10]

Wilson began an expansionist project to pursue the Labour modernisation plan. However, the government soon faced major difficulties in the implementation of its policies and was forced to abandon its expansionist projects. The crucial point in understanding Thatcherism can be found in the lessons learnt by the Conservatives at the expense of the Labour government. The inability of Harold Wilson to implement effective corporatist policies such as the prices and incomes policies, and the national and industrial policies, made the Conservatives doubt the validity of the modernization strategy. Many influential elements within the party turned against modernization policies, which eventually led to the growth of the New Right faction in the Party.[11]

The 1960s witnessed the quickening pace of cultural changes, the launch of the New Right and the beginning of the phenomenon of Thatcherism in Britain. The New Right Conservatives not only rejected state interventionism, but also were worried about British values such as the family, law and order and national identity. They attempted to focus on internal issues and began to challenge the Party leadership in shaping the outcome of various policies.[12]

[9]*Op cit*, chp 4
[10]See S. Robin-Letwin, *The Anatomy of Thatcherism* (London: Fontana), 1992, chp3
[11]See D. Kavanagh, *Thatcherism and British Politics: The End of Consensus?* (Oxford: University Press), 1987
[12]For a more elaborate analysis see P. Hennessey and A. Seldon, *Ruling Performance: British Governments from Atlee to Thatcher* (Oxford: University Press), 1987

The New Right, far from being a coherent political movement, contained several different strands. Enoch Powell, the central figure in the rise of the New Right, managed to unite its different strands and provided a serious challenge to the more liberal Conservatives, such as Edward Heath.[13]

As early as the 1950s Powell was committed to the ideas of free market and laissez-faire economics. But the most important aspect of Powell's popularity with the electorate was his outspoken views on the question of race and immigration throughout the 1960s. Powell was the first major political figure to challenge the universal political consensus on the issue of immigration. Powell was concerned with the identity of the nation and the need to safeguard its basic character. Powell's nationalism, drawing from an old Conservative idea, therefore, became an emphasis upon the importance of the British nationhood and itscontinuity above all else (Ball and Seldon: 1996 pp 219-34).

Powell believed that the ability of the Conservative Party to be the national party and to appeal to the working class depended upon the Party's ability to safeguard the nation from its adversaries. Despite his popularity Powell was unable to produce substantive changes:

> ...its [Powellism] populism was racist and 'little Englandist', its authoritarianism was largely constitutionalist (emphasizing ... substantive rule of law) and its liberalism was Manchesterian (stressing the need for tax reductions, sound money and perfect competition).[14]

In an attempt to distance the party from Powell's extremist views, in the late 1960s, the Conservative leadership expelled Powell from the Shadow Cabinet and ensured he remained outside any leadership contest. Powell was increasingly marginalized because he was no longer able to maintain support

---

[13]Ball & Seldon (Eds.), *'The Heath Government 1970-74: A Reappraisal* (London: Longman), 1996, pp. 22-3
[14]Jessop *et.al*, *Thatcherism: A Tale of Two Nations* (Oxford: Polity Press), 1988, p.60

at the popular level for his racism, and at the level of the Establishment for his anti-European attitude.[15]

Once removed from all political responsibilities, Powell began his sustained attack upon the political Establishment. He was particularly critical of economic policies and the tripartite corporatist arrangements between the state, unions and the employers. Powell also expressed his strongest desire for Britain to stay outside the European Common Market, and became the first politician whose ideas of the free market and the strong state were to be firmly on the agenda of the New Right in the 1970s and 1980s (Ball and Seldon:1996 pp 262-3).

Phase Two: The Road to Power

For two important reasons Powellism was crucial for the rise of Thatcherism. It was responsible for creating two crucial 'alternatives' for the emerging New Right. Firstly, it showed that there was a coherent intellectual alternative to the modernization project within the context of a social democracy. Secondly, it laid the foundation for an alternative politics of support to the Conservatives. If the old political agenda was to be invalidated, there remained an alternative opportunity to implement a new strategy (Ranelagh:1991 pp182-4).

The 1970s saw the rise of Edward Heath and his neo-liberal political and economic program which remained firmly within the parameter of post-war social democracy. Heath's election victory was followed by the abolition of many institutions which the Labour government had previously set up, such as the Ministry of Technology. Heath's administration was committed to leading Britain into the common market, anticipating the opening of the British economy to the European competition. The European commitment was seen as an integral part of a project to modernize the British economy. European membership was also viewed as embarking upon a new age of economic cooperation in the post-imperial epoch (Ball and Seldon: 1996 pp 259-284).

---

[15]This issue is discussed in more detail by R.Letwin, *The Anatomy of Thatcherism, op cit*, p. 278

Heath successfully led Britain into the EEC, but he faced massive domestic difficulties, particularly over the trade unions. Heath's policies produced staggering unemployment and a crisis for law and order. The miners' strikes of 1972-74 were some of the most crucial events with important implications for the future of Britain.[16]

Heath's attempt to introduce the Industrial Relations Act provoked a unified union resistance, forcing the Government to adopt several changes of policies. By 1974 even the CBI admitted that the new Act had damaged the Government's credibility. Essentially the Act aimed to combat the growing problem of unofficial strikes, by giving greater power to the national executives. The unions refused to endorse such a proposal, hence worsening the relationship between the unions and the Government (Marsh: 1992 p.21). Between 1970 and 1974 Heath was forced to declare five states of emergencies. The government confronted the trade union movement on industrial and political issues, and was defeated on both fronts. The trade union movement successfully defeated the Industrial Relations Act and the Government seemed unable to govern the country. Heath called an election on the basis of 'Who Governs Britain' and failed to win a parliamentary majority. Consequently, the Labour Party formed a minority government and in the general election of October 1974 they won a small parliamentary majority.

Heath's economic and social experiment proved to be as crucial as Powellism in the emergence of Thatcherism. His unsuccessful experiment with political and economic issues produced dissatisfaction in all sections of society. Ironically Heath aimed to introduce a Thatcherite plan hoping to reduce the responsibilities of the state in the last phase of the modernization project of the 1960s.[17]

After the 1974 election defeat a Conservative leadership

---

[16]See D. Marsh, *The Politics of British Trade Unionism: Union Power and the Thatcher Legacy* (London: Macmillan), 1992, pp 23-33
[17]See E.J. Evans, *Thatcher and Thatcherism* (London: Routledge) 1997. Evans presents a brief but useful appraisal of the Heath's government

contest became inevitable. The most senior figure in the campaign against Heath was Keith Joseph. Joseph was fiercely critical of Heath's loss of authority and set out to challenge his policies. In a series of speeches, Joseph urged the Conservatives to rediscover their roots and began to develop a free market and monetarist project. In an attempt to articulate the ideology of the New Right, Joseph and Thatcher set up an alternative source of policy advice, the Centre for Policy Studies.[18]

However, Joseph's self-destructive speech on the issue of birth control for lower income groups effectively ended his chances of becoming the new Conservative leader. The way was cleared for Thatcher, the Education Minister in Heath's Cabinet, to challenge Heath under a new set of rules drawn up by Lord Home (Letwin: 1992 p.84).

Thatcher managed to gain the support of all those who did not want her as leader but hoped that her victory would persuade Heath to resign. Subsequently, in the first ballot she defeated Heath by 11 votes, and in the second ballot won 146 votes against other challengers and was declared the Leader of the Party.[19] It was, therefore, almost by chance that the New Right movement, for the first time, reached its highest platform in the Conservative Party.

Phase Three: Thatcher in Power

After her election as the Conservative leader, Thatcher attracted considerable attention, not only because she became the first female leader of a major political party, but also because of her distinctive approach in responding to the crises that undermined the authority of the Labour administration. It soon became clear that she had her own objectives and political beliefs. Thatcher's style as the leader of the opposition encouraged the attention of popular and intellectual forces in support of her New Right project. She favoured a radical project armed with an ideological

---

[18]It is not surprising, therefore, that Mrs. Thatcher dedicated one of her books, *The Path to Power*, to the 'memories of Sir Keith Joseph'

[19]For a more detailed, and highly interesting, account of the 1975 Conservative leadership challenge refer to: R. Behrens, *The Conservative Party from Heath to Thatcher* (London: Saxon House), 1980

crusade against socialism.[20]

On foreign policy, Thatcher's stance marked a shift away from the EEC and a new commitment to the Atlantic Alliance. Thatcher's new economic policy adopted the monetarist approach, with Keith Joseph being appointed to the Conservative Research Department.[21]

Joseph and Thatcher were critical of the Keynesian approach, but while Joseph sought an intellectual justification in favour of the new economic strategy, Thatcher was preoccupied with finding remedies for high inflation. Meanwhile, the crisis of the Keynesian welfare state, and Labour's inadequate strategy, remained unresolved throughout the 1970s. In this period there emerged significant economic, political and ideological dissatisfactions which, partly, facilitated the ascendancy of Thatcherism. There were several campaigns such as the Festival of Light or the National Viewers' and Listeners' Association to make the voice of the non-corporate business in Britain more audible. Similar organizations, such as National Federation of the Self-Employed, the Association of Self-Employed People, and the Association of Independent Businesses were also involved.[22]

The radical right also became more organised through associations such as GB75, the Civil Assistance and the National Association of Freedom which functioned as its ideological organ. These rather scattered forces, together with the financial circles in the City, formed the new 'power bloc' for the Thatcherite project. After her victory in the 1975 leadership contest, Thatcher offered a new hope to these disparate organisations. She believed that the essential problems were the state, trade union power, the Labour Party and 'creeping socialism'. The Conservative manifesto for the 1979 election asserted:

The crippling industrial disruption which hit Britain last

---

[20]Mrs Thatcher's speech, Party conference, January 19, 1976
[21]See D. Elles, 'The Foreign Policy of the Thatcher Government', in K. Minougue and M. Biddiss (eds), *Thatcherism: Personality and Politics* (London: Macmillan), 1987
[22]See B. Elliott & R. McCrone, 'The petty bourgeoisie and conservatism in Britain', *Sociological Review*, 1987

winter had several causes: years with no growth in production; rigid pay control; high marginal rates of taxation; and the extension of trade union power and privileges. Between 1974 and 1976, Labour enacted a 'militant charter' of trade union legislation. It tilted the balance of power in bargaining throughout industry away from responsible management and towards unions.' (Quoted in *Times Guide to House of Commons*, 1979, p.284)

Unlike Powell and Heath, Thatcher mobilized the support of the middle classes as well as ordinary people through her stance on strong state and key material issues such as tax cuts, council house sales and opposition to inflation. On the social issues Thatcher promised to defuse and stop the increasing influence of the trade unions. In taking sides with capital Thatcher began her program of restructuring the welfare state and mobilizing popular support against its crumbling status.

The 'Winter of Discontent' in 1979 ruled out any possibility of a second Labour government. The crippling strikes staged by public sector employees demonstrated the government's mismanagement of economic and social policies. Consequently, the political initiative rested entirely with the Conservatives and they won the election in 1979.[23]

Thatcherism was a historically specific phenomenon partly because of the following reasons. It connected various sectors of the fragmented and unorganised petty bourgeois' discontent against the post war settlement. It also mobilized the working classes, through their dissatisfaction over the mismanagement of the political economy by the Labour and Conservative governments in the 1960s and 1970s. It also provided a new platform for the growth of capital as it clearly sided with the economic policies favourable to the 'City' and other major economic institutions in Britain. This stance was also favourable with the upper middle classes, hence their growing support for the project. Furthermore, she had a charismatic, and inspiring,

---

[23]This theme is explored by Ian Gilmour in his excellent book, *Dancing With Dogma* (Lonodn: Simon & Schuster), 1992, chp V

impact upon a large section of the female voters in the country.[24]

Thatcherism combined these forces and mobilized them behind a new political project. As a leader of a major political party she acquired a certain political legitimacy and credibility which Powell could not achieve. This popular mobilization, however, could not be achieved without an appeal to the territory of the mind, in order to create a particular common sense view of the way things should be done. The Thatcherite mission went beyond a mere assault against institutions. It reinforced an individualistic rather than a collectivist view of life. Each person living in society was to be charged with responsibility for his or her own destiny, an ethos captured neatly in the words of Norman Tebbit about his father who, when faced by unemployment, had jumped on his bike.[25]

At the social level, Thatcherism attempted to reinforce a particular view of the way the world should be. Although there were various approaches to this notion, essentially it was to be an acceptance of an individualist rather than a collectivist view of social life.

At the political level, as Andrew Gamble argues, the Thatcherite project has to be assessed as both a politics of support and as a politics of power, aimed at creating support for the Conservatives based on their ability to win votes in the battle of ideas as well as on successful management of the economy and the state.[26]

At the ideological level Thatcherism sought to shift the emphasis away from certain policies and concentrate on others. The most important areas which the Thatcherite project focused upon were the explanations of the Labour Party's policy shift on

---

[24]During Mrs Thatcher terms of office there were a growing number of female public figures who clearly chose Mrs Thatcher as a role model. The most notable example is Lady Porter, the former –and disgraced- leader of Westminster Council.
[25]See N. Tebbit, *Upwardly Mobile* (London: Weidenfeld & Nicholson)
[26]Source: A. Gamble. *The Free Economy and the Strong State,* Op cit. pp 208-212. In an interesting discussion Gamble provides a detailed analysis of the Thatcherite hegemony. Although we aree with Gamble's general approach, his analysis is comprised of a rather uncritical usage of Gramsci's concept of hegemony. Moreover his theoretical claims lack empirical substantiation

many issues, the sale of local authorities' housing, the legacy of privatisation policies, changes in the industrial relations laws, new forms of taxation, particular policies in foreign relations and the European Community.

The ideological impact of Thatcherism was partly consolidated by the phenomenal support provided by the media, particularly by the press. It is crucial to note that the press provides most of the newsworthy materials, and helps to set the agenda for debates and reports on television. The apparently active support given by the press to the government was an important factor in sustaining the momentum of Thatcherism and projecting its policies as the only right and possible ones.[27]

At the economic level, Thatcherism sought to promote a complete integration of Britain into the global economy. This process was to be achieved by the promotion of capital and the gradual marginalisation of labour via a fundamental restructuring of the economy. Thatcherism assured the creation of a 'free economy', a strategy for accumulation that radically broke away from the Keynesian economic management which advocated state interventionism and state welfare (Evans: 1997, pp 107, 112).

Denationalization, together with monetarism, marked the entire economic strategy, even though it did not appear as such in the 1979 manifesto. Accordingly, Thatcherism aimed to reduce the influence of the trade unions in the policy making process and to avoid committing itself to the formulation of an industrial strategy (Marsh: 1992).

Through lack of investment and training, the project was obviously indifferent towards the role of the manufacturing industry by not developing a strategic priority to maintain its continued function. Instead, the service industries acquired priority as the possible replacement for manufacturing. As the position of manufacturing declined the position of the trade unions also began to decline. Mass unemployment decreased union membership by 5 per cent. Several important industrial relations laws in 1980, 1982 and 1984 severely tightened the ring

---

[27]Gamble, *ibid*, p.222

Table 1 The number of injunctions served against unions – 1970s and 1980s

Sector	1971 – 75	1980 – 87
Printing	4	38
Transport	15	21
Public Sector	10	14
Others	2	21

of control over trade union activities and made them vulnerable to court actions and financial penalties.[28]

The latter parts of this study will assess how the major strikes culminating in the 1984-85 miners' dispute were crucial for Thatcherism to assert its authority over the trade unions.

Victory after victory against organized labour encouraged Thatcherism to introduce and reinforce new industrial relations, in which unions would either be absent entirely or would act in the capacity of company unions willing to accept no strike agreements and fully commit themselves to the success of their companies. The strategy to split the unions, the establishment of the Union of Democratic Miners, the growth of 'the new realism' associated with unions such as Amalgamated Union of Engineering Workers, AUEW, were all seen as aiding the break-up of the traditional labour movement and increasing the flexibility of the labour market.

It is evident that from September 1980 to April 1989, 92 per cent of injunctions requested by the employers were granted. Furthermore, as Table 1 indicates, from 1980 to 1987 in three sectors alone there were 80 injunctions issued against the unions.[29]

---

[28]Source: TUC, 'Working for Your Future', (TUC: London), 1993
[29]Sources used for this research:
  Labour Research, October 1985, October 1987, September 1988, October 1989
  TUC, *Bargaining in Privatised Companies* (London: TUC), 1989
  B. Weeks et.al., *Industrial Relations and the Limits of the Law* (Oxford: Blackwell)
  E. Wigham, *Strikes and the Government 1873-1974* (London: Macmillan)
  Journal of Industrial Relations

Table 1 demonstrates a clear increase in the juridification of industrial relations in the 1980s. The period since the 1979 election has seen a marked increase in the number of legal actions brought by employers against unions. This remarkable, and unprecedented, process found a new facet in the context of the 1984 miners' strike and will be further assessed in chapter Four.

For several crucial reasons Thatcher was rather keen to deal with the miners issue. Economically, coal had to be integrated into global capital and the coal industry had to compete on the international markets. Ideologically, the coal strike would be useful to divide the opposition and shift the balance of power away from the labour and in favour of capital. Politically, during the year long strike, Thatcher attempted to reorganise the state, and strived to project an image of neutrality by pretending to be outside the dispute and adopting an impartial posture.

In such circumstances, the media, particularly the press industry, were the dominant vehicle in which Thatcherite ideas were propelled further forward. Indeed as it will be empirically demonstrated this study will suggest that the great majority of the national press adopted the Thatcherite political and social mission as their own by indisputably lending a hand in the establishment of the new beliefs championed by Thatcher.

The next section aims to outline and critically analyse some of the most important attempts in theorizing Thatcherism. Although this book is not an attempt to theorize Thatcherism as such, a review of various theoretical approaches to this phenomenon, however, may shed light upon some of the theoretical aspects of this work. Amongst others, Stuart Hall's 'Authoritarian Populism', and Jessop's 'Two Nations' will be critically examined. Ultimately, it will be argued that whilst there are some valid points in these approaches, they are not fully rounded and fail to capture the complexities of the Thatcherite mission. In the final section the concept of the 'multi-faceted populism' will be offered to provide a new conceptual paradigm for studying the Thatcherite phenomenon.

Theorizing Thatcherism

This section will critically review some of the major theories of Thatcherism, including those which have emerged in the latter part of the Thatcherite epoch and were influential in the formation of the theoretical position of this work. Here there will be a discussion of a range of theories offered by commentators from various ideological persuasions but, it will be argued, their efforts have invariably drawn on radical theories and analyses. A major part of this section, however, is devoted to a detailed assessment of the following sociological theories of Thatcherism; Alan O'Shea's Cultural Theory of Thatcherism', Raymond William's 'Mobile Privatization', Stuart Hall's 'Authoritarian Populism' and Bob Jessop's 'Two Nations'. Prior to this assessment, however, this section begins with a brief revision of some other theories of Thatcherism.

Economic-oriented theories of Thatcherism

Most theories of Thatcherism attempt to explain its economic dimensions. These analyses focus on the commitment of Thatcherism to monetarism, the market economy and neo liberalism. They emphasize that Thatcherism expanded the economic interests of the capitalist framework. This section begins by reviewing some of these approaches.

A wide range of analyses of Thatcherism focus on the New Right theories of academics such as Milton Friedman or Friedrich von Hayek, the research studies of the Institute of Economic Affairs, the Adam Smith Institute, or the Centre for Policy Studies. Although these analyses are useful in some respects, they neglect 'the relation between ideology, policies and the consequences of Thatcherism, and misleadingly reduce Thatcherism to its intellectual history.' (Jessop *et al.* :1988, p.28)

In his empirical study of the economic effect of Thatcherism, John Ross (1983) claims that the Thatcherite economic mission was based upon the promotion of the interests of a 'great complex of firms based on foreign investments, banks and suppliers of the internal working class market.' Ross goes on to argue that the financial contributions to the Conservative Party reflects the profit levels and the Thatcherite structural economic shifts:

> *Certain sections of the capitalist class have gained enormously from the Conservative Party in general and Thatcherism in particular and continue to finance the Tory Party to a high degree.*[30]

Ross' theory of the Thatcherite economic mission is provocative and raises some important issues within its general parameter. However, Ross tends to ignore the complexities of political struggle and the relative autonomy of the State. In doing so, Ross overlooks the political significance of the economic shift from Keynesianism to monetarism. Furthermore, it is widely accepted that Thatcher sought to make publicly felt the impact of her own particular experience and convictions. She depicted that task as being fundamentally moral: 'Economics are the method; the object is to change heart and soul.'[31]

In a more sophisticated study Bhaduri and Steindl (1983) approach Thatcherism from the point of view of its services to the 'interests of one specific section of capital' in the larger context of the political economy of Britain.

> *...monetarism serves as an antidote against Keynesian ideology which assigns to the banks the role of instruments of the governments full employment policy.*[32]

This study emphasizes the shift in economic power from industry to the 'City' promoted by the importance of monetarism, a process which occurred through the rise of European markets and the banking business. The problem with this approach is its attempt to bond Thatcherism to monetarism.

---

[30] J. Ross, *Thatcher and Friends* (London: Pluto Press), 1983, pp 40-1
[31] Interview of May 1981, quoted in Martin Holms, *The First Thatcher Government, 1979-1983: Contemporary Conservativism and Economic Change* (Brighton: Wheatsheaf), 1985. p.209
[32] Bhaduri & Steindl, 'The Rise of Monetarism as a Social Doctrine', Thames Working Paper in Political Economy, London, 1984, p.14

It is well established that Thatcherite economic policy shifted away from monetarism in the early stages of its development.

In a detailed analysis, Tom Nairn (1981) maintains that the Thatcherite economic strategy was to use the recession to accelerate and solidify the dominance of finance capital and the interests of the multinationals. This is linked to the increasing globalization of the British economy, which required a general reorganization of the social and political order:

> ...*the metropolitan heartland complex will become ever more of a service-zone to international capital the conveniently offshore location for investment or reinvestment, insurance and speculation, granted by both public and private institutions underwritten by a famous social stability.*[33]

Although Nairn's excellent polemic captures the strength of the dominant hegemony rooted in civil society and parliamentarianism, his account of the Thatcherite economic strategy is narrow in focus and factionalist in approach. In considering Thatcherism as reflecting the logic of capital, Simon Clarke (1987) attempts to argue that Thatcherism should not be regarded as a simple tool of some specific interest, for it pursued widespread and global capitalist policies. In relation to monetarism Clark argues:

> *The term monetarism indicates the central thrust of this politics: all things must be answerable to money. And, of course, the power and values embodied in money are the power and values of capital, which dominates the circulation of money and of which money is the most abstract and most general form.*[34]

The 'logic of capital' approach can mistakenly be seen as a singular and decisive factor for the success of Thatcherism. There

---

[33] T. Nairn, *The Break-Up of Britain* (London: Verso), 1981, p.388
[34] S. Clarke, 'Capitalist Crisis and the Rise of Monetarism', *Socialist Register*, 1987

were, as we shall see later, other factors involved in the project. This analysis also fails to explain the different forms which political and economic restructuring take in different societies. The economic conditions of countries such as Japan and France with their more statist path differ from the more corporatist approaches of Sweden and Germany.

With a much more politically oriented theory, Joel Krieger (1986) regards Thatcherism as abnormally fierce in ideological conviction and highly statist in nature. In a comparative study, Krieger stresses that both Reaganism in America and Thatcherism in Britain emerged when political chances coincided with the crisis of the Keynesian welfare state.

It was far easier before the political implications of the global recession of the 1970s were as obvious as they are today, and before Reagan and Thatcher, to be lulled by the seeming permanence of the thirty year reign of Keynesianism. (Krieger: 1986, p. 189)

Once in power both aimed to disorganize the political opposition by implementing a crude power politics for a fundamental restructuring of state institutions. Thatcherism, by resorting to the policy of de-integration, made it difficult for groups such as the ethnic minorities, women, the unemployed and the low-paid to partake in political decision-making. Krieger goes on to conclude that Thatcherism derived its sectional support for its policies such as business values and the sale of council houses rather than relying on a mass support for its radical politics.

The problem with Krieger's analysis is in his approach to the question of 'economic crisis.' At best, Krieger is concerned with the symptoms of crisis without addressing the source of this crisis, or why there was a crisis in the first place.

Having outlined, albeit very briefly, some of the influential economically oriented theories of Thatcherism, it is important to note that although these approaches provide valid contributions to the study of Thatcherism, they miss an important social and ideological dimension. The next section, therefore, will review some of the major contributions in these fields for a better grasp of the social, political and ideological impact of Thatcherism.

Alan O'Shea's Cultural Theory of Thatcherism

Alan O'Shea's Cultural Theory of Thatcherism (1984) analyses the Thatcherite project as a populist movement.[35] Thatcherism, O'Shea points out, is a combination of different ideological strands unified under a new philosophical umbrella and a more or less coherent set of identities. This is materialised through a discrete combination of two forms of populism. Firstly, an antagonistic discourse which mobilized the public against the ideas of social democracy and secondly, 'a more neutral concept of consensual, non-antagonistic people which submerges their identities and antagonisms.' (O'Shea: 1984, pp.19-44).

For O'Shea, Thatcherism represents a combination of 'national popular' identity and the construction of a distinctive historical identity for the project, through which highly complex economic measures were assembled through simple moral ideas. Considered as a populist discourse Thatcherism was concerned to identify and mobilize a new Thatcherite subject 'the individuals' right to protect their freedom' as well as a distinctive historical identity for Thatcher (O'Shea: 1984, p.21).

The importance of O'Shea's analysis, as Jessop has shown, is his approach to the issue of ideology in the construction of the Thatcherite hegemonic project. For O'Shea, not only does each ideological strand have its limits, but it also possesses its own history and cannot be redeployed at will.[36] By treating ideological elements as active, rather than passive resources, they are an important part of the construction of the Thatcherite hegemonic project.

O'Shea's approach, however, suffers from several important defects. Firstly, O'Shea's approach lacks empirical evidence. For O'Shea, the impact of Thatcherism cannot be assessed through empirical research since its real influence is at the level of

---

[35] A. O'Shea, 'Trusting the people: how does Thatcherism work? In: *Formation of Nation and People* (London: Routledge & Kegan), 1984
[36] Jessop *et.al., Op cit.* p.44

political agenda. One way of research into the problem of Thatcherism, this thesis argues, is by assessing the role of the national press for their promotion of the Thatcherite political and social ideas.

Secondly, O'Shea treats Thatcherism as an 'unbroken' and continuous project since 1979. The Thatcherite ideological ground, for O'Shea, was formed between 1968 and 1979, and since then not much changed on the Thatcherite ideological terrain. However, as it is now well documented, Thatcherism continuously modified its ideological position to adapt to policy crises.

Finally, O'Shea treats Thatcherism as a unified system formed through subtle combinations of contradictory elements. In an empirical discussion of Thatcherism, it will be demonstrated that the project was highly selective and influenced by shifting priorities.

Raymond Williams' Mobile Privatization

A useful way of approaching the rise, and popularity, of Thatcherism was shown by Raymond Williams. In an article published in the *'New Left Review'* (1983), Williams attempts to study the impact of Thatcherism across the boundaries of classes.[37]

Originally, in his *Television: Technology and Cultural Form*, (1974) Williams utilized the concept of 'mobile privatization' to examine the development of radio and television as part of an attempt to characterize the form and content of cultural identities associated with a range of social and technological developments in industrial capitalism.[38] Specifically, he argued that the decline of smaller forms of settlement and productive labour had resulted in both an increasing potential mobility for individuals and a withdraw from extended family units and traditional communities towards a more privatized nuclear family. The material base for this can be traced in the increasing diffusion of mass-produced household goods for home-centred consumption by the majority. Under such circumstances,

---

[37] R. Williams, 'The problem of the coming period', *New Left Review*, 140 (July-August 1983), pp 7-18
[38] R. Williams, *Television: Technology and Cultural Form* (London: Fontana), 1974

moreover, the welfare provisions are also undermined. The novelty of Williams' approach is in his focus on the forms of cultural identities associated with these social transformations:

> ...at most active social levels people are increasingly living as private small-family units, or disrupting even that, as private and deliberately self-enclosed individuals, while at the same time there is a quite unprecedented mobility of such restricted privacies.[39]

This identity is then dependent upon certain external conditions such as cheap and easy credit to buy consumer durables, and the availability of full employment for an expansive version of mobile privatization to encompass most of the population. Within this social arrangement, however, the consciousness was never deeply formed by the preconditions for its own realization. Indeed, no matter how deep the crisis of modern capitalism, there will always be an ever increasing number of individuals who willingly joining in to pursue an apolitical lifestyle. In applying this analysis to the rise of the New Right in Britain, Williams provides an alternative approach for he identifies some of the material bases for the appeal of Thatcherism. In this approach Williams, at least in part, explains the reception mechanism for the Thatcherite discourse.

Similarly, Hall's approach stresses the need to explore the material connections between discourse and social changes.

Hall's Authoritarian Populism

In a theoretical analysis, Hall argues that the project of Thatcherism rested upon the concept of 'Authoritarian Populism.'[40] The concept, Hall argues, condenses a wide range of popular dissatisfactions with the post-war political, economic and social order and gathers them around an authoritarian, right-wing solution to the economic and political crisis in Britain.

---

[39]R. Williams, *Television: Technology and Cultural Form*, op.cit
[40]Hall and Jacques, (Eds), *The Politics of Thatcherism* (London: Lawrence & Wishart), 1983

For a better grasp of Hall's analysis, there is a need to locate his arguments in the following context. The emergence and success of Thatcherism must be seen in terms of a general shift in the 1970s towards the coercive, disciplinary aspect of state power at the expense of consensual politics. This situation arose out of the erosion of the Conservative hegemony in the 1950s and the inability of the Labour movement to seize power. This crisis, therefore, gradually deepened just as the class struggle began to intensify. By the late 1960s 'law and order' was firmly on the political agenda. Meanwhile, Edward Heath's return to the political arena was marked by two defeats at the hands of the miners. In 1974 a new Labour Government was formed but having performed so dismally, grounds were prepared for the emergence of the radical Right represented by Thatcher. Thatcher came to power, Hall further argues, because of three significant trends. These were the collapse of the third post-war Labour Government, the resumption of the new Cold War, and most importantly, the long term structural decline of the British economy.[41]

The fundamental problem with the concept of Authoritarian Populism is its over emphasis upon the ideological aspect of Thatcherism, which in turn is related to a rather unsophisticated usage of the concept of hegemony. Part of the confusion in the proper usage of the concept of hegemony is related to Gramsci himself. Gramsci focused mainly on the politics and ideology of class leadership and neglected the structural determinations of hegemony.[42] It is therefore not surprising that in his argument Hall is concerned with hegemony, and not with changes in the structural aspects of capitalist formations.

Hall attempts to focus upon a form of 'discourse' analysis which regards 'language and discourse' as an autonomous entity. In doing so, Hall creates a theoretical analysis which leans effectively on the function of ideology. Furthermore, Hall's theory of the Thatcherite discourse uses the concept of hegemony in terms of how Thatcherism reshaped the relations

---

[41] Hall & Jacques, Op.cit, pp. 218-323
[42] See P. Anderson, 'The Antinomies of Antonio Gramsci', *New Left Review*, no.100, 1976, p.74

between the public and the state. In this sense, Thatcherism is theorized in terms of its ability to gather public support through implementation of policies such as freedom of choice, individualism and the rule of market. The problem then remains of how one can account for the other essential elements of the Thatcherite project and the relationship between the economy and the state and the support provided for the project among both the public and power blocks.

The concept of Authoritarian Populism, although useful in our understanding of the changing role of the mass media in the ideological sphere, is an insufficient analytical base for the complexity of the Thatcherite project. The crucial problem with this approach is that it sees Thatcher's mission as appealing to people across all social boundaries. By focusing on the ideological incorporation, Hall wants us to believe that Thatcherism had an excessively unified base, and that it derived its support from all sectors of British society for the same reason. It goes without saying that the support for Thatcher was subjected to some volatility and considerable fluctuation, not only periodically, but also geographically.

The present study aims to argue that Thatcherism, far from having a unified image, should be seen as a combination of different groups, or actors, gathered around a self-contradictory mission. Further, it is necessary to assess the methods used to incorporate these specific groups behind the general themes of 'strong Government', 'national interest', 'patriotism', and 'curbing the power of the unions'. Not only may this enable us to understand the rift amongst these groups and within the Thatcherite camp, but we may also be able to utilize this understanding for the strength of the Thatcherite mission.

Jessop's Two Nations

I think that the country is more divided now than it was, and I think that there is a penalty to be paid for all that. She isn't a One- Nation Conservative. James Prior[43]

[43]Quoted in H. Young & A. Sloman, *The Thatcher Phenomenon* (London: BBC), 1986, p.141

Jessop's theory of 'Two Nations' aims to capture the political and ideological complexities of Thatcherism by concentrating on the notions of 'politics of power', 'politics of support' and the working classes support for Thatcherism. This approach argues that by disposing of the old Tories, Thatcher broke away from the 'One Nation' strategy and began her political agenda for the 'Two Nations' approach.

Jessop and company begin their approach with a detailed criticism of Authoritarian Populism, whilst also stressing that there are some useful ideas behind it. This approach, they emphasize, may be used in understanding the apparent irrational support by the working class for the Thatcherite project, for it also recognizes the complex conjuncture to which Thatcherism relates. However, they argue that the concept is derived from an uncritical aspect of Gramsci's idea of hegemony and is, at times, incoherent and provides inconsistent explanations (Jessop *et al.*: 1988, pp 68-92).

Methodologically, the concept fails to recognize some potential contradiction and tension within the Thatcherite camp and over emphasizes its cohesion. Jessop, on the other hand, views Thatcherism as an essentially contradictory project ridden with internal struggle. To theorize the project with an image of cohesion is to simplify a highly complex movement, and risk theoretical and methodological validity. Furthermore, in dealing with Hall's approach, Jessop argues, we are faced with an analytical confusion as the concept is used with apparent contradictions.[44] These contradictions may be seen in terms of trying to match two seemingly contradictory terms. The apparent mixture of 'people' with 'authority' is analytically difficult to sustain. At times Hall relies on the coercive and authoritarian aspect of the concept whilst at others he emphasizes its popular, populist and consensual aspect.

In emphasizing the inconsistencies of Authoritarian Populism, Jessop notes that at times Hall sees Thatcherism as a result of dual and passive revolutions from *'above'* and *'below'*.

---

[44]Jessop in an article published in the *New Left Review*, 1984, extensively explores this aspect of Hall's analysis

It is a passive revolution from below because it is populist, popular and contains consensual aspects. It is also a passive revolution from above because it is authoritarian, disciplinary and coercive. At other times when the authoritarian aspect of the concept is emphasised, it implies a strong state with social discipline, and embodies coercive measures and opposes democratic institutions. When the populist aspect of the concept is used it implies a set of popular notions, redefining the boundaries of being British and addressing national interests. The concept of Authoritarian Populism, useful as it may be, conceals the real sources of support for the Thatcherite project.

Before presenting Jessop's own theoretical approach, a brief account of his introductory analysis is in order.

The essential problem with the social democratic movement in Britain, Jessop argues, must be located in the distinctive cross class and inter-party consensus that emerged from the wartime coalition government, which inhibited both the development of a strong, right-wing bourgeois party such as the Gaullist movement, and the development of a nationally hegemonic Brandt/Schmidt type of social democracy in Britain.[45]

The crisis of social democracy cannot be entirely blamed for Thatcher's assault, for the system also had suffered from structural flaws. These flaws stem from the fact that the post-war welfare system in Britain was constructed under the conservative political and ideological consensus which aimed to survive under economic constraints imposed by the City and other major economic establishments.

As the structural weakness of the British economy in the 1970s became increasingly severe, the entire structure of the welfare state became shaky. The first miners' strike of 1972, although offensive, in tactical terms, by the corporatist movement, failed to bring about a systematic reorganization of capital and power in favour of the Labour movement. The third post-war Labour government witnessed a period of relative stability. However, before the 'Winter of Discontent' dawned on the government, the Right prepared itself for a political and

---

[45] The same point is made by Barnett in 'Iron Britannia', *New Left Review*, 134, p.46

ideological offensive. Thatcherism provided the most convenient focal point around which the counter-offensive mobilized. Indeed Thatcher's agenda aimed for immediate political stability by showing the structural problems of the welfare state.

The novelty of Thatcherism, Jessop argues, is in its ability to offer a 'dual-strategy' with the help of which Thatcher addressed the problem of working class discontent in Britain. By disposing of the old Tories, Thatcher broke away from any notion of 'One Nation' or 'Right progressive' issues. When Edward Heath was ousted, Thatcher had clear policies for her government. However, despite the resolute images of a strong state, we witnessed Thatcher on several occasions adopt U-turns in the light of changing circumstances. Working class conservativism is not a new phenomenon in Britain. There always has been a large Conservative support amongst the working classes. However the novelty of the Thatcherite plan was to mobilize two kinds of working class support; deferential voters and self-seeking voters. Thatcherism appealed to a large section of the working classes because of what it could offer them. Lower taxation, sales of council houses, rising living standards and lower inflation.

In his analysis Jessop aims to concentrate on the politics of power and Thatcherism's support within the dominant classes. The Authoritarian Populism approach, Jessop argues, diverts attention from the power bloc in Britain and the shifting relations within this so-called Establishment. There is little doubt that Thatcherism had a major impact upon the state, which in turn is an essential factor in organizing a power bloc. However the state does not constitute the power bloc simply through some act of will or some political project. Given Mrs. Thatcher's distaste for the concessions involved in building a power bloc and by the contradictions in the sources of support for her project, she established a new power bloc. The general support for the project stemmed from the City, had mixed blessings from industry, and divided the opposition from organised labour. The City continued to expand independently of the crises of the domestic economy, and the growth of the small business ethos of economic liberalism became a part of the creation of the new power bloc in Britain (Jessop et al.: 1988 pp 91-2).

Jessop's Two Nations approach is an important theoretical analysis which captures the political and ideological complexities of Thatcherism as there is compelling evidence to accept the Thatcherite 'dual strategy.' However, despite being influenced by this approach, this study will argue that Jessop's theory suffers from several weaknesses. Firstly, in his attempt to present a more political and institutional analysis, Jessop plays down the crucial dimension of the economic factor involved in the Thatcherite phenomenon. It has been established that certain sections of the business community had gained enormously from the Thatcherite project, and remain the main body providing funding for the Conservative party.

Secondly, upon reading the 'Two Nations' perspective one feels that the levels of political and ideological struggle are not clearly distinguished as concepts which are crucial for locating the specificity of these levels, are missing from the analysis. Accordingly, the issue of law and order, implied in the 'Two Nations' approach, is a highly complex debate. The initial policies of Thatcherism provoked civil right activists, professional opposition, and some working class resistance against the new approach to law and order. These resistances include the riots of 1981, the miners' strike and the poll-tax riots.

Thirdly, Jessop maintains that Thatcherism involved a passive revolution rather than mass mobilization (Jessop *et al*: 1988 p.43). This assertion, I believe, is particularly mistaken. The 'new model' trade unions such as Electrical, Electronic, Telecommunication and Plumbing Union (EETPU) and The Union of Democratic Mineworkers (UDM) are only two examples used in this study to demonstrate the new realism of Thatcherite industrial relations and union practices. The gradual reduction in strikes and industrial disputes since 1985 has proven that the new model of trade unionism has effectively changed the nature of British industrial relations. Further, the continuous restructuring of the Labour Party indicates a gradual erosion of the foundation of the opposition. The Labour Party was split over issues such as union leaders, the EEC, income policy, and nationalization issues.

It must be made absolutely clear that this study has no

intention to align Thatcherism with any notion of fascist mass movement. Since Thatcher years, however, Britain began to generally move towards a form of presidential system. Government legitimacy became dependent upon the popular prestige of the prime ministers and their ability to appeal directly to the people.[46]

The New Right gradually became a popular mass movement, particularly after the Falklands conflict. The mass movement mobilized behind such a project was not only amplified, but indeed systematically 'popularized' by the media. The press industry aided the Thatcherite mission by imposing its definition of 'political agenda' and consolidating its political and social visions.

More importantly, the Thatcherite delivery of economic concessions was positively 'popularized' by the press industry. There have been some significant studies in this area which will be assessed later in this section. This thesis will maintain that to a large extent, Thatcherism stabilized itself with the help of an unlikely alliance of 'actors' in the economic sphere who were seemingly united because of their particular material interests. The economic interests of the City, the promotion of laissez-faire in the financial markets, received ideological and political approval by Sir Keith Joseph's 'conversion' to monetarism and anti-statism, plus its backing by leading City commentators and specialist financial journalists as the organic intellectuals of a new economic strategy.[47]

The CBI happily approved the promises of lower inflation and tax cuts for businessmen. The unions were to be excluded from the policy making process, which was warmly received by the City and other key industrial sectors. The trade union movement's inability to have an effective contribution in the formulation and implementation of an effective income policy is perhaps because of the separation of the industrial and political

---

[46]In the latter stages of this chapter it will be shown empirically that Mrs Thatcher utilised presidential advertising strategies. Also, for an interesting debate on the 'presidentialization of British politics', see Sue Pryce, *Presidentializing the Premiership*, (Basingstoke: Macmillan), 1987

[47]W. Keegan, *Mrs Thatcher's Economic Experiment* (Harmondsworth: Penguin), 1984

wings of the Labour Party and the dominance of the City's interests within the Conservative Party. The pursuit of monetarism by Thatcher was presented to the voters in terms of its potential tax cuts, reduced inflation and increased incentives. This economic strategy coupled with the crisis of representation within the Labour Party created a special form of 'populism'. Thatcherism was not concerned with an active mobilization which, as Jessop argues, would be threatening to its decisional autonomy. It concentrated on disorganizing any form of opposition inside and outside the Conservative Party, and attempted to represent people directly. In this context any form of opposition was deemed as undemocratic. ' In this sense Thatcher speaks in the name of people against all sectional interests, including those in her own party.'[48]

Populism and prerogative power enabled Thatcher to enhance her government's decisional autonomy. However, we witnessed several policy errors and political embarrassments, one of which brought the entire system down with the poll tax riots. Therefore, decisional autonomy does not necessarily guarantee good government.

Thatcherism, backed by the media, offered justification for public expenditure cuts, and by doing so effectively diminished the credibility of alternative economic approaches. It also managed to convince many that future benefits would follow the suffering. At some crucial points, dissatisfaction with its policies was contained within manageable bounds.

Politically, after Heath's defeat in 1974, it became clear that the Conservative Party needed to sort out its electoral support. Thatcher's attempt to break away from consensus politics developed a new appeal. Despite its obvious plans to plunge Britain into a deeper polarization, Thatcherism had a pragmatic appeal to those people who were linked to the productive sector of the economy. Better salaries and lower taxes for the skilled manual workers became the new weapons in the reconstruction

---

[48]Keith Middlemas, 'The Supremacy of Party', *New Statesman*, 10 June 1983. Chapter Six of this thesis will demonstrate how the concept of 'democracy' was used by the pree against the NUM's procedures in the miners' strike of 1984-85

of the Tory support. The Labour movement's crucial weakness was its inability to recapture the support of the skilled workers, and its weakness became a reflection for Thatcher's strength. The increasing support amongst this particular class enabled Thatcher to reverse the structural decline in Conservative support.[49]

However, the Conservative voting skilled working class proved to be the most volatile, hence the eventual dissatisfaction of this group with Thatcher's local government policies.

The Falklands crisis was another crucial political factor. The conflict consolidated Thatcher's personal position and the policies with which she is identified.[50] She went on to restructure the state in such a manner that the impact of these policies was institutionalized. Indeed, Blair's first Government had to deal with a state which had been Thatcherized for over fifteen years. To reverse some aspects of these transformations did prove to be extremely difficult. The transformations had been through civil service structural reorganization, politically motivated promotions, the enhancement of Treasury control over all areas of government, and a radical centralization of government and the assault on local government.

Having briefly discussed these issues, the next section of this chapter aims to develop the concept of 'multi-faceted populism' to capture the meaning of a historical phenomenon which cannot be simply reduced to a one dimensional analysis.

Thatcherism As a Multi-Faceted Populism

In the previous sections, Thatcherism was identified as 'a highly contradictory and complex political, social and economic program. A specific project that continually modified itself in the face of dilemmas and policy failures, and with the help of which

[49]For a useful summary of trends see J. Ross, *Thatcher and Friends*, op cit.
[50]Baroness Thatcher unveiled her coat of arms for the first time with which she depicts her victory in the Falkland war. A. Hamilton, ' Baroness rampant hails her Falkland victory', *The Times*, Friday 18 November 1994

alternative solutions were produced.' Thatcherism also sought ways of blocking concessions given to the demands of the working class which previous Conservative government had deemed as necessary.

The concept of 'multi-faceted populism' aims to incorporate an analysis of Thatcherism with that of the British press as the medium of ideological change. Thatcherism's 'multi-faceted populism' is defined by this study as:

a historically specific Conservative political movement which successfully mobilized multi-class support for its neo-liberal social, economic and political agendas.

This paradigm aims to highlight three issues. Firstly, Thatcherism, as argued above, connected the fragmented and disorganized middle class discontent against the post-war settlement. It also mobilized various sections of the working classes, through their dissatisfaction of the mismanagement of the political economy by the Labour and Conservative governments in the 1960s and 1970s.

Secondly, the market mechanism rewarded those involved in its functions, whilst the 'unproductive' groups were condemned for not being able to contribute to the profitable processes of the market. The economic aspect of such an ethos was justified by arguing that lower income and deteriorating conditions would eventually force some to help themselves by entering the productive sphere of the market. Thatcherism, therefore, was successful in its effort to recompose the conservative working class in a secular, instrumentalist, privatized direction. It also produced a more productivist attitude in the trade union movement. The combined effects of Conservative legislation and mass unemployment eventually imposed a new realism upon the trade union movement. The defeat of the miners had some major implications, as it will be demonstrated later, for both the miners and Thatcherism.

Thirdly, the Thatcherite project remained unopposed because both the unproductive class and the Labour party remained highly fragmented for over a decade. It is ironic that it was the revolt of the unproductive group together with a general discontent over the state of the economy which led to the downfall of Thatcher. The law and order issue, plus the local government taxation system provoked civil libertarian and professional opposition.

To complement the study of the popular support for Thatcherism, as Jessop has done, we need to show that it was able to constitute a new 'power bloc' for its project. As argued before, the Falklands War marked the end of the initial step of Thatcherism and the beginnings of its stabilization. Following the general election victory of 1983 there were more coherent, long term strategies to regenerate economic needs and political reconstruction. The new Thatcherite power bloc, as defined, earlier persisted with general support from the City, industry, and the divided opposition.

The crucial point is that Thatcher's new power bloc consolidated itself on the inability of the Labour Party to develop a coherent and unified response. Furthermore, Thatcherite populist appeal depended for its success upon more general social restructuring. The decisional autonomy that Thatcher acquired rested upon an uneasy alliance of interests between disparate groups in society.

It is true that opinion polls show that most people in Britain have not been converted to the Thatcherite creed. But it is also true that in three successive elections they have not been willing to elect other alternative political parties. Ironically, in its attempt to appeal to the electorate the Labour Party accepted most of the Thatcherite 'settlement'. Blair governments have not restored public ownership, repealed the antiunion legislation, nor restored the power and independence of local government. Instead the Labour Party has become a late convert to the merits of the European Union, seeing in its Social Charter the best hope of defending the sort of collective social-democratic values that it no longer feels able to champion vigorously in Britain.[51]

---

[51]The popularity of the Thatcherism in Eastern Europe in the early 1990s is explored by P. Levy who attempts to show the negative consequences of Thatcherism in Britain, in 'Thatcherism', *Socialist Alternatives*, no 1&2, Spring 1992

Above all, 'multi-faceted populism' is particularly useful in understanding the changing role of the mass media, especially the popular press, in the ideological struggle. The next section examines this theme in a more detailed manner.

Thatcherism and The Media: The Underlying Traits

This section briefly examines the 'special relationship' between Thatcher and the media in general and the press industry in particular. It will argue that the media were the dominant feature in Thatcher's mission to reconstruct the relations between state and civil society. The reconstitution of the state was at the heart of Thatcherite policies, which on the surface was a 'reduction' of its boundaries, but in reality was a selective reduction in public services together with substantial centralization of political control of many areas of civic life and the weakening of dissenting centres of potential checks and balances. The role of the media in this setting was of crucial importance and can be distinguished in three patterns; the rightward tendency of the national press in the Thatcher years; the extraordinary pressure exerted upon the media by the Thatcher governments to reflect and disseminate its views; and the unprecedented campaign to establish, and strengthen, government's own publicity and press relations activities. This section will now examine each of these themes in more detail.

Thatcherism and the National Press
The general rightward tendency of the national and provincial press in the Thatcher epoch is now regarded as the dominant feature of that era and indeed post-war British political life. Throughout this period eleven out of seventeen national press were explicitly pro Conservative, with only two papers leaning to the social democratic left. Ironically, shortly before the 1979 Conservative victory the Royal Commission on the Press expressed concern over this issue, which became acute in the 1980s by the rightward shift of Rupert Murdoch and his papers which served both ends of the market, *The Times* and the *Sun*. It

Table 2 The newspapers' support for the Conservatives: Titles and Circulation a week before the general elections – Figures in 000s

Title	1979	1983	1987
The Sun	3,492	4,155	3,993
Daily Express	3,255	2,458	1,936
Daily Star	880	1,313	1,289
Daily Mail	1,973	1,834	1759
Daily Telegraph	1,358	1,289	1,147
The Times	Not published	321	442
Total Circulation	9,731 (66%)	10,843 (75%)	10,372 (71%)

Sources: Audit Bureau of Circulations, and, D. Butler, *British General Elections Since 1945* (Oxford: Blackwell), 1989

now seems that the pattern of the press support for Thatcher was an example of the press supporting the Prime Minister rather than a uniform support for the party in power. An empirical examination, shows that the national press 'personalized' support for Thatcher in the 1987 General Election was only matched by the support for Winston Churchill at the height of his popularity in 1945.[52] In a more general pattern, Table 2 demonstrates the extent of the national press' support for the Conservatives during Mrs. Thatcher's premiership.

The national press' support for Thatcher, as suggested by Table 2, reached a high of 75% of total national newspaper output a week before the 1983 general election. A more graphic empirical evidence is provided by an impressive study by Miller *et al*. In their study, conducted in Scotland alone, they show that between 1986 and 1987, amongst those who read quintessential low-brow tabloids like the *Sun* and the *Daily Star*, the support for Thatcher increased by about 34%, while the support amongst readers of quality papers only rose by 7 per cent, and 12

[52] See this study's content analysis chapter on the miners' strikes of 1972-74 and 1984-85

per cent among readers of 'middle brow tabloids' such as *Daily Express*, *Daily Mail*, *Daily Mirror*. They also show strong evidence that the press had more influence than television on those voters who did not change their opinions.

Elsewhere William Miller produces more observed evidence which reinforces his earlier findings. 'As the [1987] election approached readers of right-wing tabloids, particularly those who had weak or non-existent party preferences in the mid-term, swung heavily towards the Conservatives while other readers did not. Most of that swing occurred between our Mid-Term Wave of interviews in the early summer of 1986 and our Pre-Campaign Wave in March 1987.'[53]

With this pragmatic evidence it will not be out of context to argue that within the press industry most of the national editors and journalists reinforced the crucial links between the press owners and the external political sphere. Their words, texts, editorials, photos, analyses and ideas were mostly favourable for the dominant political mood. Thatcher in turn expressed her appreciation by handing out honorary titles and other social and economic rewards. During the Thatcher epoch an unprecedented number of national press editors and owners received knighthoods. In 1980 Larry Lamb (*Sun*) and John Junior (*Sunday Express*) received knighthoods for 'their services to journalism'. In the same year Victor Matthews at the *Daily Express* was ennobled 'for keeping the paper in being and true to the Tory party when its losses were enormous.'[54] In 1982, David English (*Daily Mail*) was awarded knighthood. Towards the end of the 1980s Nicholas Lloyd (*Daily Express*) and Peregrine Worsthorne (*Sunday Telegraph*) received their knighthoods.[55]

Throughout the 1980s, however, it was the special relationship between Rupert Murdoch and Thatcher which symbolized the cooperation of powerful political actors with

---

[53] W. Miler, *Media and Voters: The Audience, Content, and Influences of Press and Television at the 1987 General Election* (Oxford: Clarendon Press), 1991, p.216
[54] S. Jenkins, 'The more Things change...Fleet Street's half-hearted revolution, op.cit.p.55
[55] Source: A, Neil, *Disclosure*,op.cit. And J.Tunstall, *Newspaper Power*, op.cit

economic and cultural actors in order to encourage, and nurture, a mutually beneficial social order. Commenting on the more general significance of this William Shawcross argues:

> *Throughout the 1980s Murdoch and Thatcher had a symbiotic relationship in which the one consistently and almost constantly encouraged and reinforced the other. The Thatcherite revolution strode hand in hand across a decade.*[56]

In a similar expression of concern, Harold Evans, the former editor of *The Times* (1981-82), comments:

> *The secret of Murdoch's power over politicians, of course, is that he is prepared to use his newspapers to reward them for favours given and destroy them for favours denied. His machinations are almost Jacobean in their strategic cunning.*[57]

The former Conservative National Heritage Secretary, David Mellor, in an interview with the *Guardian* (30 August 1994), saw the expansion of the influence of Murdoch's News International as 'an unfortunate development for the future of our country.' Mellor went on to say:

> *No one in their right mind would want any more organs of opinion owned by News International. That things had got to the present state was one of the great self-inflicted wounds of Britain in the 1980s.*

The 'special relationship' between Murdoch and Thatcher will be examined further in the next chapter with a particular reference to the struggle for ownership of Times Newspapers.

---

[56] W. Showcross, *Rupert Murdoch: Ringmaster of the Information Crisis* (London: Chatto & Windus), 1992, p.210
[57] H. Evans in an interview with Rob Brown in *Scotland on Sunday*, June 26, 1994

Thatcher and Media Pressure

The second pattern can be described as the remarkable pressure exerted upon the media by the Thatcher governments to reflect and disseminate its views. This strategy included suppression of 'unfavourable' news, misinformation and disinformation. The BBC, in particular, found itself fighting a losing battle for its editorial independence with a Prime Minister who became increasingly hostile to the Corporation's political programs. The most notable examples of this pressure were the banning of a feature on the Zircon spy satellite and a subsequent raid by the Special Branch on BBC offices to seize files in 1987, and the attack from Norman Tebbit, Chairman of the Conservative Party, over the BBC's reporting of the American bombing of Libya in 1986. In a letter to the BBC, Tebbit argued: 'The BBC did not offer objective evidence so much as a highly flavoured editorial view. It prompts charges of professional incompetence or, even worse, prejudice. This could be held to have arisen either through bias or incompetence. Given the pressures under which the broadcasters operated a serious shortfall in professional and editorial standards is much the easier alternative to accept.' (Tebbit: 1988, p.256) Tebbit was convinced that his criticisms of the BBC 'struck home and that members of the editorial staff began to look more critically at their own work.' (Tebbit: 1988, p.256)

The BBC was not the only target. In the 1980s the media coverage of Northern Ireland was full of instances of censorship and attempted censorship. The most well-known instance was the legally imposed ban which prohibited the broadcasting of direct statements by representatives of eleven Irish political and military organizations. This was introduced in October 1988 and lifted in September 1994 in the aftermath of the peace process.[58]

With special reference to the Falklands conflict, Michael Cockerell (1985) points out that the official managers of political

---

[58]Source: D. Miller, 'The Media and Northern Ireland: Censorship, Information Management and the Broadcasting Ban' in G. Philo (ed), *Glasgow Media Group Reader*, Vol 2: *Industry, Economy, War and Politics* (London: Routledge), 1995

news are too often allowed to dictate the agenda so that the machinery of government news management operates with the active collaboration of the press and broadcasters. With important exceptions, there was too much complacency in the media instead of passion for disclosure that could match Whitehall's passion for confidentiality: '...all this explain why newspaper coverage of political news is as it is. But Journalists have a wider obligation. We have failed to build an adequate information base for the voter. Until we do, the British political process will remain a pastiche of democracy.' (Cockerell *et al.*, p.11).

Thatcherism and Publicity Strategy

The third, and most crucial pattern, is the way in which Thatcher's governments began the unprecedented campaign to establish, and strengthen, its own publicity and media relations activities. This section will examine the crucial role of important elements in Thatcher's publicity campaign such as Gordon Reece, Tim Bell, Saatchi and Saatchi and Christopher Lawson.

From the 1979 election Thatcher and the Conservative Party increasingly adopted public relations techniques normally associated with American electioneering. Great care was taken on the stage setting, colour, design and use of music and the parading of celebrities for Thatcher's keynote speeches. Thatcher was the first Prime Minister to use the telepromptor, with its two screens either side of the speaker, which allows the speaker to look directly at the audience in the venue. Gordon Reece, one of Thatcher's close advisors, was originally a producer of television light entertainment programs. From 1979, Reece influenced the choice of her speech-writers and, on the basis of market research, set out to change her image, with attention to voice, dress and hair style.[59]

Reece made important connections for Thatcher in the

---

[59]See J. Ranelagh, *Thatcher's People: An Insider's Account of the Politics, the Power, and the Personalities* (London: Harper Collins), 1991, p.146 and p. 214

media, notably with the advertising agency Saatchi & Saatchi, which acted as a 'think tank' for ideas and provided information and analysis. This formed the beginning of some effective advertising campaigns which included the 1979 slogan, 'Labour Isn't Working'. The agency, started in 1970 from a modest background, expanded rapidly to become one of UK's top 500 companies in 1990. The Thatcher–Saatchi & Saatchi relationship lasted until 1987 when, after the general election, the agency resigned the account (Ranelagh: 1991 pp 212-15).

Thatcher's connection with Saatchi & Saatchi saw the rise of a new influential figure in Thatcher's advertising and publicity campaign. Tim Bell joined the agency in 1970 as media director. In the years that followed Bell became the public face of the agency, and the point man on the Conservative party account. Bell and Reece worked closely together and both were regarded favourably by Thatcher. Bell's success with the Conservative account was crucial in the City's support for the international expansion of Saatchi & Saatchi.[60] Crucially, from this thesis' point of view, in the late 1970s, Reece and Bell became close friends with Larry Lamb, the *Sun*'s editor during the 1979 general election.

> *At regular meetings Lamb was given the freedom to expound at length on the merit of himself and the paper at communicating with the readers, and about how he and KRM (Murdoch) understood both the 'folks' thesis and the importance of television. Bell and Reece would nod sagely.*[61]

In 1985 Bell left the agency and set up his own company and in the 1987 general election campaign, he was called in by David Young to second-guess Saatchi & Saatchi, the official Conservative Party publicists (Lawson: 1992 p.698).

Tim Bell's contribution to the Thatcher's publicity and

---

[60]See Lord Young, *The Enterprise Years* (London: Headline), 1990, pp 198-201
[61]Source: P. Chippindale & C. Horrie, *Stick It Your Punter: The Rise and Fall of the Sun* (London: Heinemann), 1990, p.60

advertising policies is of immense importance. In her memoirs Thatcher writes:

> *Tim had a more sensitive set of antennae than most politicians. He could pick up quicker than anyone else a change in the national mood. And, unlike most advertising men, he understood that selling ideas is different from selling soap.*[62]

Through the years, Bell became a trusted assessor of public opinion and moods and was a crucial figure to each of Thatcher's successful general election campaigns and was, therefore, rewarded a knighthood in Thatcher's resignation honours list.

More interestingly however, both Tim Bell and Gordon Reece, important figures closely linked with the government, were consulted by the National Coal Board to advice on public relations during the miners' strike of 1984-85. Thatcher makes an explicit reference to this issue:

> *It was clearly very important that the NCB should do everything possible to get its case over to those tempted to give up the strike and return to work. On my recommendation, Tim Bell, who had given me so much good advice on presentation in the past, had begun to advise Ian MacGregor (NCB's Chairman).* (Thatcher: 1995 p. 354)

Another important figure in Thatcher's public relations team was Christopher Lawson, who in 1982 became the Conservative Party's first-ever Director of Marketing and was knighted in 1984. Lawson was extremely familiar with President Reagan's techniques of marketing political persuasion and had a business career that involved the selling of Mars bars. He had also been a Conservative local councilor in Hertfordshire where he first met Norman Tebbit and Cecil Parkinson.[63]

---

[62]Margaret Thatcher, *The Downing Street Years* (London: Harper & Collins), 1995, p. 354

[63]Source: M. Cockerell, P. Hennessy, D. Walker, *Sources Close the Prime Minister: Inside the hidden World of News Manipulation* (London: Macmillan), 1985, pp.190-99

Lawson was asked did he think that there was a difference in principle between marketing Mars bars and promoting the policies of a political party and selling them to the electorates?

I think there is a slight difference... I mean we had a saying in the old days that marketing involves everything from conception to consumption. I think it does in product terms. I think the big difference in marketing party political policies is that of course one has much less to say about what goes into the product than one did then but apart from that I think it's more or less the same. It's communication. (Cockerell et al., 1985 p. 198)

In this interview, Christopher Lawson reaffirms Thatcherite belief that party leaders and policies are seen as products which have to be sold to the voters. By 1988 Thatcher's government was spending £200 million on publicity and advertising, a figure which was only matched by Unilever and Proctor and Gamble in the private sector. Most of this sum was spent on promoting major privatization ventures. The government spent £42 million to publicize the privatization of the water industry and a further £100 million for the electricity privatization campaign.[64] In 1987, The *Financial Times* pointed out that:

When Mrs. Thatcher came into power in 1979, the Government spent a mere £31 million on advertising, on things like road safety campaigns. But a decade which has seen record unemployment levels, the selling off of State assets, and the emergence of diseases such as AIDS, has pushed the Government into the forefront of the advertising world... it was perhaps hardly surprising that her government should try to use the techniques of persuasion to convince the public that her policies were right.[65]

---

[64]Source: *The Observer*, 3 September 1989
[65]Quoted by A. Mattelart, *Advertising International: The Privatization of Public Space* (London: Routledge), 1991, p.192

The selling of British Petroleum is an interesting example of the government's publicity campaign in the 1980s. Both BBC and ITV ran news reports that mirrored the government's own political advertising. In other words, the publicity campaign became a news item and, in effect, making television news a space for free advertising. Indeed a media event was organized involving Royal Marines climbing down the side of the BP building to reveal the price of shares posted there. All this news coverage took place alongside interviews with government ministers, oil experts, and City analysts. Thus the ITN item on 15 October 1987 concluded: 'The issue is not likely to fail – today's razzmatazz was just to make sure of success.' In 1990, Mrs. Thatcher honoured (Dame) Sue Tinson, associate editor of ITN, in her resignation honours list (Ranelagh: 1991).

However, four days after the event on the infamous 'Black Monday', the price of BP shares on the Stock Exchange plummeted to well below the £3.30 at which the government was offering its own shares for sale.[66]

Having outlined these major characteristics of Mrs. Thatcher's propaganda policy, the next section of this chapter will now examines the role of the Prime Minister's press secretary as the crucial link between the media and the Prime Minister and whose contribution is worthy of a more detailed analysis.

The Prime Minister's Press Secretary

For most people mass media are the only significant sources of finding out about the events in parliament or No 10 Downing Street. The role of the Prime Minister's press secretary, therefore, is of immense importance since he does much to set the tone of the government. Bernard Ingham was appointed as Mrs. Thatcher's press secretary in November 1979 and remained in that post throughout her term. He was a journalist and

---

[66]Source: G. Philo, 'Political Advertising and Popular Belief', in G. Philo (ed), *Glasgow Media Group Reader*, Vol 2: *Industry, Economy, War and Politics*, op.cit., pp210-12

Labour activist in the 1950s and 1960s, entering the civil service as press officer for Harold Wilson's Prices and Income Board in 1965. He became Thatcher's press secretary through normal civil service procedures. Ingham left Number Ten in November 1990 when Mrs. Thatcher resigned and was subsequently knighted in her resignation honours list.

Bernard Ingham describes his duties as the Prime Minister's Chief Press secretary:

> *A Chief Press Secretary in Number 10 has three major tasks. They are to: 1 serve as spokesman for the Prime Minister and, as the occasion requires it, the Government as a whole; 2 act as advisor to the Prime Minister on his or her presentational program and to the Government as a whole on the overall presentation of its policies and measures; and to 3 co-ordinate, at official as distinct from Ministerial level, the Government's presentational program – to conduct the Government's communications orchestra.*[67]

For many journalists the Prime Minister's Press Secretary is a regular source of information and a crucial link between the government and the media. Accordingly, few people were granted a better and more complete view of what was going on in Government than Bernard Ingham. Ingham seemed to live a charmed life, for Mrs. Thatcher's prompt, and at times devastating, criticisms of her ministers and of other senior civil servants were legendary. Ingham, however, received a different treatment from the others. His loyalty was never in question and for that reason if he committed an error, she would always criticize the press and the journalists for getting it wrong; Ingham, she absolved from blame.[68] Ingham gave the impression that he was serving in a presidential government. In doing so he was of course acting fully in accordance with the Prime Minister's desires; otherwise he would not have held his office so

---

[67]Bernard Ingham, *Kill the Messenger* (London: Harper Collins), 1991, p.177
[68]See R. Harris, *Good and Faithful Servant* (London: Farber & Farber), 1990, pp121-23

long, nor would Thatcher have been so emphatic in her praise of him. Above all, Ingham was given wide 'license to leak' differences of opinion within the cabinet. From 1979 to 1981, in particular, he told lobby correspondents stories of the Prime Minister's stunning victories, some of them mythical, over her cabinet colleagues (Harris: 1990 p. 122). Through his 'leaks' Ingham played a major part in the rift between Thatcher and her cabinet colleagues (Economist: 20 June 1981, Lawson: 1992 pp 469-70).

The Thatcher-Ingham act was based on the agreement that while Thatcher was vigorously defending a colleague in the House of Commons, Ingham, speaking with the Lobby correspondents upstairs, might be giving an opposite version under the protective cloak of anonymity. Francis Pym, John Biffen and Geoffrey Howe, amongst others, were the target of the Thatcher-Ingham act (Harris: pp 89-91, Ingham: 1991 pp319-33).

Yet despite this peculiar use of the lobby system most of the national press remained loyal members of the lobby – only *the Guardian, the Independent,* and *the Scotsman* withdrew from Ingham's unattributable briefings. (Kavanagh and Seldon: 1989 pp294-95)

The Thatcher-Ingham partnership has drawn much criticism. Thatcher's former Defense Secretary, Sir John Nott, called Ingham's use of the lobby 'sickening, deplorable and malicious'. Edward Heath argued that 'the press office at No 10 had been used in a way which can be described as corrupt – in a way which went far beyond not only the achievements but even the aspirations of any previous government' (Harris: pp 175-92). Nigel Lawson, Chancellor of the Exchequer, 1983-89, critically describes Ingham's impact in the 1980s:

> *One of the most self-defeating aspects of the Thatcher regime was Margaret's excessive and increasing reliance on Bernard Ingham.... A blunt, sometimes thug-like, xenophobic Yorkshire man, Ingham became a tremendous admirer and promoter of the Prime Minister and her activities.... He was only really at home with the*

tabloids – above all the Sun – and once rebuked a newly appointed Press Secretary of mine for wasting time lunching with senior Financial Times writer, instead of cultivating those who really mattered. At quite an early stage, Margaret decided that she had no time to read the newspapers during the week. Instead, Ingham would get into Number 10 very early each morning, go through the papers himself, and prepare her a crisply written press summary. This had a selection and a slant that was very much his own. It would usually start with the Sun, the paper he himself was closest to and which he had taught Margaret represented the true views of the man on the street. It was also the paper whose contents he could most readily influence. This led to a marked circularity. Margaret would sound off about something, Ingham would then translate the line into Sun-ese and feed it to that newspaper, which would normally use it. This would then take pride of place in the news summary he provided for Margaret, who marveled at the unique rapport she evidently enjoyed with the British people.[69]

Mrs. Thatcher's press office was subordinate not just to party but to personal advantage. By the abuse of the lobby system which shields the identity of the briefer, the news was being managed and massaged for the benefit of the Prime Minister.'[70]

The Thatcherite communication strategy was, therefore, successful in the popularization process of its 'political and social agenda'. This study will empirically argue that this popularization process was partly 'manufactured and presented' by the media, particularly the national press. Accordingly, it will be argued that Thatcherism was a political and social mission, which contributed greatly in minimizing the role of organized opposition and labour in the process of income policy.

However, in an approach away from the deterministic idea of

---

[69] Nigel Lawson,*The View From No. 11: Memories of a Tory Radical* (London: Corgi Books), 1993, p.467
[70] See J. Ranelagh, Op.cit., pp 234, 248, 254-256, 291

'blanket indoctrination', it will be shown that Thatcherism derived its new 'power bloc' from an unsettled and volatile alliance of different actors who found it suitable for their own gains and interests, thus, acquiring the label of 'multi-faceted populism'. In this context, an instrumental analysis which ignores the relative autonomy of the state and the complexities of political struggle will be avoided. It will be taken into consideration the shift in economic strategy in Britain from Keynesianism to monetarism and the political significance of this shift in strategy.

At the same time, the complex political conjuncture and the discursive strategies whose effects benefited some more than others will not be forgotten. There is a valuable point in Jessop's assertion that the political and ideological context of Thatcherism is the discontent of the middle classes; small and medium capital against the economic and social impact of the Keynesian welfare state.[71] The social basis of Thatcherism in both the middle and working classes meant that the Tories had to make some significant acquiescence to these groups. These allowances were not only economic but also political and ideological.

To conclude this section, it has been argued that the task of this study as a whole is to provide a new approach to the problem of modern culture. The term Thatcherism, in this study, is used to assess the processes whereby its approach as a suitable solution to Britain's social, political and economic crises was accepted by the majority. This particular view, moreover, was diffused to all sections of society by the way of a capital intensive culture industry of which the press industry has been selected as an independent unit of analysis. On the theoretical level, therefore, the concept of 'multi-faceted populism' was proposed and expanded upon. Connected to this concept, the central hypothesis of this book relates the Thatcherite project, its inception and expansion, to one aspect of the culture industry, i.e. the national press. The empirical sections of this study (Chapters Three and Four) aim to show that Thatcherism

[71] See Jessop *et al*, Op.cit., p.58

provided new definitions for 'the way things should be', in which it had no class or partisan belonging, but informed the attitudes, activities, and loyalties of people from various classes and partisan constituencies.

Thatcherism will be regarded as a project which articulated an alternative idea of the national popular interest with the specific policies necessary to secure its realization. However this project had a lesser emphasis on the ideological incorporation of the masses, for it was mixed with a 'dual action' of political economy.

Furthermore, Thatcherism provided a new political agenda with new issues and political priorities: greater economic freedom, individualism as opposed to collectivism and consolidating the state machinery in its new, more restricted role.

In terms of popularity, Thatcherism had a set of specific strategies for economic regeneration and expansion. The 'privatization' scheme was deployed to launch an anti-statist rhetoric of freedom and responsibility. The popularity of denationalization and share ownership which supposedly transcended class barriers may be helpful in grasping the economic project's specificity. Policies such as union reforms, public spending cuts, higher defense spending, and the attack on local government autonomy, had a popular justification for their implementation.

Related to this issue Thatcherism, created new 'electoral perspectives' by which party leaders reconciled the electoral ideologies of rank-and-file activists and the views of the mass electorates as a precondition of winning office. With the leadership of Thatcher there was certainly a significant shift in the Conservative Party in its greater emphasis on populism in their mass electoral appeal. This was particularly clear in the 'realigning election of 1979 but less obvious in 1983, 1987'. In all cases, nonetheless, popular elements were articulated with other themes, such as neo-liberalism, egoism and nationalism'.[72]

---

[72]Gamble distinguishes between 'electoral ideologies' and 'electoral perspectives'. Electoral ideologies refers to the electoral line of a political party which are articulated among party activists and committed voters. See: A. Gamble, *The Conservative Nation* (London: Routledge & Kegan), 1974, pp 8-9

Thatcherism, by its popular appeal, reorganized the state by placing emphasis on law and order, the consolidation of the state apparatus, the concentration and centralization of power, the increased central state influence over education, youth training and welfare.

Having proposed these theoretical issues, the next section aims to deal with the methodological-indicators-model.

The Indicators: Methodological Approach

One of the crucial objectives of communication is to persuade. Persuasion is a special instance of social influence in which a person or a group attempts to change another person or group by communicating 'information' supporting the desired change.[73]

For many years we were led to believe that the mass media have minimal influence in the process of political socialization and relatively no effect on voting behaviour. One reason to question these assumptions is that in a substantial amount of research conducted in the USA and in Britain, the mass media were not included as either 'dependent or independent' variables.[74]

The present study has sought to use the 'press industry' as an important 'independent variable'. Although this focus is limited yet it is broad enough to provide a sound basis for a sociological research on the crisis of modern popular culture.

The press should not be seen as a simple source of 'stimulus' which reinforces predispositions. This view fails to account for increasing evidence that media use is a highly structured activity. People form habits of media use, and these habits are often formed because an individual consciously decides to use the media to serve certain purposes or desires. These habits are adjusted to an individual's everyday routine. When political

---

[73]See: A.S. Tan, *Mass Communication: Theories and Research* (NY: Wiley and Sons), 1981
[74]S. Kraus and D. Davis, *The Effects of Mass Communication on Political Behaviour* (Pennsylvania Press), 1976

events, issues and personalities are given extensive coverage by the mass media, we can expect that they receive mass attention by the general public. It is possible that certain ways of presenting news about particular events may have more or less immediate consequences for political, social and economic processes. Indeed certain issues may be communicated so that they are perceived as being highly salient by a majority of the public. This may affect the consequences for a particular political issue, personality or other social processes.

The presentation by the mass media, particularly the popular press, of the Thatcherite project was greatly influential on political and social behaviour, which resulted in a salient perception of it. In recent years there have been a number of empirical studies which attempted to examine the relationship between the popular press and Thatcherism. Some concentrated on the economic aspects, others on the political and social sides. In the following section, some of these significant studies will be mentioned in an attempt to construct a distinct methodological stance. Patrick Dunleavy and Chris Husbands, in their study of the voting patterns in Britain, argue that the press exerted a very clear effect on voting patterns during the 1983 election.

> *Within all the class categories used the Conservative vote is some 30 percent lower amongst people primarily exposed to non Tory messages than it is amongst readers of the Tory press, a high level of association that has few parallels amongst either social background or issue influences. The difference is even more marked when we compare the two extreme groups, those exposed to a predominantly Tory message and those receiving a predominantly non-Tory one; the difference in Conservative support range from 36 to 58 points.*[75]

---

[75] P. Dunleavy and C. Husbands, *British Democracy at the Crossroads* (London: George Allen and Unwin), 1985, p.115

Ken Newton in his study uses a different methodology in establishing the influence of the press on the attitude of readers. In a small scale study, Newton examines the extent of the 'newspaper effect' by considering only 'cross-readers': those respondents whose newspaper reading does not 'match' their voting opinions whilst controlling for attitudes towards election issues. By using this methodology, Newton avoids an important analytical problem of whether there is any way of definitely establishing how far newspapers influence their readers. Newton's finding is rather interesting. Overall, he argues, the figures confirm the hypothesized major impact of attitudes and the more minor impact of newspapers after the effect of attitudes has been taken into account.[76]

In a relatively large scale study, David Sanders attempted to examine the correlation between the influence of the 'popular press' on the portrayal of the British economy, 1979-1987.[77] The study produced some interesting results suggesting that there is a considerable amount of evidence to argue that the political preferences of voters are influenced by the condition of the domestic economy. In their study, Sanders *et al.*, examined the proposition that in Britain, at least, the connection between macroeconomic change and public perceptions of the government are mediated by the way in which major national daily newspapers cover economic news. Using an aggregate data-analytic approach, it is shown that there is a moderate correlation between the economic coverage of most national dailies and the condition of 'real economy'. They also show that although press coverage of the economy fails to exert a direct effect on government popularity, it does exert an indirect effect through its impact on the overall level of personal financial optimism and pessimism. They undertook a systematic description of the

---

[76]See Ken Newton, 'Do People Read Everything They Believe in the Papers?' in I. Crew and P. Norris (eds), *Newspapers and Voters in the 1983 and 1987 Elections*, British Parties and Election Yearbook, (London: Simon & Schuster), 1991
[77]D. Sanders, D. Marsh, H. ward, 'The Electoral Impact of Press Coverage of the British Economy', 1979-87,*British Journal of Political Science*, 1993, Vol 23, April, pp.175-210

daily coverage of economic issues provided by seven national newspapers. Using the method of 'content analysis', five types of economic categories were set up. These were Unemployment, Inflation, Exchange Rate/Balance of Payments, Public Borrowing, and General Economic. By utilizing statistical methods Sanders and company show that the balance of economic coverage by the press gradually tended to be more and more sympathetic from the middle of 1981 onwards. The data supported the view that a large segment of the British national dailies tended to be broadly supportive of the Conservative party in their presentation of economic news. The important point here is that, confronted with the same objective economic circumstances, certain newspapers consistently contrived to interpret events in a manner broadly sympathetic to the government. This is compelling evidence showing the way in which the party political predispositions of the major British newspapers inform their coverage of economic news.

Another important result by the Sanders team is the finding that the pro-Conservative press did tend to provide more sympathetic coverage for the government during 'election campaigns', though these effects were much more pronounced in 1983 than in 1987.

In all of the studies outlined above, with the exception of Hall's Authoritarian Populism, the 'popular press' was used as an independent variable, together with some dependent variables which tended to be economic. Hall's study tended to be more political and social. However, since this study attempts to concentrate on the issue of the Thatcherite 'multi-faceted populism', with a special reference to the outcome of certain Thatcherite policies, political and social issues will form the dependent variables as portrayed by the independent variable, the popular press. This approach also aims to take into account the role of the press industry in the popularity of the Thatcherite project at the cultural level.

The national press was chosen as a unit of analysis for two reasons. Firstly, by the 1980s, the British public read more newspapers proportionally than any comparable

Western nation.[78]

Furthermore, it is the newspapers which provide so much material and help fix the parameters for debates and news reporting on television. As argued above, the national press, during Thatcher's era displayed a significant partisanship unequalled in the recent history of British mass democracy. This has made the 'relative objectivity' and pluralism of the television output stand out in comparison. The combined circulation of the tabloid press in Britain at times exceeded seven million copies per day. This is a good reason to concentrate on the 'popular press', although this research will demonstrate that some quality newspapers were not far off the standards set by the populars.[79]

Press consumption and entertainment is a significant part of Britain's cultural intake, and as contended by the Frankfurt School theorists, the distraction, messages and journalistic style of the popular papers has an important ideological dimension. As early as the 1950s Hoggart sensed the danger posed by the press:

> *most mass entertainments are full of corrupt brightness, of improper appeals and moral evasions ... they assist a gradual drying-up of the more positive, the fuller, the more cooperative kinds of enjoyment, in which one gains much by giving much. The popular press was contributing*

---

[78] The newspaper reading habit: an international table; circulation per 1,000 inhabitants:

SWEDEN	526
UNITED KINGDOM	479
NORWAY	459
DENMARK	367
NETHERLANDS	325
WEST GERMANY	324
UNITED STATES	282
ITALY	238

(Source: United Nations Yearbook – 1985)

[79] This figure was produced by calculating 'published' figures of Four daily tabloids and 2 middle range national newspapers. It is important to note that this figure is for those people who actually bought these newspapers in one day. We believe that this figure would be substantially higher if we calculate those who don't actually buy these papers but invariably come in contact with them. For example reading a friend's or partner's or in a waiting room or in libraries, etc.

to the erosion of the decent local, personal and communal way of life of traditional working-class culture.[80]

Although one might think that the excessive entertainment contents of the popular press may not be connected to the political domination and manufacturing consent, according to Adorno and Horkheimer they essentially embody the dominant ideas and common sense. The seemingly harmless pages decorated with colourful pictures and editorials of the tabloid industry provide a fragmented, atomistic view of the world, compelling people to neglect crucial and topical issues such as class struggle, echoing the Thatcherite motto that 'there is no such thing as society.'[81]

Despite the confirmation of the Frankfurt School's theory of culture industry, the connection between the politics and the entertainment of the press industry is not wholly perfect. The stress upon the notion of an 'active audience' is quite crucial here as it reinstates a perception of the audience as people for whom the mass media are merely one part of some complex patterns of life and ideas. People choose to read entertaining materials. They are not simply being fed with them.

Curran and Sparks rightly assert that the tabloid press, in their pages, does not simply impose a picture of the world on its audience, but rather starts from their experiences and interests and works them into a form that is pleasurable and entertaining. Since the majority of the tabloid readers are working class and experience life in a way that is partly different from the representations of reality within the dominant culture, this generates tensions and contradictions within the pages of the popular press.[82]

To empirically validate these aspects of representations and contradictions created by the press, this thesis has chosen to study the fortunes of the miners to demonstrate the effects of the

---

[80] R. Hoggart, *The Uses of Literacy* (London: Chatto & Windus and Harmondsworth), 1957, p.244
[81] D. Steel, 'Why I Have a Few Regrets', *The Observer*, May 15, 1988
[82] J. Curran & C. Sparks, 'Press and Popular Culture', *Media, Culture and Society*, 1991, Vol;13, (2), p.232

Thatcherite project on two distinctive levels. Firstly, the growth and development of the Thatcherite 'multi-faceted populism' and its impact upon the working class. Secondly, the erosion of the organised opposition and the process of creating internal conflict and division in the working class organizations such as the NUM.

In an attempt to establish a correlation between the miners' defeat in 1985 and the attitude of the press, and its role in facilitating this defeat, this thesis shows how the 'power of resistance' by working class organizations was undermined.

In Britain, the erosion of popular political organizations and the concentration of political life into forms directly related to the media have contributed to an increasing drying up of the ideological wells of resistance.[83]

Furthermore, the miners constituted a real threat to the initial phases of the Thatcherite project. They were regarded by the Tories as old class enemies. The defeat of Heath's administration at the hands of the miners had a significant negative impression on the Conservative Party. There was no better way for Thatcherism to renew its momentum than a victory against the miners. Indeed to take on the miners, who had a history of working class solidarity, would have shown that the miners are not invincible after all and which would be a warning to other working class organisations that industrial action would prompt the Government to react severely. By defeating the NUM, the Thatcherite views nurtured a new realism amongst the trade union movement in Britain. For the purpose of reliability and validity, a historical and comparative dimension to this study is necessary.[84]

Accordingly, the role of the press industry in the miners

---

[83] J. Curran & C. Sparks, *ibid*
[84] Here we found the Weberian approach to history useful. Weber studied history mainly in order to make comparisons. His case studies are strewn with references to other situations and with generalisations or hints at possible generalisations. Weber has shown that the ability to compare different situations aids enormously the analysis of any given society, and particularly the discovery of causal relationships.

strikes of 1972 and 1974 and the subsequent defeat of Edward Heath's government will be examined. The dependent variables used here remain the same as those to be used in the 1984-85 miners' strike. These are the attitude of the miners and other sections of the working class and the portrayal of Heath's economic and social policies by the national press.

The inclusion of the miners' strikes of 1970s will highlight the following themes. Firstly, an analysis of the NUM's position is crucial in our assessment of the 'solidarity and values' of a large section of the working class in both periods of Conservative power (Heath and Thatcher). Accordingly, the way in which different Conservative governments responded to the strikes staged by the NUM, and the attitude of the general public, is crucial in our understanding of the complex relationship between the press industry and the ruling ideas.

Secondly, both the Conservative governments of Heath and Thatcher entered office when Britain was going through a severe economic recession. This study is concerned with the problem of how and why one government collapsed whilst the other not only survived but also managed to hold on to power for two further elections.

A systematic 'content analysis' of a sample of national dailies will form the methodological tool of this thesis. The empirical chapter of this study will assess the problems and the usefulness of this method, and a new proposal will be offered for enhancing its effectiveness and reliability.

Conclusion

This chapter aimed to establish a link between concepts and indicators. Theoretically, it was argued that, the problem of 'Thatcherism' should be viewed as a particular form of 'populism' with a multi-faceted dimension. Thatcherism became a popular project because of its appeal to disparate groups in different sectors of society. At the economic level it appealed to the economic 'mega'actors in the City and other major economic centres, at the political level it made sense to those floating voters across the country, and at the cultural level it pleased the newly revived patriots, lower, upper middle and the working classes.

Methodologically, it was argued, the notion of 'multi-faceted populism' as opposed to 'Authoritarian Populism' or 'Two Nations' allows us to examine Thatcherism from different angles and points of departure. Above all, the concept is particularly useful in understanding the changing role of the mass media, especially the popular press, in the ideological struggle. Accordingly, the relationship between the Thatcher governments and the media were examined and the underlying characteristics of media and advertising policies were explored with a particular reference to the crucial 'mega and collective' actors who facilitated those policies in the 1980s. It was shown, empirically, that some of these important actors clearly connected to the government, were also utilized to assist the National Coal Board in its conflict with miners in the 1984-85 strike.

The inclusion of a comparative study of the miners' strikes in this study may shed some light on the way 'principal ideas' of Thatcherism were introduced and cultivated. It will be proposed, and empirically assessed, that this was based upon a tactical strategy to undermine opposition, be it internal or external to the Conservative Party.

In this chapter several theories of Thatcherism were considered. Some were deemed as redundant, some were perceived as influential in the formation of a theoretical position of this study

In an attempt to further develop the theoretical arguement of this book, the next two chapters are devoted to a detailed examination of the economic and structural organization of the national press industry in the 1980s.

THREE

THE PRESS INDUSTRY IN THATCHER'S YEARS
A Model for British Culture Industry?

Introduction

This chapter aims to examine the role, and the impact, of the press industry in the Thatcherite epoch, in light of the Thatcherite 'multi-faceted populism'. During the 1980s, it will be argued, the industry further expanded its role as the supporting sector of the hegemonic capital. At its height, the 1980s witnessed the phenomenal integration of the British press into the core sectors of financial and industrial capital. This chapter will argue that modern popular national newspapers in Britain either have, or are controlled by, a major interest outside the industry. Accordingly, this chapter will examine some of the social, political and economic factors involved in this process and demonstrate that the growing business interests of the press empires in modern Britain have created a whole set of delicate networks of co-operation between the press and other giant multinationals. Accordingly, this chapter will further develop the analysis of *macro* and *collective agency* in the internal and external spheres of the press. Consequently, the role of the modern media proprietors and other business leaders in restructuring the modern British press will be further examined .

Mass media cannot be studied independently from their content, nor can there be a sociology of mass culture that does not examine communication technology. The underlying aim of this chapter is to show that technology and culture (form and content, medium and message) are inseparable and mutually interrelated. Mass culture and mass media, therefore, must be examined together. Indeed, through an examination of the consequences of the technological changes which occurred within the press industry, it will be argued that it is not the *technological determinism* which matters, rather *technology and agency* complimenting each other in producing the effects which are the indispensable and permanent features of the modern press industry. This chapter will pay particular attention to the most striking developments within the press in the 1980s and the following four issues will be considered. Firstly, the *unprecedented* increase in the concentration of capital with the significant integration of the modern press into the core sectors of financial and industrial resources. Secondly, the technological transformation in the contemporary press industry. Thirdly, the increasing polarization between quality and popular, national and provincial newspapers and finally, the increasing partisan role of the press industry.

This chapter is, therefore, comprised of two closely related parts. The first part is an analysis of the continuity and development of concentration of capital in the press during the Thatcher years. Appropriately, the chapter strives to examine the role of Rupert Murdoch in order to assess the contribution of modern press barons to the structural development of the industry. The second part will examine the impact of the new technological progress and its effects upon the industry in the Thatcher era. The purpose here is to assess the impact, and the consequences, of technological developments within the industry and the social, economic and political effects outside it.

In the course of these analyses, the role of agency in these structural developments will be assessed further. By considering the role of the political, economic and institutional actors in the Thatcher epoch, this chapter will demonstrate that these actors played a significant role in the way the press industry was mobilised to enhance, and further cultivate, the Thatcherite multi-faceted populism as a part of the process of sustaining a social order favourable to the interests of all those involved. It would be naive, however, to argue that this involvement occurred in a uniform pattern and always without conflicts and contradictions. It will be maintained that at times these groups of actors were, in fact, internally and externally disunited and in conflict with each other.

This chapter will now assess the role of Rupert Murdoch as an example of modern press proprietors and will strive to demonstrate how these *mega actors* in the internal sphere were to render their services to the Thatcherite political, economic and social ideology, and how these ideas were transmitted by the press and were shared, and consumed in '*standardized*' form, by multitude of readers across the country.

The 'Murdoch' Factor in the British Press:
Macro Agency in the Internal Sphere

> *When all allowances have been made for variations within the industry, its most striking feature, and possibly its greatest problem, is its dominance by a small number of highly individualistic proprietors with their own personal interests and philosophy of management.*[1]

This section will examine the institution of press ownership in modern Britain. It will be maintained that despite the radical changes in the sphere of press ownership, modern press proprietors remain powerful mega actors with considerable social, economic and political power.

The modern epoch has witnessed the emergence of new forms of press owners who are inventive and partisan businessmen. The prime objective for modern press barons, such as Rupert Murdoch and Robert Maxwell, was the acquisition of more publications and other media properties. The driving force for them is profits, growth and financial performance. Political influence, however, provides an added incentive, not least because it may be turned to commercial advantage.

The most notable, and perhaps most significant, example of modern press barons is Rupert Murdoch. Murdoch has not only built an empire, he also is a risk-taking entrepreneur with an

[1] Private Management Inquiry – commissioned by newspaper publishers- 1966

eccentric management style which may involve political motives.[2]

Murdoch's talent for *acquisition* began in 1950s with one daily newspaper in Adelaide, South Australia, which he inherited from his father. He subsequently built an Australian empire which included the Channel 9 television franchise in Adelaide and Sydney's *Daily Mirror*. By the late 1960s Murdoch was a major Australian media baron.[3]

In 1969 Murdoch began building his empire in Britain. He first acquired the *Sunday News of the World*, then the daily *Sun*. By 1973 the *Sun*'s circulation had risen from one to three million and was generating enough profits to fuel Murdoch's American adventure. There he began with newspapers before switching to magazines, a Hollywood production studio and a chain of television stations.[4]

By 1990 he was the leading newspaper baron in both Britain and Australia, owner of the massively circulating US weekly magazine – *TV Guide* – and five other major magazines and owner of two book publishing interests Harper & Row in the US and Collins in the UK. There is a steady trend to larger and larger acquisitions. The 1988 purchase of *TV Guide* for $2.85 billion was the largest deal in publishing history.[5] In Britain, his acquisition of the *Sun*, the *News of the World*, and later the *Sunday Times*, proved extremely profitable and partly responsible for his international expansion. Before discussing Murdoch's other interests, a brief analysis of the manner of his acquisition of *The Times* and *Sunday Times* is necessary, not least because it remains a remarkable example of the collusion between Murdoch and the Thatcher government and marks a reciprocal relationship between the mega actors within the press industry and those in the political sphere. This collaboration began in 1979 and lasted almost to her last days in office. Here,

---

[2]See J. Tunstall and M. Palmer, *Media Moguls* (London: Routledge), 1991
[3]Source: M. Leapman, *Bearfaced Cheek: Rupert Murdoch* (London: Coronet), 1983, pp. 24-32
[4]See: S. Regan, *Rupert Murdoch: A Business Biography* (London: Angus & Robertson), 1976
[5]See: *Business Week* (Europe), 22 August 1988, 'Murdoch adds a few megatons to his arsenal'

we will outline and discuss three significant examples of this extraordinary relationship, and will refer to this theme in the latter parts of the chapter.

Thatcher–Murdoch Reciprocity: The path to the ownership of *Times* Newspapers

Prior to the acquisition of *The Times* Newspapers, Murdoch was already in control of the *News of the World* and the *Sun* and had met Mrs. Thatcher on several occasions before he committed the support of the *Sun* during her winning election campaign of 1979.[6] The 1979 General Election witnessed the transformation of the old Labour-supporting *Daily Herald/ Sun* into the new Murdoch version of the *Sun* which in 1979 'voted' Conservative for the first time. The *Sun*'s front page editorial, on the election day, was headlined:

> 'Vote Tory This Time. It's The Only Way To Stop The Rot.'

A great deal was at stake when the grapple for ownership of Times Newspapers began. Murdoch's interest not only entailed a greater concentration of the ownership of the national press, but it could also tilt the balance even more towards support for Thatcher in both the tabloid and quality markets. Murdoch's proposal could have been referred to the Monopolies Commission, since it threaten to erode the foundation of a pluralist media. In 1981, when the Times Newspapers went up for sale, the bidders included, amongst others, Robert Maxwell; Lord Mathews; Lord Rothermere, owner of Associated Newspapers; and Rupert Murdoch. Harold Evans, who was then editor of the *Sunday Times*, and William Rees-Mogg, then the editor of *The Times* were also in contention to purchase the titles on behalf of the management and journalists.[7] Thatcher,

---

[6]A very interesting account of this event appears in L. Lamb, '*Sunrise*', op.cit. pp 150-60
[7]Source: J. Eldridge, J. Kitzinger and K. Williams, '*The Mass Media and Power in Modern Britain*', op.cit, pp34-5

however, supported Murdoch's bid and agreed with his fictional claim that both *The Times* and *Sunday Times* were loss-making newspapers in danger of collapsing which therefore should not be referred to the Monopolies Commission.

Murdoch fiercely opposed such a course of action because there were always the danger that the Monopolies Commission would find several grounds on which to oppose the acquisition. On 22 January 1981, Thomson British Holdings announced that Murdoch had been successful in his bid to purchase *The Times* and *Sunday Times*. Ironically, the unions backed Murdoch on the grounds that he had successfully built up the *Sun* and created more employment.[8]

Once in control of the Times Newspapers, Murdoch met Evans and offered him the editorship of *The Times*. Frank Giles replaced Evans as editor of *The Sunday Times*.

This avoidance of the Monopolies Commission is the most remarkable example of how Thatcher was able to use the vague wording of the monopoly law for her own political purposes. Moreover, this episode also exemplifies the general acquiescence of many journalists and of the trade unions. The journalists on the two newspapers eventually failed to follow through on their intention to take the issue to court.[9]

Once again, in 1987, when Murdoch purchased *Today* (founded in 1986) from 'Tiny' Rowland of Lonrho there was no reference to the Monopolies Commission. This time a government Minister, Jonathan Aitken, argued that the matter was not to be referred to the Commission because it did not constitute 'a going concern'.[10]

The last gift by Thatcher to Murdoch happened only a month before she was forced to resign in November 28, 1990. On October 29, Murdoch visited Thatcher and informed her of the forthcoming merger of the two satellite services, BSB and SKY. This merger actually contravened the provisions of the

---

[8] The Print unions backing for Murdoch's bid was an ironic decision. In the light of the events at Wapping, which will be discussed in detail later, this decision by the unions was one of the most intriguing events of the 1980s.
[9] See: H. Evans, *'Good Times, Bad Times'*, op.cit.
[10] Quoted by J. Tunstall, *The Newspaper Power*, op.cit, part V

Broadcasting Act. Nonetheless, Thatcher agreed to the merger, and did not hand on the information. The BSB/SKY merger was agreed and announced on November 3, 1990 six days after Thatcher was first informed.[11]

Outside Britain, Murdoch's highly profitable British trio of the *Sun*, *News of the World* and later *The Sunday Times* enabled the News Corporation to acquire more and more interests in American media. Murdoch's global empire now includes over 100 papers stretching from Hong Kong, the USA and Australia, as well as ownership of the very successful Sky Channel and major shareholder status in the publishing group Collins. In this respect Murdoch's company strategy increasingly saw the British newspapers as 'profit-generators'. This strategy can be seen in the sale based of the *Sun*, and the News of the World, the advertising based of the *Sunday Times*, as well as in the frequent mood and editor changes at *The Times*.[12]

Murdoch's newspapers, in return, became increasingly partisan from 1979 onwards. As a matter of methodological necessity the next section will examine editorials and political comments of the *Sun*, the *News of the World*, and *The Times* to determine the extent of the partisanship in Murdoch's newspapers throughout the 1980s.

Murdoch–Thatcher Reciprocity: Content Analysis of the Sun, the *News of the World* and *The Times* – 1979-87

This section will empirically assess the extent of Murdoch's increasing political partisanship, in the 1980s, as displayed by three of his newspapers in Britain. It has been established that the *Sun*, the *News of the World* and *The Times* were Conservative supporters in all three general elections, involving Thatcher.

---

[11]Sources: Newspaper reports on this merger: *The Guardian, The Independent and The Observer.* M. Palmer, J. Tunstall, *Liberating Communications: Policy-Making in France and Britain* (Oxford: Blackwell), 1990. J. Tunstall, 'Newspaper Power', op.cit.

[12]See J. Tunstall, *Newspaper Power*, op.cit.

(Miller *et al.*, 1990 and 1991; Dunleavy and Husbands 1985). This study, however, will present a new approach to assess the extent of the support for the Conservatives as demonstrated by Murdoch's papers in these periods.

The Sample
The sampling procedure for this research is as follows:

1. Three newspapers, which were randomly selected, are Murdoch's major national papers the *Sun*, the *News of the World* and *The Times*.
2. The time-frame for this research is two weeks prior to three general elections since 1979. The first period includes 20 April to 3 May 1979, the second period includes 28 May to 9 June 1983 and the third period include 1 to 11 June 1987.
3. The front page headlines and comments, the editorials and political comments of the above-mentioned papers were quantitatively and qualitatively content analysed.

The Categories
Three sets of categories were used by this study to assess the extent of partisanship presented by Murdoch's national papers. These are the categories of **'supporting'**, **'campaigning for'** and **'crusading against'** and each are measured at the level of individual articles and editorials examined here. Since we are comparing the extent of partisanship within the chosen papers, these categories are 'internally coherent' with the objective of this research.

The category of **'supporting'** denotes a simple political support for the Conservatives such as:

'VOTE FOR MAGGIE TO GIVE YOU AND YOUR CHILDREN A BETTER BRITAIN' (The *Sun* June 1983)

'I BELIEVE! THIS COULD BE OUR LAST

CHANCE TO BUILD A BETTER BRITAIN' Mrs. Thatcher (The *Sun* 12 April 1979, Front page)

'The mums back Maggie: The women of Britain have given... Maggie Thatcher an overwhelming vote of confidence.' (*News of the World* June 1983)

The category of **'campaigning for'**, which is measured here at the level of individual article or editorial, denotes a biased support for the Conservatives with some access to the opposing views and policies, such as:

'TUC pact won't fix for Jim' The P.M.'s new agreement with the TUC... stands little hope of achieving its main objective – restoring Government authority' (*News of the World*, 1979)

HELL OF A JOB: Labour leader Michael Foot startled his party last night by admitting they had "a hell of a lot to do to catch up". But he insisted Labour still has "a chance of winning." (*News of the World,* June 1983)

'The illiberal policies of the Labour Party... But they insist... these are good for Britain'. (*The Times* June 1983)

'Why It Pays to Buy a Council House'.(The *Sun* June 1987)

The category of **'crusading against'**, also measured at the level of individual article or editorial, denotes a very strong political bias towards the Conservatives with no access to the opposing views and policies. This category is 'usually' accompanied by *derogatory* words for the opposition such as:

'JIM'S BIG CON'... 'Don't be fooled by the Labour Party's cosy General Election manifesto. It is window dressing designed by the P.M. to con the electorate.' (The *Sun* April 1979)

'BLOODY BATTLE SET TO BURY LABOUR CORPSE' (*News of the World*, June 1983)

'Special Nightmare Issue- Life Under The Socialists' or 'Why I'm Backing Kinnock, By Stalin' (The *Sun* June 1987).

Having outlined the main points of this research the next section will outline the findings. The 'quantitative' results are presented in three separate tables for the General Elections of 1979, 1983 and 1987. This inquiry will also present some editorials, or political comments, published in a *standardized* format, for each period to illustrate the quantitative dimension of the research. This analysis begins with the role of Murdoch's papers in the 1979 election.

The 1979 General Election

In 1979 the *Sun* and the *News of the World* provided a support for the Conservatives which was clearly defined in their coverage of the campaign. Each displayed their partisanship by giving positive support to the Conservatives, while treating Labour and the Liberals in a pejorative fashion, or ignoring it. *The News of the World*, in particular, concentrated on the voting intentions of first time voters:

'YOUNG BRITAIN SWINGS OVER TO THE TORIES' (April 8 1979).

After a long series of clashes between management and unions, Times Newspapers suspended publication of *The Times* and the *Sunday Times*. For the 1979 election, therefore, *The Times* is excluded from this research.

As suggested by Table 3, 59 per cent of the *Sun*'s output, prior to the 1979 General Election, fell in the 'support' category, 28 per cent of its material was categorized as 'campaigning for' the Conservatives. For the category of 'crusading against' the

Table 3 1979 General Election

	Supporting	Campaigning For	Crusading Against
The Sun Editor: L. Lamb	59%	28%	13%
The News of The World Editor: B. Shrimsley	61%	30%	9%
The Times Editor: W.Rees-Mogg	Not Published		

opposition, the sample produced only 13 per cent of the total material examined. The *News of the World* followed a similar pattern with less than 10 per cent of its material crusading against the opposing political views. To put these figures in a 'qualitative' format the thesis will now present an editorial published by the *Sun*:

The *Sun*, Wednesday May 2, 1979- Page 2: 'The *Sun* Says'
The Sun has a bigger post bag than any other newspaper. We know that millions of traditional Labour voters have a sense of shame and outrage about the failures of Their government and the wild antics of Their party. At the same time, we understand the feeling of some of them that they still cannot bring themselves to vote Tory. But the only real alternative to five more years of drift IS Margaret Thatcher. A vote for Liberals, or any fringe party, is really a vote FOR Jim and against common sense. You cannot vote for a hung Parliament.. nor can you vote for the centre..if you would rather vote for a Social Democrat you will find that the only ACTIVE ones are now in the ranks of the Conservatives. The Sun's advice is: if you cannot bring yourself to vote Tory tomorrow, stay at home.

The 1983 General Election

In the general election of 1983, as suggested by Table 4, there is a marked increase in the partisanship of Murdoch's newspapers. Overall, these papers printed their political preference in a cruder manner than at any recent election. This claim is substantiated by the increasing percentages for the category of 'crusading against' the political parties other than the Conservatives.

In 1983, *The Times*, the *Sun* and the *News of the World* followed two primary themes; an attack on the dangerous extremism of Labour and a comparison of the leadership qualities of Mr. Foot and Mrs. Thatcher. To support this claim here is a selection of the 'standardized' material published by Murdoch papers.

> *The Times*, June 1 1983 - Page 12
> *Bernard Levin on the stark choice ahead: why we can all take hope for Labour's ruin.' 'The sight of Mr. Foot hanging himself higher and higher with every shifty, gaseous, unfinished, verb less, unintelligible sentence he emitted like ectoplasm in reply to Mr. Brian Walden's patient, courteous, deadly questions on Sunday's WEEKEND WORLD was so distressing... that I switched off two-thirds of the way through. I felt like a member of Greenpeace watching a month-old seal pup beating its own brains out. It is impossible not to experience a spasm of disbelief and the recollection that the opposition... decided four-fifths of the way through the twentieth century and in a free and secret ballot, to select this quavering old Struldbrugg as the most fitted to challenge Mrs. Thatcher's conservatism, and to govern the country in the event of that challenge succeeding.*

> *The Sun*, Thursday June 9, 1983 - The Sun Says: 'Vote for Maggie'
> *Don't waste your time on these no-hopers.' 'The General Election is a one-horse race. The only undecided question*

Table 4 1983 General Election

	Supporting	Campaigning For	Crusading Against
The Sun			
Editor: L. Lamb	41%	28%	31%
The News of The World			
Editor: B. Shrimsley	48%	32%	20%
The Times			
Editor: W. Rees-Mogg	59%	27%	14%

is who finishes second, the Socialists or the Alliance. Our advice: Don't waste your vote on either of these no-hopers. They have nothing constructive to offer a Britain that needs positive leadership... That is why The Sun's fervent wish is that the voters will grant her today the overwhelming mandate she has so richly earned. Carry on Maggie! All the way to the GREAT Britain that a great people deserve.

News of The World, **June 5, 1983 - COMMENT: 'Give her a chance to finish the job'**
The next four days will see a massive push to advance the Alliance's present poll rating of around 28 per cent by five or six points- putting up to 100 seats in jeopardy. It must not be allowed to happen. Only political confusion, with the ill-sorted crew of the Alliance holding a spurious balance of power, can thwart Britain's onward march towards peace, pride and renewed prosperity. The alternative ultimately could open door to the loonies of the Left already massively rejected by the British people. Strong majorities make for strong governments. Go out next Thursday and give Margaret Thatcher the chance to finish the job.

The 1987 General Election

The 1987 general election coincided with the settlement of the 'Wapping' dispute in favour of Murdoch. As will be shown in the latter parts of this chapter, Thatcher fully endorsed Murdoch's plans to move to Wapping. Murdoch's papers, in return, followed a basic theme to the 1987 election; the incompetence of the Labour Party and a well prepared smear campaign against individual politicians. In comparison with the 1983 general election, as shown by Table 5, there is a marked increase in the category of 'crusading against' political parties other than the Tories.

This research will now outline some of the *'standardized'* editorials by Murdoch's paper during the 1987 general election campaign.

The Times - June 10, 1987- page 17
In this campaign they [Tories] made a thoroughly good stab at... Mr. Kinnock's "red Rose" policies on taxation and defense... Conservative candidates all over the country have exposed Labour's confiscatory creed for British industry, its determination to bring back the secondary picket, its plan for schools in which it is the parents who must be seen and not heard.... In the word of the final Tory slogan, Britain can indeed be said to be great again. But it hangs on its greatness by a thin thread. Keeping it anything like as rich and great as its people want it to be will be no easier in the next 5 years than it was in the last. It will very likely to be harder. Only strong, determined government has a chance. This is not a simple election. The issues have touched the core of the British character and posed searching questions about our national life. For that very reason, however, it is emphatically not an election in which newspapers can sit on the fence, comforted by pious reflections about how no one single party matches its very aspiration... The Tory manifesto, with which the campaign began, contains critically important policies for enlarging the rented sector

Table 5 1987 General Election

	Supporting	Campaigning For	Crusading Against
The Sun Editor: K. McKenzie	47%	17%	36%
The News of The World Editor: D. Montgomery	40%	25%	35%
The Times Editor: C. Wilson	49%	31%	20%

of the property market, for splitting the ownership of decaying municipal estates, for extending the freedom of parents and schools.

The *Sun*, Wednesday June 10, 1987 - The *Sun* speaks its mind: WE'RE HALF-WAY THERE

....*When she became Tory leader 12 years ago, she said her vision was of "a man's right to work as he will, to spend what he earns, to own property, to have the Sate as his servant not his master. Mrs. Thatcher has found a response in the British people who are at their best as individuals. Mrs. Thatcher has given freedom back to the people. The Sun chooses freedom. We hope and pray that our readers will also choose freedom. Lets give Maggie FIVE MORE GREAT YEARS!*

News of The World, June 7, 1987

They [Labour party] didn't give a damn about their inefficiency and squandering taxpayers' money. They just enjoyed the power without personal responsibility. Profit was a dirty word, and still is, for Labour. But the bigger the profit the greater the modernisation and improvement for the consumer. Labour doesn't understand this. That's why Labour is pledged to take control of the big privatized industries again. Never mind the loses for the millions of ordinary shareholders, now the owners. Or that throughout the world Socialist control of industry has been proved a poverty-making disaster. Labour wants to get back to the dead world of Marx and Stalin. It makes them feel important.'

The editorials presented here demonstrates a marked increase in the political partisanship by Murdoch's newspapers in the three general elections involving Thatcher. As shown above, after the 1979 General Election, at the level of individual articles and editorials examined in the sample, Murdoch's national papers increasingly published cruder, more partisan and standardized materials than the previous election. In the latter parts of this chapter this reciprocal relationship between Murdoch and Thatcher, mega actors in the political sphere and the press, will be further analysed through an examination of the Wapping phenomenon. The next section, however, will examine Murdoch's proprietorial style for a better understanding of his business interests and the source of his political partisanship.

Murdoch's Proprietorial Style

Andrew Neil, former editor of the *Sunday Times* describes Murdoch's proprietorial style:

Rupert expects his papers to stand broadly for what he believes: a combination of right-wing Republicanism from America mixed with undiluted Thatcherism from Britain and stirred with some anti-British Establishment sentiments as befits his colonial heritage. The resulting potage is a radical-right dose of free market economics, the social agenda of the Christian Moral Majority and hard-line conservative views on subjects like drugs, abortion, law and order, and defence.'[13]

[13] A. Neil, *Full Disclosure*, op.cit. p.165

Generally, a press owner's political bias is not their salient' characteristic. As history has shown, before being a political partisan, Murdoch is, primarily, a businessman and defends whoever is in power to protect his interests, even though he may prefer right-wing policies. This claim can be substantiated by the *Sun's* support for Blair in the 1997 General Election. However, since the 1970s, as Murdoch himself became increasingly rightwing, his papers followed that direction. The *Sun* moved away from Labour to become a Conservative supporting paper after the 1974 General Election. This is despite the fact that over half of its readers were Labour supporters.[14]

Murdoch's direct and interventionist style, in some respect, could be seen as the return of the prewar press lords: ' ... in one of our editorial meetings he said that he did not come all this way not to interfere. He wanted to read proofs, write a leader if he likes it, change the paper about and give instructions to his staff.'[15]

The considerable pressure exerted by Murdoch's constant interference, led the first two editors of his *News of the World* to resign after spending only a few months in charge of the paper. Barry Askew recalls: 'He (Murdoch) would come into the office and literally rewrite leaders which were not supporting the hard Thatcherite line.'[16]

In contrast to the way he wished to run the *Sun* and the *News of the World* Murdoch approached *The Times* and *Sunday Times* with a rather different style. When he acquired these papers in 1981 he denied any intentions of changing their character. However, as Frank Giles recalls, although Murdoch never issued direct editorial instructions, as he did with the *Sun* and *News of the World,* he made his views forcibly known. He would jab his fingers at some materials and snarl 'what do you want to print rubbish like that for.'[17] Andrew Neil explains:

---

[14]In the 'pilot' content analysis of the *Sun* during 1974 general election this study detected certain ambiguity in the paper's political orientation. However, the paper shows definite signs of changing political allegiance towards and after the election.
[15]Quoted by Stafford Summerfield, Editor of the *'News of the World'*
[16]B. Askew, himself, was the editor of the paper for nine months only
[17]Giles was editor in Chief of the *Sunday Times* whose retirement paved the way for Andrew Neil. See: F. Giles, *'Sunday Times',* (London: Murray), 1986

> *When you work for Rupert Murdoch, you do not work for a company chairman or chief executive: you work for a Sun King. You are not...a manager or an editor: you are a courtier at the court of a Sun King – rewarded with money and status by a grateful King as long as you serve his purpose, dismissed outright... when you have ceased to please him. The Sun King is everywhere... He rules over great distance through authority ... and fear. He can be benign or ruthless, depending on his mood or the requirements of his empire.*[18]

The former editor of *The Times*, Harold Evans, also remembers,

> *The aura he [Murdoch] created in 1981-2 was one of bleak hostility to Edward Heath and the Tory rebels, and contempt for social democrats. He did this by persistent derision of them at our press meetings and on the telephone, by sending me articles marked worth reading which espoused right-wing views, by jabbing a finger at headlines which he thought could be more supportive of Mrs. Thatcher...*[19]

Under considerable pressure Evans resigned in 1983. He later described the events which led to his resignation:

> *Early in 1982 ... Murdoch went to see the Prime Minister, Mrs. Thatcher. They shared a problem: it was me. I was the editor of The Times and Murdoch's difficulty was how to dispose of me. The Times was supposed to be protected from political interference, and its editor from dismissal, by a spectacular series of pledges Murdoch had given in 1981. The irony was still fresh on them: they were given to Mrs. Thatcher's government and they were her justification for sparing Murdoch an investigation by the Monopolies Commission.* (Evans: 1983, p.17).

---

[18] A. Neil, op.cit. p. 160
[19] See; H. Evans, *Good Times, Bad Times*, op.cit. p.28

Evans concludes the account of his editorship at *The Times* by arguing:

> *Editorial guarantee are a paltry defense and they may be delusive as well. Times Newspapers enabled an air of respectability to be given to an unnecessary and hazardous extension of monopoly power.* (ibid, p 489).

Murdoch sought to have an indirect control of *The Times* by avoiding the fixing of an editorial budget. Evans therefore required permission for editorial affairs which involved significant spending. Murdoch's style of management was being replicated at other places in Fleet Street, most notably by Victor Mathews and Robert Maxwell.

Other Press Barons in the 1980s

Victor Mathews led the take-over by Trafalgar House of Beaverbrook Newspapers and became chairman, a position he was to hold until 1985 when United Newspapers purchased the group (now renamed Express Newspapers).

Trafalgar House launched the *Daily Star* in November 1978, the first new national newspaper for 75 years. The paper was planned to compete with the *Sun*; and managed to reach a 1.42 million sales mark in 1981. The *Sun*, however, fought back in 1981 with bigger bingo prizes and a price cut. The result was a 9 per cent increase in sales for 1980-82 period.[20]

During his years as chairman, Mathews was greatly influential in fighting the Fleet Street print unions. At one stage, this even involved closing down production and barricading the building with scaffolding and wire mesh.[21] Mathews was created

---

[20]See: D. Griffiths (ed), *'The Encyclopaedia of the British Press: 1422-1992'*, (London: Macmillan), 1992, p.187

[21]See: J. Lawrenson & L. Barber, *'The Price of Truth: The Story of the Reuters Millions'*, (London: Sphere Books), 1986

a life peer in the 1980 New Year Honours List, and later that year following the closure of the *Evening News* was elected chairman of the new *Evening Standard* company, 50 per cent of which was owned by Trafalgar House and 50 per cent by Associated Newspapers.[22]

Like Murdoch, Mathews also aimed to target a 'downmarket', mostly Labour-supporting audience. Five weeks after he took over, Roy Wright was replaced as editor of the *Daily Express*. Derek Jameson, Wright's successor, was a highly regarded tabloid expert from the *Daily Mirror*. His appointment appeared to confirm Mathew's belief that what the *Express* needed was more headlines and less small print.[23]

Mathews' approach for the *Daily Star* was that the paper must acquire a Conservative and partisan attitude rather than function as a market-oriented venture. Consequently the *Daily Star* adopted a complete Conservative line in the 1983 General Election, even though only 21 per cent of its readers actually supported Thatcher.[24]

Robert Maxwell controlled the Mirror Group with a similar domineering style. When he acquired the Group in 1984, Maxwell changed the autonomous editorial style of the previous owners, Reed International. Tom Bower writes "Roy Greenslade (the *Daily Mirror* editor) refrained from printing Maxwell's offer of a scoop – that six ministers would resign in protest against Margaret Thatcher's refusal to stand down after her failure to pass the threshold vote in the Conservative leadership election on 20 November 1990. 'Just print it!' Maxwell had shouted. 'I am your publisher!.'[25] Greenslade was eventually dismissed by Maxwell in 1991. This sort of crude interventionism was always being tolerated by some journalists.

---

[22]Source: D. Griffiths, op.cit. p.407
[23]Source: L. Chester and J. Fenby, *The Fall of the House of Beaverbrooks* (London: Andre Deutsch), 1979, p. 242
[24]An example of such stance is provided by Peter Grimsditch, the editor of the *Daily Star* who recalls, on reading a lead story by the paper which was critical of the Thatcher Government's first budget, Mathews angrily phoned him 'there are no poor in this country, you can take my word for it'.
[25]Source: T. Bower, *Maxwell: The Final Verdict* (London: Harper Collins), 1995, p.80

The conflict between critical journalists and proprietors reached its height during the 1980s when they encountered pressures to provide more favourable attitudes for the government. In 1983, a group of journalists at the *Daily Mail* sent a letter of complaint to their editor about the paper's one sided coverage of the general election. The same resistance occurred at the *Sunday Times* following Murdoch's take over. The most spectacular of these resistances came at the *Observer* in 1981. Tiny Rowland was forced, like Murdoch, to accept new Articles of Association and independent directors designed to stop him from interfering editorially. However, in a highly publicized row, the editor, Donald Telford, was backed by all his staff and independent directors for his refusal to withdraw an article which clearly did not agree with Rowland's business interests. Tiny Rowland was, eventually, forced to retreat.[26]

It is known, however, that press owners usually choose the editors they want. Indeed the editors' autonomy is usually limited by the budget allocated to them, the formal policy and their traditional journalism in that particular paper. Also, conforming to the owner's wishes has rewards beyond a mere salary. Good assignments, promotion and social prestige are a few of them. Indeed, the structure of news gathering and the professional code of conduct socializes journalists into a value system which attaches particular emphasis to powerful sources of news and consequently legitimizes their dependence upon them.

To sum up, this section assessed the role, and the impact, of the institution of press ownership in modern Britain with a particular reference to Murdoch's contributions in this field. Through an empirical inquiry the reciprocity and cooperation between mega actors in the press and those in the political sphere was further analysed. It was shown that the modern epoch has seen the emergence of inventive and partisan businessmen whose prime objective is acquisition of more publications and other media properties. The next section will underline this theme with a particular 'quantitative' reference to the increasing concentration of press ownership in Britain.

[26] See: R. Cockett, *David Astor and the Observer* (London: Andrew Deutsch), 1991

The Pattern of Press Ownership in Post-War Britain

This section will argue that after World War Two, the concentration of national press has dramatically increased. This trend continued its expansion during the Thatcherite epoch. In 1987, Murdoch, Maxwell and Stevens controlled 75 per cent of national dailies and 83 per cent of national Sundays. Table 6 illustrates this increasing trend by comparing the concentration of ownership of three leading corporations in 1947 and 1985.[27]

As Table 6 suggests, at the national level in the mid-1980s the three leading press conglomerates dominated the industry and dramatically increased their share of the market. At the regional level, by 1985, the leading five owners increased their market share by 275 per cent. Table 7 shows the increasing concentration of ownership in the provincial press. The five

Table 6 Concentration of ownership of dailies and Sundays 1947 and 1985. The three leading corporations' shares of

Year	Total Daily & Sunday Circulation	Total Daily Paper Circulation	Total Sunday Circulation	National Daily Circulation	National Sunday Circulation
1947	42%	42%	66%	62%	60%
1985	58%	55%	79%	75%	83%

Table 7 The five leading owners' shares of

Year	Regional Evening circulation	Regional Morning circulation	Local Weekly circulation
1947	44%	65%	8%
1985	53%	73%	30%

[27]Sources: These figures are produced by the Royal Commission on the Press, 1947 and 32nd Annual Report of the Press Council, 1985

Table 8 National dailies and Sundays: Major group ownership

Group	1947	1957	1967	1977	1987
Associated Newspapers	10	13	8	6	12
Beaverbrook	15	17	20	-	-
Mirror Group	18	23	43	-	-
News of the World	18	16	16	-	-
Kemsley	13	10	-	-	-
Odhams	16	14	-	-	-
Thomson	-	-	5	5	-
News International	-	-	-	28	34
Reed	-	-	-	36	-
Trafalgar House	-	-	-	17	-
Maxwell	-	-	-	-	27
United	-	-	-	-	16
Total	67	70	87	87	89

Sources: Royal Commission on the Press 1947; Press Council Annual Report- all figures in %

leading owners are: the Pearson, News International, Reed International, United Newspapers and Pergamon.

The leading publishers of the regional papers had their biggest gains in the weekly press. In an increasing number of sub regions extensive monopolies were created, in which nearly all papers were owned by the same group. To put this trend in a historical perspective, as Table 8 suggests, by 1987 the four largest groups controlled 88 per cent of the total dailies and Sundays market. The table also demonstrates the increasing pattern of the press concentration in Britain since 1940s.[28]

As suggested by Table 8, while in 1947 there were six groups sharing 67 per cent of the market, in 1987 there were only 4 conglomerates taking 89 per cent. The increasing pattern of

[28] See: C. Seymour-Ure, *The British Press and Broadcasting Since 1945*, op.cit.

concentration of ownership of newspapers in Britain during the 1980s indicates the trend towards a more centralised control over the entertainment industries in general. Companies such as the Pearson Group, News International, Reed International, United Newspapers and Pergamon Holding Foundation controlled over 40 percent of book sales, 45 per cent of television transmissions, half of total video rentals, records, cassettes, and compact disc sales, and over three-quarters of daily and Sunday paper sales.[29]

The next section will be a more detailed examination of the role of capital in the modern press industry.

The Function of Capital: Macro Agency in the External and Internal Spheres

The process of increasing diversification of the modern press industry, we believe, was sponsored by the mega actors in both the internal and external spheres of the press, and has firmly placed the industry within the domain of hegemonic capital. The close working relationships amongst the modern press barons – in the internal sphere – and other key conglomerate directors – in the external sphere – has given way to a new ideological and business culture shared by the press industry and other businesses.

For many media analysts, such as Colin Sparks and James Curran, Britain is an example of a country whose press is predominantly owned by conglomerates and multinational companies, whose main profits and concerns are in other industries. Since the late 1960s, they argue, Britain has become the leading example in the world of a pattern of ownership previously found in interwar Germany and France, and in more recent years in Latin America and Italy.[30]

Over three decades, from the 1960s to the 1980s, nine

---

[29]Pearson Group is controlled by the Cowdray families. Pergamon Holding Foundation was controlled by Maxwell. United Newspapers was headed by Stevens.
[30]See: J. Tunstall, 'The British Press in the Age of Television', in H. Christian (ed), 'The Sociology of Journalism and the Press', *The Sociological Review Monograph*, October 1980

Table 9 The business diversification of 'Four' major National Newspapers

Company	Main U.K. Press interests	Selected other media interests	Selected non-media interests
News Corporation (Murdoch)	*Sun, News of the World, The Times, Sunday Times, Today*	B Sky B, Harper Collins, Fontana, Channel Ten, Sydney, *Herald,* and Weekly Times Group, Australia, Fox TV, USA, Harper & Row, USA	Ansett Transport, Santos Natural Gas' News, Eagle Oil, Australia
Pergamon	*Daily Mirror Sunday Mirror Sunday People Daily Record Sunday Mail*	British Cable Services TF-1 –France Merril Publishing –USA Magyar Hirlop-Hung	E..J Arnold Furniture, Holis Plastics, Paulton Investments, Jet Ferry International Panama, Milthorp machinery (Australia)
United Newspapers (Stevens)	*Daily Express, Sunday Express, Daily Star,* United Provincial, Press, United magazines	TV-am, Asian Business Press, Singapore, Specialist Publications (Hong Knog), Capital Radio, Inter Media Group, USA	JBS properties, M G insurance, Moncroft Finances, PRN Holdings –USA, David McKay-USA
Associated Newspapers (Rothermere)	*Daily Mail, Mail on Sunday,* Weekend Northcliffe Newspapers	London Broadcasting Company,*Herald Sun* TV, Australia, Esquire Magazine Group, USA	Bouverie Investments, Canada, Consolidated, Bathurst, Canada, Transport Group Holdings, Jetlink Ferries

Sources: Who Owns Whom 1988: Company Reports: Press Council Annual Report 1990- Also quoted by Curran et.al, in: Power Without Responsibility-1990

multinationals bought over 200 newspapers and magazines with a total circulation of 46 million. Media tycoons such as Murdoch, Maxwell and Stevens started in the printing business and gradually extended their business interests to other fields such as gas, engineering, transport and banking. However, some other figures were outside Fleet Street when they began to extend their activities into the press industry, such as Lonhro which had constructions interests in Kenya and Zimbabwe.[31]

The most crucial point here is that, in accordance with the basic principles of the culture industry thesis, the British press industry gradually became a supporting part of the hegemonic capital. Table 9 demonstrates the diversification of business interests of the British press industry in the 1980s.

The growing business interests of the press industry in modern Britain, as Table 9 indicates, has created a delicate network of cooperation between the press and other conglomerates. The similar social origins, shared educational patterns and close working relationships amongst the modern press barons – in the internal sphere – and other top directors and captains of industry – in the external sphere – has given way to a new ideological and business culture shared by the press industry and other businesses.[32] As argued in the last chapter, the press in Britain are involved with the international oil industry, and the state is commercially and directly involved with the oil industry. This may be seen as the point where the state and the press industry may share a mutual business interest.

In recent decades the press industry has become a legitimate venue to protect the interests of giant multinationals. This process was facilitated by closer proprietorial interventions. Indeed, the industry became the facilitator of politically aligned conglomerates. These businesses aimed to sustain and support, financially and verbally, the only political party which they believed best served their business interests, the Conservatives in

---

[31]See J. Anstey & J. Silverlight (Eds), *The Observer Observed* (London: Barrie & Jenkins), 1991
[32]G. Murdoch develops this notion in: 'Class, Power and the Press: Problems of conceptualization and evidence', in: H. Christian (ed), *The Sociology of Journalism and the Press*, op.cit.

general and Thatcher in particular. In the 1970s and 1980s major press groups such as United Newspapers, the Pearson and Express group, provided substantial donations to the Conservative Party.[33]

Owning a newspaper, it seems, is regarded as desirable for its social prestige. Buying newspapers at the time when they were making huge losses, clearly indicates that conglomerates were seeking more than just a quick way of making money.[34]

The Function of the Mass Market: Collective Agency in the External sphere

This section argues that the major cause of increasing economic pressure on the industry was the rapid escalation of costs. This was to lead to a polarisation within the British press industry, with the popular press adopting a tabloid format and diminishing their political and foreign output to secure more readers and retain their existing readers from other popular papers which were increasingly competing for readers. After 1945 the cost of paper and paging increased considerably, and the salary scale for the editorial and production staff quadrupled. The annual expenditure of the average London and national daily rose from £1.5 million in 1946 to £28.1 million in 1974. The industry no longer had a sheltered operation.[35] Instead it became an intensely competitive area where the expanding readership became crucial. At the same time that the industry faced rises in costs, fierce competition became inevitable as the number of national newspaper titles in the 1980s remained the same as in the 1960s and the regional press faced a declining prospect. (Table 10).

[33] Curran et al, 'Power Without Responsibility', op.cit. p.92
[34] By 1975 four national dailies and six out of seven Sunday papers made a total loss of £5.3m. In 1982 the national press were reported to have made a net loss of £29m. Source: *Financial Times*, 11 March, 1985
[35] Sources: G. Cranfield, *The Press and Society* (London: Longman), 1978
  P. Brendon, *The Life and Death of Press Barons* (London: Secker & Warburg), 1982
  J. Eldridge (ed), *Getting the Message: News, Truth and Power*, op.cit. 1993

Table 10 The number of paper titles 1961-85 (Figures in%)

NATIONAL PAPERS	1961	1985
DAILIES	10	10
SUNDAYS	8	8

REGIONAL PRESS		
MORNING	22	19
EVENING	77	75
SUNDAY	5	4
WEEKLY	1219	839

SOURCE: Royal Commissions 1947-1961 and Press Council Annual Report 1985

Under such circumstances, most dailies such as the *Daily Mirror* began to think that they had to respond to a growing taste for popular themes. From the 1950 onwards, the paper shifted its political orientation partly because of the power of the mass market. The class rhetoric of the paper's 'them and us' of the 1940s softened in the 1950s and 1960s, and by the 1980s the paper took the format of opposition to the 'Tories' rather than a positive commitment to the socialist alternative. With Maxwell, the paper's old radical motto 'Forward with the People' was changed to a more Thatcherite tone of 'Forward With Britain'. This new image, one may argue, was a response to both managerial and mass market pressures.[36]

The policy of circulation maximization was in turn to force the press industry to respond to the mass market demands at the cost of minority interests. Between 1945 to 1988 there was a remarkable reading preference for tabloid newspapers (Table 11).

As the table shows, the decade from 1977 to 1988 saw no less

[36]See: R. Greensdale, *Maxwell's Fall* (London: Simon and Schuster), 1992

Table 11 Date of adopting tabloid format - National Press[37]

Year	Newspaper
Before 1945	DAILY MIRROR- SKETCH
1962	SUNDAY CITIZEN
1969	THE SUN
1971	DAILY MAIL
1974	SUNDAY PEOPLE
1977	DAILY EXPRESS
1978	DAILY STAR
1982	MAIL ON SUNDAY
1984	NEWS OF THE WORLD
1986	TODAY-SUNDAY TODAY- SUNDAY SPORT
1987	NEWS ON SUNDAY
1988	THE POST

than eight national dailies and Sundays adopt the tabloid format, some of which closed shortly after their launch such as the *Sunday Today* and *News on Sunday*. The mass market expressed preference for human interest stories and certain entertainment features such as gossip, cartoons and horoscopes. Political and public affairs, it is argued, were of limited interest to women and young people. The industry thus responded to the mass demand, and began to devote more and more space to features with a common denominator appeal. The important distinction here, as noted by Colin Sparks, is that the popular press provides a form of immediacy and totality in its contents. This immediacy is achieved by resorting to a direct appeal to personal experience. The popular conception of the personal becomes the explanatory framework within which the social order is presented as transparent.[38]

In the last twenty years, this personal experience has meant

---

[37]Source: C. Seymour-Ure, *The British Press and Broadcasting Since 1945*, op.cit. p.33
[38]C. Sparks, 'Popular Journalism: Theories and Practices', in: P. Dahlgren (ed), *Journalism and Popular Culture* (London: Sage), 1992, pp 36-8

that features such as home politics and industrial news took up less space than sport in nearly all papers in Britain. This included some of the qualities such as the *Observer* and *Daily Telegraph*.[39] According to this data, the two most prominent features of the dailies by 1976, were entertainment and miscellaneous such as cartoons, horoscopes and competition. By the early 1980s, prompted by the objective to increase their circulation, the industry's standards of journalism also began to decline. Headlines at all costs meant to print well-publicized excesses such as any stories about the marriage of Prince Charles and Princess Diana, as well as fabrications of stories and photographs to stimulate the interest of the mass market. Other examples are the Falklands War and its aftermath and the phenomenon of the 'Yorkshire Ripper'.[40]

The structural trend over the past thirty years, therefore, has been for a polarization of the press between the quality and the mass circulating tabloids, at the expense of those middle range or serious papers. Furthermore, market pressures also brought about another striking feature of the modern press industry.

There were qualitative differences between the way popular and quality papers were financed. The quality papers relied more upon advertising revenues which did not necessarily depend upon the recruitment of non-elite readers. This meant that they were not pressurised into changing their editorial styles to attract more readers from other classes. The implication here is that the collective actors in the advertising circles – the external sphere- gave the middle class minorities the power of easier representation in the press industry than those reading popular papers, because they had insufficient pulling power amongst advertisers.[41]

The popular press industry needed the sales revenue from large circulations to cover their costs. Advertising revenue would help, but much of it went to the paper production costs of printing the advertisements. However the quality press relied on

[39]Source: Curran *et al.*, *Power Without Responsibility*
[40]See: J. Taylor, '*Shock! Horror! The Tabloids in Action*', (London: Bantam Press), 1991
[41]This point can be sustained by looking at the way in which *The Times* increased its circulation by 69 per cent between 1965 and 1969 through more popularised features and news which was backed by a forceful advertising strategy

the greater purchasing power of their readers, some of whom spent corporate money, as well as their own personal incomes, enabling the quality papers to charge far higher advertising rates and to break even at circulation levels completely unrealistic for the populars. Indeed, the economic and market pressures upon the popular mass papers increased even more with the introduction of a new printing technology which began in the 1970s, and reached its highest point in 1980s. The 1980s was a decade dominated by battles over new technology and the establishment of new titles. When proprietors sold, either anticipating amalgamation or a continuing future, they did so because of decreasing interest or energy, or because they did not have the resources to turn around a weak paper in an increasingly competitive market.[42]

Technological Reformation in the British Press Industry: Macro Agency in the Internal Sphere

It was only a few months since I reproached Mrs. Thatcher on this score: 'You have done nothing for Fleet Street. I am putting my trust solely in Eddie Shah.' Ooh, she said fervently. so am I, so am I![43]

This part of the chapter will continue the analysis of the role of macro agency by focusing upon the introduction and the impact of modern technology in the press. By examining the consequences of the technological changes within the industry, it will be argued that this is not an appraisal in favour of *technological determinism*, rather it is a portrayal of *technology and agency* complementing one other in producing the effects which are the inseparable and permanent features of the modern press industry. This section argues that the primary rationales

---

[42]This notion is extensively explored with a particular reference to the fortunes of the *News on Sunday* in P. Chippindale and C. Horrie, *Disaster! The Rise and Fall of News on Sunday: Anatomy of business failure* (London: Sphere Books Ltd), 1988
[43]P. Johnson, *The Spectator*, December 21, 1985

for the introduction and use of new press technology were generating greater profit margins and further accumulation of capital. Within the larger theoretical context of this thesis, the implementation of new technology could be seen as the further intensification of 'formal rationality' within the press industry. The arrival of new press technology, supported by Thatcher, provided the dominant actors in the internal sphere with further opportunities to consolidate their power, to rationalize their modes of operation, to mass produce more editions in a quicker and efficient manner, and to valorize capital in more productive ways. Apart from Murdoch, Eddie Shah is another crucial mega actor whose innovative idea began a new age for the press during the Thatcher years. Shah, a publisher of free sheets in the northwest, became famous for his victory over the National Graphical Association (NGA). In 1985, he announced that he intended to set up a new national daily and Sunday paper in a green field site, far from Fleet Street, using the latest in print technology. Shah's new concept in the industry marked the beginning of a new era. Not only did it revolutionize the social organization of press production and defeat the powerful print unions, but it also lowered wages for production workers, and produced a simplified, mass producing printing system replacing the old discontinuous process in which the shop-floor was effectively controlled by the unions.[44]

The year 1986 has been regarded as year zero of the Fleet Street reformation. In the course of just one week at the end of January, Shah successfully concluded the first dummy run of his new colour daily, *Today*; Robert Maxwell, having reduced the workforce at Mirror Group Newspapers by 2000, told advertisers that they could expect cuts of up to half in his paper's advertising rates, United Newspapers formally confirmed that it wanted a one-third reduction in manning at the Express Group, and, most dramatic of all, Rupert Murdoch's News International produced *The Times, Sunday Times*, the *Sun* and the *News of the World* from behind a fortified printing plant at Wapping while locking out 5000 members of the traditional print unions. The

---

[44]See D. Griffiths (ed), *The Encyclopedia of the British Press: 1422-1992*, op.cit. p.514

speed of change was bewildering and, as we shall see later, the transition was neither smooth nor painless. Vested interests on all sides affected the process quite dramatically.

When Eddie Shah began to implement his new ideas, most other industrialised countries were already in the vanguard of the information revolution, exploiting new electronic technology. In Britain the power of the unions in Fleet Street and, to a lesser extent, in the provincial sector had a significant impact upon the belated advent of the print technology.[45]

The economic savings, which were inherent in the new idea, had several consequences. Firstly, the 'hot metal' type could be dispensed with by using a computer with which journalists and others could key in their materials directly. This process meant that a whole layer of composing, lithographic and paste-up staff were no longer necessary. The new powerful, web-offset machines could considerably reduce staffing levels. Facsimile transmission further reduced distribution costs and allowed for a more profitable use of printing presses. This was done by simultaneous production at satellite printing plants.[46]

The economic advantages of the new technology, it was then argued, enabled even groups with limited resources to set up new papers, hence increasing the diversity of the industry. Ian Aitken, political editor of the *Guardian* (Founded in 1821), believed that the new technology could help the emergence of 'entirely new newspapers representing all points of view'. Only the unions, he went on to say, might stop this process (*Guardian*: 21 November 1985). Robert Taylor, the political editor of the *Observer*, believed that 'with the new technology, the tyranny of the mass-circulating press, with its mindless formula journalism appealing to the lowest common denominator, will be weakened.' (Melvern: 1986, p.5).

Murdoch, of course, was the most influential figure in the development of the press technology. His multi-million pound plant in Wapping, as promised to the printing union, was first to be used to print his new local daily. In fact the plant was big

---

[45]See D. Jameson, *The Last of the Hot Metal Men* (London: Ebury Press), 1990
[46]*ibid*, pp 20-38

enough to print all of his national papers. To complete his plan for a strike-free operation, Murdoch reconstituted his Wapping plant as a separate company so that picketing by his Fleet Street staff outside Wapping would be technically illegal.[47]

Legally, the 1980 and 1982 Employment Acts were not particularly concerned with the press industry, but the 1980 Act restricted 'closed shops' and lawful picketing, and the 1982 Act tightened the provisions. However, these Acts became useful weapons for those who wished to challenge the 'closed shops' of the National Graphical Association (NGA) , National Union of Journalists (NUJ) and SOGAT 82 in the sphere of the press industry. In early 1983 Eddie Shah used the new laws to challenge the unions. That autumn, Shah's plant at Warrington was mass picketed, preventing his delivery vans from going out. The riots received nightly television and media coverage. With the aid of legal protection, Shah won the battle. He then went on to set up his technologically advanced national daily *Today* in London. Although the paper was eventually sold, Shah pioneered the method of using the law to effectively marginalize the unions.[48]

Murdoch, in a more spectacular fashion, confronted the powerful print unions and paved the way for a slim line non-unionized operation at Wapping. Murdoch's approach in Britain was ruthless and swift. In the USA, for example, Murdoch's News Corporation met with more effective resistance from the unions than was the case in the UK.[49] The Wapping dispute, this book will argue, is another example of the reciprocal cooperation between Thatcher and Murdoch. It epitomized Thatcher's desire to reduce the unions' role in the policy-making process and to assert its authority, and therefore its image of governing competence. The Wapping episode also captures a proprietor's desire to publish mass circulating national papers in a more cost effective, efficient and non-unionized method. The outcome of

[47]S. M. Littleton, *The Wapping Dispute* (Aldershot: Avebury), 1992, p.62
[48]See: B. MacArthur, *Eddy Shah: Today and the Newspaper Revolution* (Newton Abbot: David and Charles), 1988. Also see C. Wintour, *The Rise and Fall of Fleet Street*, (London: Hutchinson), 1989
[49]Quoted by B. McNair, 'New Technology and the Media', in A. Briggs and P. Cobley, *The Media: An Introduction* (Edinburgh: Longman), 1998, p.174

the Wapping phenomenon, in other words, was beneficial for both mega actors in the internal and external spheres of the press. This momentous event in the history of the British Press will now be examined in the light of the close cooperation between a government dedicated to curb the unions influence in policy-making and an entrepreneur in search of maximizing profit margins and business expansion.

The Wapping Dispute: Collective Agency in the Internal and External Spheres

The Wapping dispute remains an important event in the development of the press in Britain. Indeed, by analysing the events at Wapping, the this study aims to demonstrate how the growing business interests of the press empires have created a whole set of delicate networks of co-operation with other large multinationals. Wapping also highlights the impact of collective actors from the external sphere of the press in facilitating Murdoch's success. This was a process whereby the corporate interests of those in the internal sphere were greatly influenced by those in the external sphere who, in return, had some vested interest in the proceedings. Earlier, this chapter demonstrated empirically that the collusion between Murdoch and Thatcher became a reciprocal relationship between the mega actors within the press and those in the political sphere. This section will continue that discussion and will argue that Murdoch's defeat of the powerful print unions was greatly assisted by the revised network of Conservative employment and trade union laws.

In 1977, News International purchased an eleven acre site in the London Docklands. Construction began there two years later. Murdoch's original intention was to keep the company's editorial base at Fleet Street and to create a new facility to print the *Sun* and the *News of the World*. In 1981, when Murdoch acquired *The Times* and *Sunday Times,* the company began to discuss the proposed site with its employees. Two years later negotiations began with the union officials concerning the manning of the new plant.[50] By 1984, the Wapping plant was completed at an estimated cost of £72 million. In September, the unions were invited by the company for fresh talks based on a twenty-four per cent manning reduction for the machines, and a twenty-nine per cent reduction for the rest of the plant. After several years of negotiations, no significant agreement had been reached concerning the comprehensive operations at the facility. News International openly expressed disgust regarding the attitude of one senior member of the Society of Graphical and Allied Trade -SOGAT – who was quoted as saying: ' when will you get it through your thick heads, we will never let you use it, you may as well put a match to it – or we will do it for you.'[51]

At the same time as negotiations were being conducted with the unions, Murdoch began secret plans to expedite News International's operations at Wapping without the unions. Murdoch's plans would become increasingly complex and detailed over the next year. News International continued both to engage the unions in negotiations and to secretly develop an alternative strategy of operating Wapping without the participation of the Fleet Street unions.[52]

By January 1985, a twelve foot high spiked fence was constructed around the site, giving it an awesome fortress shape. During the same period when some managers were meeting with the unions, Murdoch was meeting key executives to outline his intentions for Wapping. At this time, he instructed his company's New York office to order a $10 million newspaper computer terminal system for Wapping from the Atex Corporation.[53]

Talks with the unions concerning the proposed move of production of the *Sun* and the *News of the World* continued into March. At that time, the General Secretary of SOGAT was reported to have claimed that News International was asking for 'quite unrealistic' manning levels.[54]

[50]O'Neil, the Company negotiator, was regarded asa tough negotiator and one of Murdoch's nest assistants. He was also the Vice President for News America Publishing Inc.
[51]See: C. Wintour, *The Rise and Fall of the Fleet Street*, op.cit. 218-19
[52] *ibid*, Introduction
[53]S.M. Litleton, op.cit. p62
[54]D. Goodhart and R. Snoddy, 'London paper battle possible', *Financial Times*, 11 March 1985

During March 1985, Murdoch publicly announced News International's intent to enter the London evening market with a new publication to be entitled the London Post. Murdoch argued that, if successful, the London Post would become a twenty-four hour paper publishing for London nightly and for all of Britain each morning. At this time, Murdoch contracted the services of Christopher Pole-Carew, described as 'the pioneer of nonunion newspapers in Britain' to head the 'post project'.[55]

The unions, watching developments at Wapping, also suspected that Murdoch was having numerous meetings with leaders of firms which manufactured printing equipment. During March, he began the creation of several News International 'shadow' companies. By restructuring the company's critical operations into decentralized smaller companies, Murdoch protected the business from union action under the 1980 Employment Act. Any future union action against these new smaller companies, which in combination carried out precisely what the single parent company did would now, under the group's new legal configuration, be considered an illegal secondary action. Indeed Geoffrey Richards, one of Murdoch's key solicitors, was named director of two of these new companies.[56]

By the end of the month, Murdoch began to explore an alternative national distribution network for his existing four publications. Thomas Nationwide Transport (TNT), a private distribution company, was contacted. Murdoch shared the ownership of Australian Ansett Transport, which in turn, owned TNT. He commissioned the company to do a feasibility study of distribution for Wapping, providing the necessary details to TNT in early April for a plan code named *'Daily Post'* to be operational for October 1985.[57]

Ultimately, TNT not only claimed that it was capable of

---

[55]Melvern, *The End of the Street* (London: Methuen), 1986, pp 215-17
[56]News International Distribution Ltd and News International Advertising Ltd.
[57]P. Wintour, 'Transport plans: Reveal Murdoch's deception', *The Guardian*, 21 July 1986

fulfilling the company's needs, but also maintained it was more efficient, cheaper and faster than British Rail. Later Murdoch signed a five year contract worth £1million a week with TNT. Murdoch was also calling on his American connections. John Keating, technical director of News America, took Pole-Carew and the National Secretary of the Electrical, Electronic, Telecommunication and Plumbing Union (EETPU) Tom Rice, on tours of several newspaper facilities in the United States.[58]

The tour was said to give Tom Rice a general understanding of the modern printing industry and an overview of the equipment. Following the trip, there were several meetings between the management and the unions to discuss manning and shift patterns needed for Wapping. Union members engaged in spying on Wapping decided it was timely and imperative that they go public with their information. They put together a display of their evidence to show at the Strand Palace Hotel, which to their disappointment, had a dismal attendance.[59]

Meanwhile, the company agreed to pay salaries of between £19,000 to £22,000 for technicians at the plant, but they were asked to be prepared to walk through picket lines. Recruiting continued via the EETPU. The reason behind selecting this union was not only that the EETPU struck a deal with the Finnish paper company for Wapping, but Eric Hammond, the union's General Secretary, was described as 'the apostle of cooperation, of no-strike agreements and of single union representation'.[60] Described by a journalist of the *Sunday Times* as 'the most important trade union leader in Britain', Hammond was depicted by the left as a traitor and the 'enemy within' of the labour movement.[61]

The EETPU became a model trade union organization for the Conservatives:

> ... *it was the EETPU, more than any other union, which*

[58] Melvern, op.cit., p216
[59] *ibid*, p.230
[60] P. Patterson, 'Murdoch should show mercy', *The Spectator*, 1 February 1986
[61] M. Chittenden, 'Hammonds' landslide vote lights up path to progress', *The Sunday Times*, 14 June 1987

was to be known as the 'New Realism' needed to prosper in a Thatcherite world ... Hammond ... talked about profits, productivity and technological change ... He also believed in flexibility of labour, joint training with management .. and the EETPU did not insist on a closed shop and ... allowing the company to respond quickly to changing market demands.[62]

Hammond and the EETPU, therefore, offered Murdoch a life-line for the Wapping operation.[63]

In July, in anticipation of the new transition, journalists at *The Times* and its supplements accepted a 'Pay and New Technology' deal that was publicly reported for training and familiarisation purposes only.

By August, training started for new employees and it was believed that the paper and ink supplies were ready. In early September, Wapping was producing mock press runs. On 30 September 1985, Murdoch met with the NGA, SOGAT and EETPU, to discuss negotiations for the proposed *London Post*. At the meeting, Murdoch openly expressed his frustration with current union practices and conditions. Because Wapping had been idle for several years, News International insisted that an agreement had to be reached by Christmas. Both sides agreed that if the talks made good progress, they would once again be extended to include discussions of the future transfer of the *Sun* and the *News of the World* to Wapping.[64]

The negotiations for the *London Post* began in October. The senior managers presented the unions with a document containing four basic requirements, which the print unions refused to discuss. Dubbed 'the serfs' charter' by union officials, it included provisions for the management's right to manage, the abolition of the closed shop, for a no-strike clause, and for legally binding agreements.[65]

[62]Melvern, op.cit, pp 191-2
[63]See: D. Marsh, *'The New Politics of British Trade Unionism'*, op.cit. pp 100-01
[64]H. Hague, 'Murdoch agreed to urge workers to join EETPU', *Financial Times*, 22 December 1986
[65]Melvern, *ibid*, p.11

In evaluating the company's position, the NGA took these non-negotiable conditions to mean that the company did not want an agreement and was at best seeking a nonunion plant, with no effective trade union representation.[66] The unions, having sensed that Murdoch was adamant about implementing revised conditions, began to accept vast changes to avoid being completely shut off from representations at the *London Post*.

The Christmas deadline saw the talks break down, and in late December Murdoch publicly claimed that the company refused to pursue any further negotiations concerning the London Post. The facility was being prepared for the launch of the *London Post* in 1986. Meanwhile, Murdoch did not hesitate to admit that his Wapping plant was capable of producing all five titles. By the start of 1986, the company maintained that the Wapping issue was closed to any further negotiations. In addition Murdoch claimed that the company would be reducing the workforce over six months from 5,500 to 1,500. In response, the unions continued their campaign to achieve a jobs for life guarantee, linked with a cost of living index for future wage scales for the Fleet Street staff.[67]

There was increasing anticipation of a conflict, and national attention focused on the company and the unions. The unions were quick to defend themselves, and began to publicly explain how the company's legally binding proposal was structured so that it would hold the unions' assets liable for claim. The unions clearly did not foresee that Murdoch already secretly held the power to produce all the company's Fleet Street publications without their participation.

On 12 January, Murdoch announced that a special advertising supplement would be produced on 18 January at Wapping for distribution with the regular Fleet Street run. Murdoch commissioned TNT, who employed members of the Transport and General Workers Union, to distribute the

---

[66]See: J. Gennard, *A History of the National Graphical Association* (London: Unwin Hyman), 1994, p.50
[67]D. Marsh, op.cit. p. 100. Also see: Brenda Dean, 'Murdoch sacks all our members' *Sogat Journali,* February 1986

supplement. The *Sunday Times* was successfully produced at, and distributed from, Wapping. News International stunned the print unions with the successful production run at Wapping. National union leaders formally requested their members not to walk out immediately, but to wait for the results of the strike ballot so that their industrial action would be legal under the Trade Union Act of 1984.[68]

Results indicated that SOGAT was five to one in favour, the NGA seven to one in favour. The unions were poised for industrial action. Meanwhile, Murdoch immediately informed his journalists to prepare for a transition to Wapping. Many of these journalists were members of the NUJ, which belonged to the TUC. However with threats of instant dismissal, offers of pay rises up to £2000 per year, and new private health care benefits, Murdoch eventually persuaded almost all of his seven hundred journalists to follow the company.[69]

Expecting to bring Murdoch to his knees, the long anticipated dispute was officially launched on 24 January 1986. After only twenty four hours, News International's Fleet Street facilities were virtually deserted. The company immediately transferred the production of *The Times*, the *Sun*, the *Sunday Times* and the *News of the World* to Wapping. The new plant reportedly operated with fewer than 600 production workers. Murdoch issued dismissal notices to all striking production workers on the grounds 'that their action constituted a repudiatory breach of their contracts of employment'.[70]

The strike and subsequent dismissals affected over five thousand News International workers, yet surprisingly the loss of these employees had little effect on the company's ability to produce its papers at Wapping. The following day, on the first run of the *Sunday Times* and the *News of the World*, the company claimed that it was able to print three million of its usual five million copies of the *News of the World*, and produced

---

[68]Linda Melvern, op.cit. pp 236-44
[69]*ibid*, p 82
[70]J. Lloyd and H. Hauge, 'Sun Journalists break ranks as Murdoch printers strike', *Financial Times*, 25 January 1986

1.2 million copies of the *Sunday Times*, only 150,000 short of its typical run. The front page of the *Sun* declared : 'A NEW SUN IS RISING'.[71] A few days later, Murdoch claimed that the Wapping plant was meeting the publishing needs of The Times, and ninety-nine per cent of The *Sun*'s production run.

The unions now foresaw that they would have little impact in disrupting News International's production capabilities inside Wapping. Instead they chose to pursue an alternative strategy, preventing the distribution of the product and discouraging the public from reading the Wapping papers. Picketing began at the Fleet Street offices, Wapping and Kinning Park in Glasgow.[72]

On 5 February the TUC General Council ruled that the EETPU must abide by six TUC directives or face suspension. Shortly thereafter the EETPU accepted the six directives.[73] In addition, the TUC called on all trade unionists not to purchase the company's publications, and decided to give 'no facilities' to any journalists working for Murdoch. A few days later the Labour Party began its boycott against News International. Throughout Britain, libraries expressed their support for the unions by refusing to display the company's publications on their racks. Despite the widespread protest, Thatcher condemned the library boycott as 'tantamount to censorship' in the House of Commons.[74]

By the time there were large organized protests outside the Wapping facility, the dispute was at the centre of national attention. Over the course of the dispute, demonstrations

---

[71]T. Gray, *Fleet Street Remembered* (London: Heinman), 1990, p.108
[72]J. Lloyd and H. Hague, 'TUC plea over Wapping Pickets', *Financial Times*, 29 January 1986
[73]The directives were:
  Not to further recruit for News International
  Not to recruit new members from those employed at Wapping
  To formally inform workers at the plant that they are doing work traditionally done by other unions
  Not to enter any agreement with the Company
  Not to enter unilateral negotiations with the Company
  Not to enter into a sole agreement where other unions would be deprived of existing rights
[74]'Ban on *Times* face court test', *The Times*, 3 March 1986

repeatedly and inevitably lead to massive groups of protesters congregating in the roads outside the Wapping plant. These groups attempted to prevent the passage and delivery of the company's products.

By the end of January, News International's lawyers sought legal recourse. In a parliamentary debate, Thatcher expressed her support for Murdoch, stating 'Fleet Street employers are fully entitled to use all legal remedies available to them'.[75] Within two weeks, the company filed numerous legal claims against the unions. Consequently, several injunctions were issued. SOGAT was asked to call off its 'unlawful' mass picketing outside the Wapping plant. If the unions failed to respond, their assets were to be liable for sequestration. The NGA and SOGAT chose not to comply and continued to picket the plant, trying to use legal technicalities against the company. SOGAT asked all its members to file formal applications for unfair dismissal, hoping to entitle them to redundancy pay.

However, only seventeen days into the dispute, the High Court found SOGAT in contempt of court, and fined them £25,000, and made an order for the sequestration of the union's £17 million in assets. Eventually SOGAT's assets were taken, severely crippling the union's ability to operate.[76]

Despite the legal difficulties, the unions had no problem generating the support of protesters outside the plant. Some groups were picketing the gates twenty four hours a day, seven days a week. By February, as many as five thousand demonstrators protested outside the heavily fortified facility. A News International official admitted that because of the disturbances outside the plant, the company was giving 'generous rebates to advertisers to take account of shortfalls on distribution across all four titles.'[77]

For the unions, however, not all picketing was desirable. All of the unions involved disclaimed violence on the picket lines. But in less than one month, 194 arrests were recorded outside

---

[75]J. Lloyd & H. Hague, 'TUC plea over Wapping pickets', op.cit
[76]P. Wintour, 'An exotic view of Wapping', *The Guardian*, 12 February 1986
[77]M. Brown, 'Murdoch sales figures sought by ad agencies', *The Guardian*, 6 February 1986

the plant. One thousand police officers were manning the dispute, most of them in riot gear and on horses to control the crowd. Thomas Nationwide Transport publicly claimed that its drivers were physically intimidated, while several hundred were injured, some with broken arms, others with glass in their eyes.[78] Wapping production workers, meanwhile, continued to achieve complete print runs. Despite the delays outside the plant, the Wapping newspapers were distributed with ease. Despite the inability to disrupt the flow of papers from Wapping, the rallies frequently provided a source of news. Media coverage was particularly heavy when there was violence outside the plant. Over one month into the dispute, in the light of constraints, violence, and sustained media attention, both the company and the unions were increasingly eager to resolve the dispute.

As the Department of Employment was making concessions to News International's striking workforce, making them eligible for unemployment benefits, the National Council for Civil Liberties began investigating complaints by local Wapping residents regarding the dispute. Violence at Wapping had reached a level whereby the Wapping area was the most densely policed area in all of Britain.[79]

On 16 April the company and the unions met again. Hoping to be recognized at Wapping and to end the dispute, the unions presented the company with a new idea. The unions suggested that the four production unions could form a News International National Joint Committee, which would have sole negotiating rights for all union workers at the plant. Murdoch had no intention of returning any of his production to traditional industrial relations. The company had already begun negotiations with its present workforce at Wapping to ensure long-term stability at the facility.[80]

Over the May Day weekend, Wapping experienced the most violent demonstration yet seen. 12,000 printers from as far as Scotland had marched for two weeks. They were joined by

---

[78]'Queen awards CBE to Murdoch's lorry boss', *Morning Star,* 12 February 1986
[79]S.M. Littleton, op.cit., p96
[80]M. horsnell, 'Print union decision is not to purge contempt', *The Times,* 22 April 1986

others throughout Britain, congregating in a massive protest outside Wapping. The confrontation between the police and protesters resulted in 81 arrests, and left 250 demonstrators and 175 police officers injured. The weekend rioting created much parliamentary and public debate. The unions publicly called for a formal inquiry to investigate police tactics outside Wapping. Consequently, meetings were arranged for the police and union leaders to discuss ways to maintain peaceful demonstrations.[81]

Within days, SOGAT moved towards what its leaders regarded as the most practical decision. The General Secretary, Brenda Dean, apologized to the court for SOGAT's contempt of court, and stated she regretted the union's previous refusal to cooperate with the court's injunction. Some officials supported Dean's action, but SOGAT's London branches representing the dismissed workers expressed 'disgust and abhorrence' toward the apology.[82]

Following the heavy violence outside Wapping, SOGAT was under increased pressure to resolve the conflict. After intense negotiations in late May, the unions were able to convince the company to raise the compensation offer from £15 to £50 million worth of benefits for the dismissed workers. In exchange Murdoch asked the unions to stop all dispute-related activities and to agree to a twelve month moratorium on discussions concerning the union representation at Wapping. The new deadline was set for 6 June as a company envoy added that 'they would regard the discussions as ended for good.'[83]

The unions began proceedings to attract the attention of their respective members. SOGAT's National Executive passed an emergency provision to send details of the company's offer to its members by mail for secret balloting. The London Machine Branch claimed that the package was formed to attract the maximum number of SOGAT strikers. They maintained the position that any resolution must include union representation and jobs. Despite the rifts within the unions, the balloting

[81]S. M. Littleton, op.cit., p 102
[82]*ibid*, p 102
[83]'Wapping warning by Sogat', *The Daily Telegraph*, 29 May 1986

continued. By early June, it was clear that the members were not willing to accept Murdoch's compensation offer. Murdoch commented that the unions did their members no favour by not pushing for a 'yes' vote. News International claimed that it would undertake no further negotiations, but that the company would approach individual employees with an offer. Furthermore the company, angered and frustrated by the failure of its compensation offer, once again instigated legal action against the unions. Writs served on NGA and SOGAT sought injunctions to stop all demonstrations, and to limit the number of pickets to six persons outside Wapping.[84]

The court granted News international several injunctions and ruled that the intimidation of News International employees should stop. The judge ruled that marches should be peaceful, disciplined and subject to the control of the police. The mass pickets at Wapping were illegal under guidelines outlined in a Department of Employment advisory code, which limited the number of official pickets to six. Failure on the union's part to accept the provisions of the rulings left the unions open to contempt of court. While the unions spent much of July defending themselves against the legal claims, the company was engaged in a better relationship with the EETPU. The company employed 240 EETPU members from Fleet Street facilities. Following their leadership advice, these electricians never went on strike again and remained fully employed by the company.[85]

By the beginning of August, with most of the company's various court actions behind them, they were once again ready to consider a settlement with the unions. However, Murdoch stressed that any proposed settlement that might affect the workforce at Wapping would first have to be approved by a ballot of his staff. In the meantime, the protest outside the plant continued throughout the summer with crowds occasionally surpassing 5000. The company wrote to the unions, in August, warning that its injunctions were being defied. This time, both the unions and the company began to talk and explore solutions.

[84]P. Bassett, 'Search for new initative at Wapping', *Financial Times*, 9 June 1986
[85]S.M. Littleton, op.cit. p. 111

But the company maintained that its £50 million offer was no longer available, and any new settlements meant new deals. After some detailed negotiations, a new compensation package was drawn up and presented by the company to the unions in September. The company was now prepared to raise its redundancy pay from £50 to £58 million, but the company maintained that the Wapping plant would not become a closed shop. Instead, a Works Committee elected by the plant would be vested with the sole authority to deal with pay, conditions and collective bargaining issues.[86]

Once again, the London based local branch activists immediately launched a campaign urging a negative vote on the compensation offer. However the TUC General Council clearly hoped the new compensation offer would resolve the dispute. On 8 October, the dismissed workers responded by voting against the deal. For the second time the company's compensation offer was turned down. During the next few months efforts were made by the unions to rejuvenate the public's concern about the issue. Since the start of the dispute an estimated £400,000 was invested by the unions toward the publicity campaign. Demonstrations continued outside the plant and, despite some efforts by the Advisory, Conciliation and Arbitration Service (ACAS) and the TUC, the Wapping dispute remained unresolved and seemed to be going nowhere.

As the new year approached, the dismissed Fleet Street employees' eligibility to receive unemployment benefits was coming to a close. The designated limit of one year for these benefits would soon arrive as Wapping's operation and dispute approached its first anniversary. Murdoch, however, insisted that sales were at an all-time high and the unions' boycott campaign was ineffective. The barbed wire around Wapping was only an annoyance. The biggest blow to the unions was inflicted on 20 January 1987, shortly before the dispute reached the one-year mark. News International delivered two writs to the High Court against SOGAT and the NGA. The company undertook

---

[86] J. Richards, 'Sogat and the NGA reject Murdoch's Wapping offer'. *The Daily Telegraph*, 9 October 1986

legal action to obtain compensation for the extra security costs since July 1986. These complaints were filed under the auspices of the Employment Act 1982. Such claims were potentially financially devastating, as there were no limits to the damages awarded under the provisions of this legislation. On 24 January, the anniversary of the dispute, Wapping experienced its worst violence yet.[87]

In the aftermath of these clashes, the print unions called for a public inquiry into the violence. A volunteer committee of twenty legal observers were witnesses to the chaos and reported to the Home Secretary, Douglas Hurd, with their criticism of police tactics. Most of the members of this committee were lawyers, and seemed to have blamed the police action for scores of injuries to non-violent demonstrators. Scotland Yard also began its own independent investigation through the Complaints Investigation Bureau in consultation their Independent Police Complaints Authority. The TUC also responded to the violence by calling a special session, in which it condemned the violence. Above all, one year after it began, Wapping was once again in the forefront of media coverage. Yet despite all the violence and disturbances, the production and distribution of the company's publications were unaffected.[88]

The company began to undertake new legal action and cited that the unions failed to abide by the injunctions granted to News International the previous July. With only one day's notice, the company's solicitors informed SOGAT's National Executives that the company intended to return to court on 6 February to pursue contempt of court charges and seek final sequestration of SOGAT's funds. The legal advice to SOGAT's Executive was to abandon the dispute immediately, or face bankruptcy. Under these terms it was no longer a question of pride or ideology and with no time to ballot its members SOGAT's National Executive voted 23-9 to unconditionally end the dispute on 5 February. The NGA, also immediately held a special meeting and reluctantly

---

[87]There were 150 injuries of these 73 who required hospital treatment 39 were police officers, two were press photographers and 32 were demonstrators and observers
[88]Littleton, op.cit. pp 118-19

decided to end its involvement in the dispute. Tony Dubbins bitterly commented that 'the company's proposed legal action ... denied our members the right to ballot.'[89] The company responded that it would drop all legal claims under process against the unions, and that it would reopen its £58 million compensation offer to all dismissed workers.

Both the NGA and SOGAT urged their members to take advantage of the company's cash offer, but many militant members said they would still picket, even without official union support. Many workers reportedly had 'feelings of anger, betrayal and disgust over the halt of the dispute.'[90] Over fifty-four weeks after the printers walked out on Fleet Street, the Wapping dispute was officially concluded.

This account, we believe, highlights several important issues. Firstly, the Wapping dispute can be seen as underlying the role of *macro agency* in the internal and external spheres of the press during the 1980s. As argued above, Shah and Murdoch could not have got so far without the reciprocal assistance provided by the *collective and mega actors* in the financial, political and legal spheres. Indeed, as shown, at times the cooperation between these institutions was at the international level. Murdoch and other Fleet Street proprietors were strongly supported by Thatcher's policies which included government deregulation of financial services which helped fund Reuters' floatation and the subsequent cash windfall for the press title-holders.

Moreover, it was Thatcher's personal intervention which allowed Murdoch in 1981 to acquire *The Times* and *Sunday Times* without an investigation by the Monopolies Commission. However, the most significant indication of Thatcher's support was three separate trade union laws in 1980, 1982 and 1984. These new laws applied to all trade unions and were first implemented to full effect against the miners' during their strike in 1984. In the case of the print unions, the court actions flowing from these laws meant that they could not financially afford to

[89]National Council end News International dispute: NGA print, March 1987
[90]H. Hague, 'Sacked strikers contemptous of 'sell-out' at Wapping', *Financial Times*, 9 February 1987

continue the dispute.[91]

Secondly, the Wapping dispute highlighted the conflict between the unions involved in the dispute. Primarily, apart from the TUC's inability to have a positive impact upon the negotiations in late 1985, there was the ineptitude of the unions' London membership to gather the support of their fellow members outside London. This was more evident in the case of SOGAT which completely failed to persuade its members in newspaper wholesalers not to handle the papers belonging to Murdoch. The NGA and SOGAT regarded the EEPTU as the miscreant in the dispute. As discussed above, Hammond was prepared to face intense hostility from other unions in return for few hundred extra members. Moreover, there were disputes between the NGA and the NUJ. In 1983 there were plans for a merger between the NUJ and NGA, but the talks had broken down. The arrival of new technology threatened the virtual abolition of the NGA, because in future the journalists, using computer technology, could do the task themselves. There were disputes between these unions in different locations over these issues and by 1985, there was considerable bitterness.[92]

The Impact of Wapping

> *Without Wapping there probably would have been changes in the British national newspaper industry – but those changes would have fallen far short of what all British publishers now enjoy ... the Wapping experience has forced the unions to be far more flexible in their approach to new working practices than they have ever been before.*[93]

During the past decade there have been numerous analyses of the nature of technological changes in British media and

---
[91] L. Melvern, op.cit. and S. Littleton, op.cit
[92] C. Cockburn, *'Brothers'*, (London: Pluto Press), 1983
[93] News International in the Docklnads, News International promotional material

communications. Authors as diverse as Schiller, Mattellart, Garnham, Webster and Robins all recognize that the enthusiastic response by Rightist governments such as Thatcher's in Britain for neo-liberal economic policies represented a political program aimed at restoring favourable conditions for capital accumulation. Accordingly, there was a renewed round of capital concentration accompanied by further transnationalization of capital under the benign patronage of the state. The onslaught on organized labour was also led by the state through its legislatively policed industrial relations policy. Robbins and Webster, argue that new information technology is not a socially neutral force whose humane and rational application will ensure a 'computopia', but an expression of relations of power. Its application in the hands of transnational corporation facilitates capital's domination of the labour process. It extends capital's opportunities to shape the mode of consumption of workers.[94]

Murdoch's success at Wapping was a major shift in power and capital away from trade unions and the labour force in favour of proprietors, management, and editors. Distribution practices, wholesaling arrangements and size and shapes of newspapers were also transformed. Murdoch's success seemed to indicate that industrial power, political influence, and profitability could be pursued simultaneously.

The Wapping episode would have happened even if Murdoch had not initiated it. Major changes in the printing and distribution of newspapers had become inevitable by the early 1980s. Thatcher's Britain valued those prepared to innovate, reorganize and confront traditional practices. Not just Murdoch, in his move to Wapping, seemed agreeable to Thatcher's new Britain. David Stevens at the *Daily Express*, and Robert Maxwell at the *Daily Mirror* followed suit. Andrew Neil writes: 'What a wonderful victory, Robert Maxwell called to say on 7 February 1987, the day the dispute ended. Well done. I trust there will be

---

[94]See: F. Webster & K. Robbins, *Information Technology: a Luddite Analysis* (N.J.: Ablex), 1986. Also, H. Schiller, *'Information and Crisis Economy'*, (NJ: Ablex), 1984; A. Mattelart, M. Mattelart and X. Delacourt,*'International Image Markets'*,(London: Comedia), 1984

no brutes outside your gates tonight.'[95] Maxwell's and Stevens' initial testimonies were businesslike, their approach to unions courageous with an obsessive determination to reduce production costs.

Robert Maxwell was in fact the first major proprietor to sack 240 NGA members of *Sporting Life* in 1985 which produced no effective response from the union. Maxwell went even further and negotiated a redundancy settlement for 2,100 employees of the Mirror Group with the NGA seven weeks before the beginning of the Wapping dispute.[96] Furthermore, in 1983 Reuters, the world news agency, was floated on the stock market. This meant that the national press which together owned 37.5 percent of Reuters each received substantial capital. The extra cash was seen by some of the publishers as added encouragement to move away from Fleet Street.[97]

In the beginning of 1983 the *Daily Telegraph* invested £105 million for new printing sites in east London and Manchester. This investment included installing an Atex computer system. The *Telegraph*'s dockland site was fully operational by 29 September 1986. By 1986, in and around Wapping the national press boosted their profit margins by drastic cuts in manning levels and costs. Murdoch claimed, "the changes that took place at Wapping have brought new prosperity to the newspaper industry, sparked off new titles and engendered the competitive atmosphere in which all newspapers, and their readers, thrive."[98]

The industry's newfound prosperity contributed to the growth of the printing and publishing sector of the London stock market, which in just over half a decade grew to ten times its former size.[99] Life after Wapping meant a new sense of cooperation and flexibility amongst the production staff and a

---

[95] A. Neil, *Full Disclosure*, op.cit. p. 157
[96] T. Bower, *Maxwell, The Outsider* (London: Mandarin), 1991
[97] J. Tunstall, *'Newspaper Power'*, op.cit. p. 19
[98] News International in the Dcoklands, op.cit
[99] Sources: J. Reed, 'The Murdoch Empire Strikes Back', *The Guardian*, 19 June, 1989
   P. Foot, 'Never has so much been owned by so few', *UK Press Gazette*, December 21-28, 1987
   M. Brown, 'Exodus from Fleet Street', *The Guardian*, 26 April, 1985

conspicuous absence of disruption. The most concrete aspect of the new era, however, was the geographical relocation of the national press. Leaving Fleet Street meant that the former cluster of publishers were now scattered around greater London, and the new production networks set up by the publishers now span all of Britain. Within sixteen months of Murdoch's move to Wapping, all national papers had either moved or announced their intention to leave Fleet Street. Only the *Guardian* and The Mirror Group retained renovated editorial facilities around Fleet Street.

The predominant configuration in the national press now consists of one site for administrative, editorial, advertising, and origination-related units, at which full pages are prepared and faxed to as many satellite printing facilities as needed to fulfill the speed and capacity needs of the paper. Printed copies then proceed to strategically placed centres throughout the country from which they are distributed. Some national titles maintain only administrative, advertising, editorial, and origination departments, and let a subcontractor handle the actual printing process. This method is used by titles such as The *Observer* which formerly maintained a full production facility on Fleet Street unused for six days a week.

The economic advantages of Wapping went beyond cheaper production costs. The City boom boosted the value of real estate in Fleet Street dramatically. The premium rent paid for a square foot of space on Fleet Street came close to £50. Selling off these premises to expanding overseas capital made the press owners £1 billion richer. The injection of foreign capital and the limited availability of property in central London created a sellers market for owners of the Fleet Street facilities. Thatcher's policy of supporting the London Docklands as a development area also enabled the Fleet Street press to obtain cheap sites for their new East London plants.[100]

The sell-off provided the substantial cash reserves needed for the modernization of the industry. By 1988, the industry had invested £1.02 billion in new equipment. It is estimated that the

---

[100] S.M. Littleton, op.cit, p.170

implementation of new technology within the industry would widen the profit margin of the national press from two to four per cent to between ten and fourteen per cent.[101]

Furthermore, this technical modernization produced several immediate effects. Most national dailies are now in colour, and the quality of reproduction was improved by the introduction of web offset technology. A greater number of pages, specialized sections and magazines were part of the increased and more diversified editorial and advertising content. The introduction of colour photography by the national press has induced important changes upon photojournalism. The utilization of digital retouching by photojournalists enables them to manipulate a piece of photography by removing, cloning, deleting or combining parts of the image with other objects, and changing their colour and brightness. Digital retouching is usually much faster than reshooting a subject and has made it possible to feed the new image directly into production. This new development in the field of photojournalism has prompted some commentators to argue that invisible manipulations of digital retouching can impair the status of photojournalism and potentially destroy the credibility of the photograph as a document.[102]

New technology has enabled most regional papers to insert their own geographically specific sections. Such additions opened up new ways for editorial coverage, and offered advertisers the opportunity to target certain localities. Both of these strategies are placing the national press in competition with the regional papers.

Automated inserting equipment has provided new methods of advertising to the public. Loose-leaf pre-printed advertising can now be inserted inside the paper. The improvements and the resulting services generate new profits from advertising revenues for publishers. Innovations such as these, some claim, have changed the 'nature of the British newspaper as an advertising

---

[101]See: C. Wintour, *The Rise and Fall of Fleet Street*, op.cit
[102]For a superb analysis of this issue see: K.E. Becker, 'To control our image: photojournalism and new technology', *Media, Culture and Society*, Vol 13. 1991, pp 381-397

medium radically.'[103]

Perhaps the most spectacular effect of the new technology, however, was its immense toll on the workforce. In 1985, prior to the Wapping dispute, the press industry employed around 30,000 people. By 1990 this was reduced by half. In general terms, workforces in composing rooms were brought down by one-half to two-thirds of their previous size. The loss of jobs contributed to what an NGA official described as, 'a colossal amount of labour simply swimming around in London.'[104] The only exception was with the introduction of the colour pages into the industry. This created a demand for highly skilled production workers in positions that had not previously existed in the press. The demand for skilled colour reproduction workers is particularly strong in the tabloid sector of the industry, which relies heavily on graphics and photographs.[105]

Those workers who managed to remain in the industry were relatively well paid. There is now a greater parity in wages among various groups of workers on the production line. Workers in origination areas were among the most highly paid, whereas machine minders in the press room were the lowest paid. The evening out of wage levels has resulted in a relative improvement in pay for machine workers.

The Wapping dispute also transformed the structure of the labour negotiation process across the press industry. The previous system of bargaining was transformed into a more structured and cohesive process in which national union officials took key leadership positions representing the interests of their members. Formerly, the diverse structure of the unions forced press management to negotiate with numerous bodies within each company, each trying to maximize benefits for its respective members. Before and during the Wapping dispute, as discussed above, the lack of cohesive structure became one of the unions' greatest weaknesses. Emphasis on labour relations in the national

---

[103] R. Snoddy, ' A leaf from the US books', *Financial Times*, 5 September 1988
[104] Quoted in 'No way in Wapping: the effect of the policing of the News International dispute on Wapping residents' (London: National Council for Civil Liberties), 1986, p.31
[105] Littleton, op.cit.p.173

press has shifted from the union negotiation of employee affairs to a greater use of in-house joint consultation, collective bargaining, and, in some cases, almost unilateral direction from the employer. In terms of titles there has been ten new papers and five disappeared titles (Table 12).

As Table 12 suggests the striking feature of the new titles since 1986 is the high number of tabloid newspapers. The only 'quality' papers which have survived are the *Independent* and *Independent on Sunday*. The national press's new status, it seems, has encouraged a decline in journalistic performance and expansion of 'tabloidization'. As argued in previous sections, the press in Britain has seldom been synonymous with 'serious journalism'. It is rather a mixture of information and entertainment. Circulation battles and cost-cutting objectives tend to marginalize materials not of mass appeal, leading to a decline in materials such as foreign affairs and political news. In America, for example, newspapers such as *Washington Post*, without close competition in the 1980s, could afford to devote more space and staff resources to political issues than their British counterparts.[106] Furthermore, in considering the above data, it seems that the Wapping revolution has not changed the character of the national press since the basic rules of publishing have not changed greatly. Establishing and running a new national title remains very costly, making it much easier for the existing proprietors and corporations to launch new titles and acquire existing ones. Shah's Today, for example required £22.5 million to be launched. Lonrho, a leading press conglomerate, injected over £24 million into the Today Group, effectively doubling its initial launching cost. Despite this, Shah eventually sold the Today Group to Murdoch in 1987.[107]

After Wapping, the News International wage bill was cut instantly by £45 million per year. As a result pre tax profits increased from £39.1million in 1985 to £165 million in 1988, which partly financed Murdoch's move into Satellite

---

[106]See: S. Jenkins, 'The more things change: Fleet
[107]For more interesting figures see B. McNair, *News and Journalism in the UK* (London: Routledge), 1994, chp7

THE PRESS INDUSTRY IN THATCHER'S YEARS

Table 12 New Arrivals and Departures since 1986

Title	Launch date	Editorial style	Exit date
Today	4 March 86	Tabloid	
Sunday Today	9 March 86	Tabloid	31 May 87
Sunday Sport	14 September 86	Tabloid	
Independent	7 October 1986	Quality	
London Daily News	24 February 87	24 hour daily	24 July 87
News on Sunday	26 April 87	Tabloid: Left-Wing	20 Nov 87
Sport (Wed)	17 August 88	Tabloid	
Post	10 November 88	Tabloid	17 Dec 88
Sport (Fri)	31 March 89	Tabloid	
Sunday Correspondent	17 Sept 1989	Quality	25 Nov 90
Independent on Sunday	28 January 1990	Quality	
*Sport (Thu)	23 August 90	Tabloid	

*The Sport's daily versions counted here as one newspaper Source: J. Tunstall, 'Newspaper Power' (Oxford: Clarendon), 1996, p25

television.[108] In considering the daily sales figures, as Table 13 indicates, the Wapping factor also failed to produce a spectacular increase in readership.

By 1988, it seems, national quality papers such as *The Times* and the *Guardian* had a marginal drop in their sales figures, whereas the *Financial Times* and the *Daily Telegraph* showed improved readership. In the tabloid section, the Sun remained the highest circulating paper, closely followed by the *Daily Mirror*. The circulation of other tabloids show a decrease in readership figures in the post Wapping era.

The new printing technology, however, did increase competition amongst the dailies and Sundays, but by no means completely transformed the economic structure of the national papers. The economic savings, however, were less than 20 per

[108]Source: P. Foot, 'Never has so much been owned by so few', op.cit

Table 13 Daily Sales, National Dailies - 1979-1988 (figures in thousands)[109]

	1979	1982	1985	1988
Guardian	390	405	440	410
Times	370	360	415	405
Financial Times	180	182	184	210
Independent	-	-	-	389
The Sun	3980	4005	4002	4000
Daily Mirror	3978	3500	3001	3005
Daily Express	2500	2000	1989	1970
Daily Mail	1980	1985	1976	1970
Daily Star	990	1350	1800	1210
Today	-	-	-	354
Daily Telegraph	1300	1280	1210	1980

cent of the total national press costs.

In other parts of the country, the new printing technology was also being rapidly deployed. The regional and local papers were rarely subjected to the degree of disruption of Fleet Street, but the new technology provided a new incentive for improvement. In keeping up with new developments at the national level, the regional publishers began the modernisation in earnest. Thomson Regional Newspapers, for example, introduced direct input technology into its ten provisional printing centres by the late 1987. In 1989, Bill Heeps, the chairman of Thomson Regional Newspapers suggested:

> ...the enemy [of the regional press] is no longer the predatory free newspaper but increasingly competitors for the advertising pound- local TV, local radio, local editions of national newspapers, and new electronic media.[110]

[109] Several sources were used for this table. Most figures are based on half yearly reports, Audit Bureau of Circulations, 1975-1989
[110] Quoted in Lawrence, 'Free for all', *UK Press Gazette*, September 15, 1989

Naturally, competition for advertising revenue has always existed, but in the late 1980s transformation of the national press began to also have an impact upon the regional press. The new technologies introduced in Wapping enabled the proprietors to 'editionize' their products, thus producing several editions of a national title suited for a particular population area in different parts of the country. Murdoch, for example, used his Glasgow plant to 'editionize' the *Sun* and the *Sunday Times* to break into the Scottish market.[111] Investment in new technologies enabled Scotland's *Herald* and *Evening Times* to improve their design, colour techniques and editionizing process. By 1990 the *Evening Times* would produce three editions between early afternoon and evening. By 1992 the *Aberdeen Press and Journal* had nine editions in circulation each targeted at specific geographical areas in Scotland.[112]

Furthermore, by implementing new technologies, the regional press were forced to improve their editorial quality in order to remain competitive with the nationals. A 1988 report by the Henley Centre for Economic Forecasting, commissioned by the major association of regional proprietors, the Newspaper Society, urged regional papers not to respond to the nationals' challenge by chasing them down-market, but to 'adopt a serious tabloid format to provide readers with local news, information and life style features which they are unlikely to get from the national press or television.' To achieve this required money for more talented journalists. Proprietors are now prepared to offer better salaries and conditions to reverse further migration of the talented journalists to London.[113]

In terms of the concentration of ownership neither of the two major national groups in 1990, Murdoch and Maxwell, was very strong in the provincial sector. Nor were the strongest provincial, United and Associated, dominant in either quality or

---

[111]Just before the general election of 1992, the *Sun*'s Scottish edition printed the headline: Rise and be a Nation Again'. A policy distinctively different from the pro-unionist, pro-Conservative editorials in England. See: B. McNair, *'News and Journalism in the Uk'*, op.cit. chp9

[112]J. Morgan, 'Sundays turn tide in sales', *UK Press Gazette*, 8 June, 1992

[113]Source: *UK Press Gazette*, 27 June, 1988

Table 14 A comparative analysis of the percentage of major groups' ownership in the regional Daily market

Press Group	Provincial Dailies	
	1976	1987
Associated Newspapers	1 0	1 2
Beaverbrook	-	-
Mirror Group	-	-
Kemsley	-	-
News of the World	-	-
Oldham	-	-
Pearson/Westminster	7	7
United	8	8
Iliffe6	-	
Thomson	15	15
News International	-	-
Reed	7	2
Lonrho	-	4
Maxwell/Pergamon	-	1 2
Total	47	60

Sources: Royal Commissions on the Press; Press Council

the popular national market. The large issues about press concentration concerned the national sector and the incorporation of the press with other media and financial interests. However, as Table 14 demonstrates, in comparison to 1976 the national press groups managed to increase their share of the provincial dailies by 13 per cent.

It is evident that the new technology has not and will not decrease the unequal competitive relationship between strong and weak papers. The popular and successful publications will acquire more revenue and lower unit costs than their rivals, because of greater economies of scale. To remain competitive, weaker papers then have to spend more and consequently will have a more vulnerable financial position. The 1977 Royal

Commission concludes "even if all newspapers accomplish the change in technology, competition may still result in some papers closing since the new technology does little to alter the relative position of competing titles."[114] Furthermore, as Garnham points out, the well publicized Wapping revolution in the 1980s was not only unable to decrease the concentration of press ownership but encouraged a reversal. The production labour costs were a relatively low percentage of total costs, and the necessary capital base for a national paper remained high. Nor has the new automation, Garnham argues, 'blocked the slide of the mass circulating press into trivia and an intense competition for a narrow range of similar stories based upon the scandal and entertainment gossip which restricts information pluralism within even narrower bounds.'[115]

Where new technology, Garnham adds, is significantly affecting the press market is with the inclusion of satellite based remote printing. This is reinforcing the concentration of control both nationally and internationally. The overseas editions of *The Wall Street Journal*, published in Europe and Asia, and the *Financial Times* published in Europe and USA are good examples of this trend. The basic economics of the press in a competitive free market leads, because of high first-copy costs and low marginal costs, to audience maximization within any given market segment. The new printing technology is now responsible for the spread of this development to ever wider geographical markets.[116]

Efficient distribution, Garnham continues, seems to be the key to the economics of the media and its output, since it is not the production of the materials that counts, but rather its access to an audience.[117] Distribution is a crucial economic factor for

---

[114] As argued before the 1977 Royal Commission also suggested that the new technology would be a better help to quality papers in reading costs.
[115] N. Garnham, 'The impact of New Information and communication Technologies: A Challenge for Press Freedom', *Unesco Publications*, no 16
[116] Colin Sparks see the internationalisation of the press as a result of the market conditions and political realities of bourgeois democracy which increasingly tend to persuade people to opt out of effective participation in the public sphere. See: C. Sparks, 'The Popular Press and Political Democracy', *Media, Culture and Society*, Vol 10, 1988
[117] Garnham, op.cit. p30

the press, because the value of much information is time-dependent, and the competition for a given audiences' attention time is therefore intense. This can be exemplified by the media coverage of the Falklands crisis in the 1980s.

Garnham concludes that despite these new technologies, 'there is a widespread evidence [in Britain] that the control and manipulation of information in their own interests by major power holders, whether in government or businesses, is on the increase and that technology gives the public little protection against this process. Ever-greater information power is in the hands of those major power holders who own the economic resources to capture and make use of the information flows'.[118]

Some commentators see the forms taken by the new technologies as fuelling a new ideology. Information has become the leitmotif of modernity, and the new technologies are taking on a symbolic value. Daniel Bell, who has been able to locate the notion of 'information society' in the wider sociological setting of 'post-industrial society' believes that the new technologies are synonymous with socioeconomic progress and the liberation of humanity. The new media technologies hold out the promise of a revival of democracy and individual freedom through the active participation of people. Individual self-expression will be ensured by the broader range of choice of entertainment and leisure. Horizontal communication will enhance social change or may, in the long run, culminate in the coming of the global village.[119]

Against this approach we need to recognize that information technology is not a socially neutral force whose implementation will ensure the ushering of a leisure society of plenty. For the Frankfurt School, the new technologies are the source of even more marked domestic inequality. Instead of taking a step forward, they have increased unemployment and made us more dependent upon machines. The new technologies will foster increased individualism and erode social cohesion, so that

---

[119]*ibid*, p.32
[120]P. Brantlinger, *Bread and Circuses: Theories of Mass Culture as Social Decay* (Cornell University Press), 1983

solidarity and social welfare will eventually disappear. They will ensure the growth of a standardized universal culture that will be based on mindless materialism.

Yet, the development of the new technologies is a very complex phenomenon for which there can be no predetermined causes. The dissemination of the new technologies is a process which includes a series of relationships between technological innovation and social innovation, and these relationships are not yet fully explored, at least not sociologically. The information society now seems to be identified by 'universalization' and 'differentiation'. The universalization can be exemplified by the new technologies infiltrating into all sectors of society. Indeed, as we argued above, they recast the economic structure of the British communications system, altering its institutional and traditional frameworks.[120]

The social relations involved in the implementation of the new printing technologies were affected and were spread from the national to the regional levels. So far, the technological tendencies point to a 'homogenization' of influences which include the privatization of the communication organization, the concentration of the media, the standardization of press materials and images, and the growth of work and entertainment values.

Conclusion

This chapter highlighted some of the processes whereby the structural changes of the press industry in the 1980s became distinguishable from other periods in the long history of the British press. It was argued that the culmination of a greater concentration of capital in a highly centralised press industry has turned it into an institution managed by a few tycoons, mostly supporters of Thatcher, whose economic and social interests

---

[120]J. Jouet & S. Coudray, *New Communication Technologies: Research Trends*, Unesco 1990 – no 105. Here the authors carefully discuss the effects of cultural imperialism which involved in the communication technologies.

were to utilize media power to provide support for the Thatcherite ethos. They formed an imperative macro agency in the 1980s, responsible for effectively nurturing the popularity of the 'New Right'.

Since the industry was no longer a mere journalistic organization, the proprietors role as social actors overlapped with their roles as economic actors which complimented one another. The industry provided a form of social prestige for the proprietors to exert enough influence not only in the social but also in the political and economic spheres.

Thatcher's implementation of labour laws provided an effective weapon to curb organised resistance to the 'efficient' output and distribution of the technologically renovated press. The section on the Wapping dispute, this study believes, highlighted the complimentary and reciprocal relationship between the political actors and other *macro* and *collective* agents in the internal and external spheres of the press industry.

Within the industry, *collective* actors such as specialist and lobby correspondents and national editors provided the crucial links between the proprietors and the external political sphere. They were, in turn, rewarded by the *mega* actors in the political sphere with lucrative contracts and honourary titles. Thatcher's gifts to Murdoch have been documented at several points in this chapter. Murdoch, in return, committed his papers to Thatcher's political and ideological views. This mutual reciprocity has also been documented in this chapter.

The Thatcher years can be seen as different in terms of the post-Thatcher restrictions imposed on unlimited ownership by any one press baron.[121] In 1995 John Major's government produced a Green Paper on Media Ownership. The basic rule, as formulated then, included the prescription that press groups with less than 20 per cent of the market share, measured by circulation, can own two ITV licenses. Those with larger shares, which currently includes News International and Mirror Group

---

[121]For a detailed discussion on the post-Thatcherite media regulation, inter-media competition, media concentration and diversity see: S.M. Beesley (Ed), *Markets and the Media: Competition, Regulation and the Interests of Consumers* (London: IEA), 1996

Newspapers, will be limited to 20 per cent of one ITV company or Channel 5 license and 5 per cent in any subsequent ITV holdings. The long term objectives include having single-media markets in which no one operator has more than 10 per cent control and that no one company should have more than 20 per cent control in any single sector. Had these rules been in place in the 1980s Murdoch would not have been able to own 35 per cent of the newspaper market and a 40 per cent share in the satellite channel BSkyB.[122]

This chapter also assessed the role of technology and its impact upon the industry. This assessment was to demonstrate the relationship between the function of the instrumental application of technology, and economic and political gain. The movement of Murdoch's press operations from Fleet Street to Wapping, it was argued, demonstrated another dimension of proprietor power which was exercised with all the resources of a multi-national conglomerate. In this context, technological changes were analysed alongside that of agency, for it highlighted the complimentary and reciprocal relationship between technology and agency. The consequences of the new technology on the print unions was assessed concluding that what Wapping represented was an overwhelming victory over the powerful print unions and that this defeat was secured by the multiple cooperation of important macro actors in different spheres of society. Above all, this chapter aimed to highlight the crucial point that the special relationship between Thatcher and Murdoch had a deeper impact not only upon the press industry but the British society as a whole In order to provide a more concrete empirical analysis of this claim the next chapter will be specifically devoted to an in depth examination of the content of the national press during the miners' strikes of 1972 and 1974 and 1984-85.

---

[122]For an examination of post Thatcher media restrictions see: Eldridge *et.al, The Mass Media and Power in Modern Britain*, op.cit, pp 41-2

FOUR

THE MINERS' STRIKES AND THE PRESS INDUSTRY
A Comparative Study of the Miners' Strikes 1972–74 & 1984–85

Introduction

This chapter outlines and analyses the empirical research conducted to substantiate the theoretical claims of this study. Fundamentally, this research is concerned with the crucial role played by the press industry during the miners' strikes in recent decades. In the 1970s as well as 1980s the miners' strikes were of immense importance for different reasons. The 1970s strikes, which ended in resounding victory for the miners encouraged the labour movement to set a new political and social agenda. The miners' triumph not only strengthened the position of the trade unions, but more importantly enabled the labour movement to launch political initiatives and form a new government headed by Harold Wilson.

The strike of the 1980s produced a qualitatively different result. The defeat of the miners is regarded as the most comprehensive in the recent history of the trade union movement in Britain. The year long conflict prepared the grounds for the advancement of the principal items of the Thatcherite agenda, to curtail the power of the organized labour and trade unionism. The victory over the historically 'militant' miners, it is claimed, was 'partly aided' by the most partisan press campaign in the modern history of the British media. It is the principal objective of this research to demonstrate that the press industry, committed to a 'manufactured schema, was greatly influential in the defeat and subsequent demise of the miners.

Working within the theoretical paradigm of the 'culture industry', this chapter is an empirical assessment of the press industry which is connected both to corporate capitalism and the political system. There will also be further assessment of Adorno's concepts which focused upon the dominant characteristics of commodified culture. Although these are diverse and have their own logic Adorno repeatedly stressed these concepts which accompany the commodification of cultural goods. These are: standardization, schematization and stereotypes. A definition, and discussion, for each one of these features has been presented in Chapter One. The qualitative section of this chapter will demonstrate empirically that in their treatment of the miners and their strike of 1984-85 the industry's editorials and leading articles were, at times, *standardized* materials accompanied with *schema* and *stereotypes* which may be regarded as an invitation for conformity and *pseudo individual* reaction by the readers.

The repetitiveness, the self-sameness, the ubiquity of mass culture tend to make for atomized reactions and to weaken the forces of individual opposition.[1]

This study intends to concentrate upon the concepts of standardization, schematization and stereotypes which are more relevant to the purposes of this reserach. The fourth aspect of the culture industry thesis, pseudo individualism, was considered by Adorno primarily in connection with commodified music and therefore, will not feature in this empirical discussion on the press industry.

The media coverage of the 1984-85 miners' dispute has become almost as controversial as the dispute itself. Ultimately, this chapter will demonstrate that during the 1984-85 miners' strike, there were no major distinctions between the 'conservative-supporting' and the 'labour-supporting' newspapers. This distinction was barely noticeable in the 1970s,

---

[1]See: Adorno, 'How to Look at Television', in J.M. Bernstein, *The Culture Industry*, op.cit

but it will be shown that, in the 1980s, the strongest Labour supporting papers, the *Guardian* and the *Daily Mirror*, were as unsympathetic to the miners in general – and the NUM in particular – as the rest of the selected papers in the sample.

To highlight these claims more effectively, it is instructive to compare the press coverage of the 1980s dispute to that of the 1970s. In doing so, the following hypotheses are presented to provide a more concrete methodological grounds:

Hypothesis 1: 'All' newspapers in the sample tended to adopt a hostile stance against the miners' dispute in the 1984-85 period.

Hypothesis 2: Most newspapers in the sample supported the miners in the 1970s period.

Hypothesis 3: The coverage of the miners' disputes by the major national press, in either period, influenced a sufficient number of their readers such that the popularity or unpopularity of the miners and their cause was significantly affected.

The following sections, explore the extent to which these hypotheses are consistent with the available evidence, using the data-analytic strategy described below.

The Methodological Principle: Overcoming Problems of Reliability

The methodological logic of this study is based upon a comprehensive utilization of 'content analysis'. Since the study is principally one of media research in retrospect, the method of content analysis seems an appropriate tool of investigation. In order to expand upon what is meant by comprehensive, a short paragraph will be presented to clarify the definition of 'content analysis' as well as its advantages and shortcomings, followed by outlining steps taken to override the operational problems.

Content analysis is the main *hermeneutic* method used by sociologists and is one of the most widely utilized research tools in media studies. As a research technique, it can be used very effectively in researching issues in social sciences. However, due to the 'scientific exterior' and essentially quantitative nature of content analysis, it is susceptible to mistaken usages. Moreover, reliability problems usually grow out of the ambiguity of word meanings, category definitions or other coding rules. The main legitimate objections directed at the growing usage of content analysis is, however, the excessive quantification of data in the behavioral sciences.[2] More specifically, there is the problem of reproducibility or inter-coder reliability. Are the same results produced when the same text is coded by more than one coder?[3] As Krippendorf points out, many investigators fail totally to assess the reliability of their coding.[4]

Nonetheless, content analysis can override these objections by incorporating three crucial strategies. Firstly, content analysis must not be regarded as an exclusively quantitative approach, but rather can incorporate a qualitative dimension for a productive and complementary methodological principle.[5] Secondly, an 'independent' opinion can be sought on the coding procedures and selection of themes and categories. Thirdly, some computer packages developed in recent years can be employed to increase the reliability of coding and word counting.[6]

[2]The following works exemplify the main objections against methodological use of content analysis:
 O. Burgeline, 'Structural analysis and mass communication', in D. McQuail (Eds), *Sociology of Mass Communications,* op.cit. pp 313-328
 J. Fiske & J. Hartley, *Reading Television* (London: Methuen), 1978
[3]See: R. Weber, *Basic Content Analysis* (London: Sage) 1990, p.17
[4]See: Krippendorf et al .*Content Analysis: An Introduction to Its Methodology* (LA, CA: Sage), 1980. pp 130-54
[5]Weber argues that the best content analytic studies use both 'qualitative' and 'quantitative' operations on texts. Thus content analysis combines what are usually thought to be antithetical modes of analysis. Op.cit.
[6]One of these packages is a toolkit named MECA. This is written in C and are available for many Macintosh PC and UNIX platforms. Additional details are available in L. Carely, 'Coding choices for textual analysis: A comparison of content analysis and map analysis', *Sociological Methodology,* Vol 23, 1993, pp 75-125. Essentially, there are ways in which newspaper texts are curremtly available in electronic form: on CD-ROMs and

Accordingly, three strategies were implemented to minimize the problem of the 'reliability' of this study. Firstly, this research study consists of two parts. A 'quantitative' section followed by a 'qualitative' analysis. Secondly, the frequency of the categories were double checked by a computer 'scanning' method and thirdly, an independent coder was employed to verify the results of the research and produce an independent, and reliable, coding of categories.

The problem of generalizability was addressed by employing two strategies: Firstly, an attempt was made to extend the scope of the research by designing a *comparative* study whereby the result of the research could be compared over three separate miners' strikes. Secondly, by examining the results of the public opinion polls published by respected organizations, such as MORI and Gallup, some degree of public opinion in relation to the miners' strike could be assessed. Accordingly, the variation of degrees of editorial hostility, both in the 1970s and the 1980s, will be analysed in conjunction with the public opinion polls published at those specific periods. The first part of the presentation of the data will demonstrate that the degrees of editorial hostility shows a significant shift in the 1980s. In the 1970s, it will be claimed, the total editorial hostility of the national press, at its height, amounted to less than 20% of the total examined in the sample. This figure in the 1980s had increased to 79% of the sample. Furthermore, and more crucially, this study will present several editorial from all the papers in the sample, which will show an *'immediate'* hostility by the national press even before the 1984 strike was due to begin. This is to argue that the national press was 'hostile' from the moment the miners began their strike. Subsequently, this research will attempt to establish a correlation between the editorial hostility of the national press and the public opinion in relation to the miners and their strike. It will also be demonstrated that the national press, including the Labour

the main on line commercial database in UK, FT Profile. However, due to the unavailability of the newspapers published in the 1970s, FT profile was used in this study as a secondary resource.

Table 15

Methodological Issue	THE OBJECTIONS	THE REMEDY
RELIABILITY	Excessive Quantification	A combined Qualitative and Quantitative analysis
	Inaccurate definitions	Usage of computer derived categories
	The problem of generalizability	Comparing the data with some external criterion: BPO ,MORI and Gallup

supporting *Daily Mirror* and the *Guardian*, began their 'hostile' campaign well before the strike officially began.

Table 15 summarizes the anticipated methodological difficulties and the strategies employed to minimize them.

The Sampling Procedure

As in most social studies, a sampling plan is of crucial importance and, as G.Stempel and Holsti argue, almost all content analyses employ a sampling strategy.[7] The sampling procedure employed by this study is as follows:

1. The time-frame encompassed by this study are three periods of the miners' strikes.[8]

---

[7] See: Stempel and Westley, *Research Methods in Mass Communication* (NJ: Prentice-Hall), 1989, p 124-149

[8] In the presentation of the data we have put the two strikes of the 1972 and 1974 together and present the results under the title of the '1970s strikes'

1st January- February 19th 1972
1st December 1973 – March 6th 1974
1st March 1984 – March 5th 1985

2. The editorial contents of 'six randomly selected national daily' newspapers: The *Sun*, *Daily Star*, *Daily Mirror*, *Daily Express*, *The Times* and *The Guardian* were examined.
3. The criterion used for inclusion of an editorial in the sample was simply its specific reference to the miners' disputes To effectively control the scope of the study it was decided to limit our research to the periods of the disputes only.[9] In an attempt to represent the days of the week equally, it was decided to include twenty-four days of each month in the sample. Four Mondays were selected randomly, four Tuesdays randomly, four Wednesdays randomly and so on. Sundays were excluded from this study.[10] If there were no editorials published on a selected day either the preceding or the proceeding days were examined instead. In all, 1467 editorials were examined and coded. They were then coded again by a research assistant.

For the purpose of reliability this study maintained the same selection of the newspapers for both periods, with the exception of the *Daily Star* which was not established until 1978. As a matter of substitution the *Daily Mail* was selected for the 1970s strikes.

For the *quantitative* section of the study a number of relevant and important categories were randomly selected and their frequencies were measured in relation to the number of editorials examined.

The results will be presented by two columns representing the results of both 'self' and 'independent' coding. The next section attempts to expand upon the procedure for assessing editorial attitude.

[9] Traditionally miners began their disputes with the implementation of 'over-time' ban, announced by the NUM, therefore, constituted the beginning of the research and ended with the first day of the return organised by the NUM

[10] Sunday papers were excluded from this sample primarily because some papers in our sample do not publish on Sundays (*The Sun – Guardian*)

Procedure For Assessing Editorial 'Attitude'

According to McQuail, there are three main ways in which 'editorial attitude' in news reports may be revealed. One consists of evaluative or interpretive comments of a tendentious kind, another of verifiable 'facts' damaging to one group or participant, a third of words and phrases which give 'colour' to an editorial and in doing so may lead to a particular judgment on the part of the reader and reflect the newspaper's attitude.[11]

This distinction is a useful strategy in assessing the attitude, or the colour, of the editorials examined. Accordingly, in the quantitative section of this study, a simple coding system was devised to assess the editorial attitude of the newspapers in the sample for 1970s and 1980s. By using McQuail's distinction, the coding system for measuring the degrees of 'editorial mood' relative to the miners cause is based upon the following scheme:

Very Favourable = 1
Favourable = 2
Middle ground = 3
Hostile = 4
Very Hostile = 5

It is important to reiterate that ultimately, the assessment, or classification, of 'editorial mood' is a matter of personal judgment, and depends on where one places the 'middle' position and on the conventions one accepts about what is fair or proper. There are no absolute standards, and this study has intended to shed some light on actual practice rather than to measure performance against an ideal. Furthermore, the classification of editorials was not made on any basis related to the possible occurrence of 'bias' but were intended to reflect normal or average performance in the period studied.

The *qualitative* section of the research, on the other hand, centres around four crucial themes of the miners' strikes.

[11] D. McQuail, 'Analysis of Newspaper Content', *Royal Commission on the Press*, Research Series 4, HMSO, 1977, Part C, pp. 149-214

Throughout the research, the repetition of certain themes which tended to occur across all the newspaper editorials in the sample was observed. These themes were then classified under **four** major headings which embody the industry's extraordinary focus upon the four issues:

1. **The miners and the press industry in a comparative perspective**: from the 'special cases' in the 1970s to the 'enemy within' of the 1980s together with a widespread usage of military and Nazi analogies.[12]
2. **'Law and order', picket violence and the role of Arthur Scargill**
3. **The depiction of trade unionism and organized labour as 'futile and dangerous'.**
4. **The encouragement of a mood of defeatism amongst miners and other trade unionists.**

According to this study's methodological principle of comparability, it will be argued that the 1970s miners' campaigns received a qualitatively different handling by the national press. To support this claim quantitative data will be presented first, followed by the qualitative analysis of the research.

Analysis of the Empirical Data: The Quantitative Dimension

The quantitative dimension of this research is divided into two distinct sections. The first part deals with a comparative analysis of the 'degrees of editorial hostility' of the national press in relation to the miners' strikes and/or their causes. We will present the most important finding of this section of the research in two separate tables and attempt to explain the emerging trend underlying the research. The remaining parts of the data will appear in the attached Appendix

---

[12]The comparative methods, we believe, lies at the heart of any sociological research that goes beyond mere description

The second part of this section deals with the frequency of the selected categories or concepts. We tried to maintain the same concepts (categories) for both periods in question. However, due to the different political and social climate of the early 1970s, some categories were not present in our sample. Therefore, a great deal of care was needed to select a group of concepts which were present in both periods of this research.

To capture the complexities of each period, on the other hand, it was decided to select certain randomly selected phrases which were particular to each period only. For example, for the 1970s, the phrase 'miners as special case' was chosen, as it occurred in that format right across the national press. For the 1980s, the phrase 'King Arthur' appeared very frequently in the national press. Therefore, this analysis contains a selection of both single words and phrases. The quantitative dimension begins with the presentation of the degrees of editorial hostility for the two periods of analysis.

The Degrees of 'Editorial Hostility'

This section presents two tables demonstrating the most important findings of the research. Each paper was analysed for the degrees of hostility in the periods studied and each editorial selected was analysed and coded. The first table in this section refers to the results of the 1970s , the second table demonstrates the results of the 1980s. The reader is reminded that for the 1970s period, the *Daily Mail* was chosen to substitute the *Daily Star* which did not then exist.

Tables 16 and 17 capture an interesting reversal of 'editorial hostility' for the 1980s miners' dispute. As indicated in the 1970s, the 'Very Favourable' coding receives 11.8 per cent of the total sample, whereas it receives less than one per cent of the sample for the 1980s. The 'Very Hostile' coding receives 3.4% of the total sample in the 1970s, but it produces a 31.4% score in the 1980s. The 'Middle Ground' coding has the highest score for the 1970s disputes, whereas the 'Hostile' section of

Table 16 A comparative analysis of the 'degree of editorial hostility' 1972-74 (All figures in %)

	Sun	Daily Mail	Daily Mirror	Daily Express	Guardian	The Times
Code 1	40	5.8	12.2	5.7	10	0.0
Code 2	22	13.8	42.8	19.2	2 8	14.2
Code 3	27	25.5	38.7	50.0	4 0	24.4
Code 4	11	41	6.1	21.1	2 2	59.1
Code 5	0.0	13.7	0.0	3.8	0.0	2.0

code 1= V. Favourable code 2= Favourable code 3= Middle ground code4= Hostile code 5= V. Hostile

Table 17 A comparative analysis of the 'degree of editorial hostility' 1984-85 (All figures in %)

	Sun	Daily Mail	Daily Mirror	Daily Express	Guardian	The Times
Code 1	0.0	0.0	3.0	0.0	0.0	0.0
Code 2	0.0	6.7	11.5	0.0	19.2	0.0
Code 3	2.8	22.9	22.3	3.8	22.9	12.7
Code 4	62.8	39.1	39.2	60.0	33.3	44.5
Code 5	31.4	31.1	30.0	36.1	24.4	42.7

the data receives the highest score for the 1980s. It is also important to note that 77.6 per cent of the editorials analysed in the sample were either between the Hostile and 'Very Hostile' categories. Comparing this figure with that of the 1970s, the figure is 30.4 per cent of the total sample falling between the two categories.

Analyses of the Categories in Each Newspaper: The Frequency of the Selected Concepts and Phrases

This section is devoted to the presentation of data in terms of the frequency of each selected concept. The categories chosen will be compared in both periods. The first table, Table 18, in this section attempts to demonstrate the frequency of each category analysed in our study for five national papers in the sample. This table will provide a source of reference and comparison between the press and the frequency of the categories. The second table, Table 19, will present an example of the method in which each of the categories were recorded and quantified.

Through the comparative and quantified analysis presented above, there are several trends that begin to emerge, which will be presented and analysed in the qualitative analyses. Each case will be outlined and discussed separately. However, on the macro level, there are two important issues that should be raised in this section of the research. The first issue deals with the 'changing focus' of the national press during the periods of the disputes. The second deals with an example of the way in which the press were beginning to respond favourably to an emerging idea of the 'Thatcherite' mission that 'there is no such thing as society'.

The next table, Table 20, shows the changing focus of the national press during two different periods of these strikes and the changing relationship between the principal actors in the miners' disputes. In the 1970s we have recorded a higher frequency of mention for the Prime Minister, Edward Heath, and a marginally lower frequency for the NUM president, Joe Gormley. In the 1980s the trend is reversed. All the papers analysed in the sample recorded a higher percentage of frequency of mention for Arthur Scargill and a significantly lower frequency for Thatcher.[13]

This table seems to confirm the national press' acceptance of

---

[13]The term 'frequency' here represents the number of times the name of the 'principal' actors were mentioned. We have merely counted the repetition of the name devoid of the context in which it appeared.

Table 18 A comparative analysis of the frequency of concepts and phrases in 'five' Papers analysed – 1984- Figures in %

Categories	Sun	Daily Mirror	Daily Express	The Times	Guardian
Militant	84	36	71	64	60
Undemocratic	75	44	67	78	54
Law/order	67	70	81	70	77
dispute	78	83	84	96	91
moderate	69	52	62	60	63
Nation	46	45	52	53	44
Britain	61	53	35	46	17
Scargill	119	84	110	139	132
Mob	73	42	57	57	29
Rule	65	12	51	64	42
Violence	78	75	71	89	66
Pickets	104	45	84	117	82
Ballot	88	62	72	101	64
Troops	46	19	39	39	7
McGregor	88	67	81	96	86
Scargillism	2.8	0	20	28	4
Thatcher	75	61	51	82	56
Political	62	53	49	81	60
Bully/ies	63	23	49	46	30
Police	79	56	51	102	57
NUM	70	64	67	58	87
TUC	52	55	21	15	59
Class war	20	15	19	30	15
Rebel miners	61	6	39	21	46
Uneconomic pits	41	22	82	59	57
General Scargill	4.7	1.5	7	0	0
King Arthur	30	9.2	15	10	14
Senseless strike	9.1	11.5	23	17	9
The Red Guards	23	0	40	8	0
Against the elected Government	27	14	35	40.8	0

Table 19 A comparative analysis of the selected categories- The Times: 1970s & 1980s

CATEGORIES	1970S Frequency	%	1980S Frequency	%
Militant/s	11	22	71	64
Extremists	8	16		39
Moderate	15	30	66	60
Undemocratic	9	18	86	78
Dispute/strike	42 / 30	85/82	106 / 136	112
Law/order	24	49	77	70
Violence	35	71	9 8	89
Picket/s	33	67	129	117
Mob	0	0	63	57
Bully/Bullies	0	0	51	46
Community	13	26	1	0.9
Nation	21	42	59	53
Britain/British	29 / 10	59/20	51 / 42	46/38
War/Battle	0 /2	0.4	62 / 40	56/36
Troops	0	0	43	39
NUM	39	79	113	102
NCB	10	20	67	61
Scargill	1	2	153	153
Scargillism	0	0	28	25
Thatcher	0	0	91	82
Thatcherism	0	0	4	4
Heath	63	128	7	6
Gormley	32	65	0	0
Rebel Miners	0	0	24	21
Class war	1	2	33	30
"Uneconomic pits"	5	10	65	59
"A dispute miners cannot win"	0	0	10	9.5
"Against the elected Government"	2	3	45	40.8
King Arthur	0	0	12	10
Senseless strike	3	2	21	17
The Red Guards	0	9	8.7	
Labour Relations	10	20	0	0
Miners as special case	18	36	0	0
Incomes policy	28	57	0	0
"Stage Three"	21	42	0	0
Pay Board	12	24	0	0
Political strike	3	6	61	55

Thatcher's claim for a non-interventionist approach during the dispute. The government repeatedly tried to depict the 1980s miners' strike as a dispute between the Coal Board and the NUM, and the government was seen as standing aloof. In the 1970s Edward Heath and his government seemed to be more targeted and received more attention by the national press, thus, confirming the involvement of his administration in the disputes, and the subsequent responsibilities arising from that involvement.[14]

Related to the theme presented in Table 20, a 1984 MORI poll assessed the public opinion. One of the findings of their research directly relates to the above-mentioned theme[15]:

Table 20 A comparative analysis of the depiction of the principal actors- 1970s and 1980s – frequencies in %

	1972-74		1984-85	
	Heath	Gormley	Thatcher	Scargill
The Sun	118	83	75	119
Daily Mail /	105	74	—	—
Daily Star	—	—	51	110
Daily Express	103	71	52	109
Daily Mirror	108	83	61	84
The Guardian	129	93	56	132
The Times	128	65	82	153

[14]This thesis has empirically demonstrated the 'indirect' involvement of the government in the dispute. Section 2.6.4- Chapter Two- has shown that both Tim Bell and Gordon Reece, important advertising consultants closely linked with the government, were employed by the National Coal Board to advice on public relations during the miners' strike of 1984-85. See: M. Thatcher: 1995p. 354 and MacGregor: 1986, p.306

[15]As part of its survey of public opinion for the *Sunday Times* at the end of August 1984, MORI used 54 sampling points throughout the country among a representative quota sample of 1,021 electors.

Q. *Which do you think is the main stumbling block in settling the miners' dispute with the NCB. Is it....*

The attitude of the NUM   52%
The attitude of the NCB   29%
The attitude of the government 28.6%
Don't Know   15%

The majority, 52%, of the respondents believed that the attitude of the NUM was the main stumbling block in settling the dispute. However the most important finding is that the government occupies the third place in ranking of the main body of actors in the dispute.

Table 21 exhibits the frequency of the term 'community' during the miners disputes. The table shows a significant decrease in the usage of the term in the 1980s. The decrease in frequency of the term 'community', this study intends to claim, captures the role of the national press in adopting the essence of Thatcherism and its quest for the assertion of individualism:

There is no such thing as society. There are individual men, women and there are families.[16]

Table 21 'The community'. The frequency of the word 'community' during the 1970s and the1980s miners' dispute. All figures in %

	1974-75	1984-85
The Sun	8	0
Daily Mail/Star	21	0
Daily Express	19	0.7
Daily Mirror	18	0
Guardian	29	1.5
The Times	26	0.9

[16] M. Thatcher, quoted in *Woman's Own*, October 31, 1987

It must be indicated that the term 'community' was only recorded when it denoted the concept of society in general. The table above shows a universal occurrence during the 1970s. The *Guardian* recorded the highest frequency, 29%, and the *Sun* with the lowest at, 8%. However, again the trend seemed to reverse in the 1980s. As indicated by the Table, the term is 'almost' universally absent. The *Guardian* produced the highest frequency, 1.5%, whereas three other national dailies shared zero-frequency. The *Times* and the *Daily Express* recorded minimal mentions.

To sum up this section of the research, the most important finding of the 'quantitative' dimension of this study shows a reversal of 'editorial hostility' for the 1980s dispute. In the 1970s the coding 'Very Favourable' received 11.9 per cent of the total sample. This trend seems to reverse dramatically for the 1980s dispute by recording less than one per cent of the sample. The 'Very Hostile' coding, on the other hand, produced a score of 3.4 per cent for the 1970s, yet for the 1980s dispute this score increases to 31.4 per cent of the total sample.

The next part of this study, the 'qualitative dimension', is a more detailed analysis of these issues and other themes which enhance the results outlined in this part.

The Qualitative Dimension

In the first part of this chapter the quantified data of this study was presented. In an attempt to make these aspects of the research more decipherable, a rather more 'qualitative' analysis will now be presented. By using the 'qualitative' approach this part of the research presents a closer scrutiny of the editorial contents of the national press. In doing so a number of themes will be developed in more depth which, in turn, will draw on some of the quantified data presented in the first part of this chapter. It is important to stress that the focus of the 'qualitative' dimension of this research will be the press and the miners in the 1980s dispute. However, there will be some references to the 1970s conflict, in order to provide either a comparative perspective or emphasis upon a particular point. There are **four** specific areas, or themes, which will receive particular attention:

1. The miners and the press industry in comparative perspective. From the 'special cases' in the 1970s to the 'enemy within' of the 1980s. The aim is to specifically show the widespread usage of military and Nazi analogies in the 1980s.
2. The miners, the issue of 'law and order', and the press. An attempt is made to widen the context of the debate by focusing upon the crucial role of the 'law', picket violence and the miners as depicted by the national press.
3. The miners, the role of the labour movement, and the press. The aim is to connect the disputes to the wider involvement of the labour movement and its treatment by the national press.
4. The role of the national press in weakening the miners' resolve and commitment to their cause.

This part of the research begins by focusing on the relationship between the miners' disputes and the press industry in a historical and comparative context.

The Miners and the Press: From 'Special Cases to the Enemy Within'

The first section of the qualitative dimension of this study aims to highlight the industry's approach to the miners' disputes in different epochs. In the first part of this study, empirical evidence was produced to substantiate the first hypothesis of this research. In this part we aim to provide a more in-depth analysis to further substantiate this claim. This section begins by outlining the extracts of two editorials published by the *Daily Express*, one in 1972, and the other in 1984, which serve aptly to enhance the clarity of our point:

> *Daily Express* **Editorial, November 2, 1972**
> *Come Ted Heath! are you listening R. Carr? Must Britain face a complete shutdown after the collapse of negotiations*

in the miners' dispute? What a tragic chilling prospect. And the crisis is so utterly unnecessary. Everyone even Mr. Carr agrees the miners deserve more money. The CB cannot offer more without direct action by the government. What then are we waiting for?.... The miners have already come down from their peak demand of a £9 week increase to £6. The Board must respond to this bargaining more .... The government should back this in cash.. Other projects enjoy state support. So should coal, which is a national asset. A doctrinaire refusal to treat the coal industry as a special case will make a lame duck out of the whole economy. That is why coal must be treated as a special case. And why Mr. Carr should call off his court inquiry.

Daily Express Editorial- May 29, 1984

Arthur Scargill increasingly looks like a commander who has lost all sense of the objectives for which the troops are fighting. ...the impression grows that this is simply one more gimmick in an increasingly crazy campaign. The NUM militants have split their union, enraged the steel men, and alienated other trade unionists. If this is a class war of Scargill's imagination, it is turning out to be a civil war pitting worker against worker.

The two examples outlined above provide an important insight into the differential treatment of the miners' strikes by the majority of the national press in two different time spans. In the 1970s, the *Daily Express* urges the employers to consider the miners in a 'special' manner, in the 1980s the same paper is convinced that the miners are an invading army, reinforcing the Thatcherite notion of the 'enemy within'. This differential treatment of the miners' disputes in different epochs will now be assessed in more detail.

The Miners as 'Special Cases'

The miners' strike of 1972 has a special place in British history, along with the dock strike of 1889 and the General Strike of 1926, as having had a major influence on British politics and society.[17]

The strike lasted from January 1 to February 19 1972. It was unusually violent: one picket was killed in a traffic accident, and in a single incident at the Saltley Coke Depot, thirty were injured, sixteen of them policemen. The strike was, for many of its leaders, avowedly political in its aims. In an interview with Robin Blackburn, Arthur Scargill, a junior member of the NUM's National Executive, argued:

> *The biggest mistake we could make is the suggestion that a wage battle is not a political battle. Of course it is... once we begin to divorce wages from politics, then we lose our perspective...*[18]

This stoppage spectacularly smashed the wage restraint policy imposed by Edward Heath's government. Arthur Scargill's role in the crucial confrontation of the strike at Saltley Coke Depot made his name, and provided a model for the use of mass picketing in the other industrial disputes of the 1970s.[19]

The NUM and the mining communities have been amongst the most politicized, and powerful, of trade unionists. Of the twenty seven members of the National Executive, in 1972, six were members of the Communist Party of Great Britain and five others belonged to the left of the Labour Party. For the purpose of an analysis of this strike, a few words must be said by way of a brief background comment. Throughout the 1960s while Lord Robens was Chairman of the NCB, cheap oil had caused a steady retrenchment in the coal industry, resulting in the closure of 400 pits and the loss of 400,000 jobs. Robens had persuaded the miners that if wages rose too high, many more pits would

---

[17] For a detailed account of the political and social climate before and during the miners' strikes of 1972 and 1974 see Appendix 2 at the end of this chapter.
[18] *New Left Review*, June 1975
[19] Scargill engineered the successful method of 'flying pickets' whereby squads of cars and mini-buses were mobilised to deny hundreds of miners to picket outside targeted collieries.

become uneconomical and liable for closure. This would have had a destructive impact upon the tightly-knit mining communities. Robens had the advantage of the adversary partnership of Will Payner, the president of the NUM. Under such circumstances the miners, by tradition a united and mutually compassionate community, accepted a decline in their position. In his autobiography Robens writes: 'without Payner I doubt it very much whether my hopes of getting the industry off piece – work and eliminating strikes... could have been possible.'[20]

Despite the political affiliation of the NUM executive, the media, in general, had played a beneficial role for the miners in previous years. In the 1970s, the public, who had no illusion about the hardships and dangers faced by the miners, were sympathetic with the miners' cause to climb back to their position as the best paid of the manual workers. The miners and their industry were in decline as a result of cutbacks in their livelihood. Every wage demand made by the miners had been met with the threat of more pit closures and less jobs. Public sympathy was bred by the media by contrasting the treatment of the miners and that of the power workers, who had a relatively safe job and who had alienated themselves from the public who had suffered from the power cuts by which they had extracted their pay rise. The NUM's success came to epitomize Britain's experience of the new industrial and political militancy which was sweeping most advanced industrial countries. The 1972 strike coincided with the infamous occupation by the Upper Clyde Shipbuilders in Glasgow, and the growing union resistance to Heath's proposed Industrial Relations Act.[21]

Two years on, the miners repeated their victory with even more far reaching repercussions. Despite the attempts made by Heath's administration to turn the build up to the 1974 strike into a witch hunt against left-wing NUM leaders, miners once

---

[20]A. Richards, *'Miners on Strike: Class Solidarity and division in Britain* (Oxford: Berg), 1996, p121
[21]The agitation against the Act culminated in 1972. A group of London Dockers – The Pentonville Five- after being imprisoned for contempt of court, were hurriedly released under the threat of a TUC led general strike

again, through their strike, challenged the government's wage restraint policy. Edward Heath responded by calling a general election on the issue 'Who Governs Britain', and was defeated by Labour.[22]

Within two years, the miners had twice shattered the government's pay policy, and precipitated the most bitter election of modern times.[23]

This section will produce evidence of the national press' 'favourable' treatment of the miners' action in 1972, as well as the 'not so hostile' approach to the 1974 stoppage. It will be shown that, contrary to popular belief, the national press industry sustained the miners' image as a 'special case' throughout the period.

Table 22 provides a comparison of the phrase 'miners as special case', used by the national press during the miners' disputes of 1972 & 1974 and 1984-5.

According to this research, the term 'miners as a special case' occurred more than 30 per cent of the time in all of the major national press' editorials during the 1970s disputes, the *Guardian* recorded the highest use of the term, and the *Daily Mirror* the lowest. In the 1980s, on the other hand, all but one recorded

Table 22 'Miners as special case' (all figures in %)

	1972-74	1984-85
The Sun	39	0
Daily Mail/ Daily Star	31	0
Daily Express	39	0
Daily Mirror	30.5	0
Guardian	48	0.7
The Times	35.8	0

[22]See Chapter Two for an extensive analysis of Heath's struggle to maintain his grip on the government.
[23]For an interesting account of the events in 1974 see: Edward Heath's autobiography, *The Course of My Life* (London: Hodder & Stoughton), 1998, pp 500-516

zero-frequency of the phrase.

The following section, is a closer examination of the editorial and page contents of the national press from early 1972 through to 1974.

From January 6, 1972, the *Sun* ran several sympathetic, if not entirely 'supportive', editorials on the miners' strike:

"*Blame Heath for jobless millions*" (Front page 21 January)

"*Why father and son (both miners) pledge: The miners must win* (Page 11 January 22)

"*Give miners what they want*" (Front page 27 January)

The *Sun* portrayed the miners as a 'special case', particularly, as it ran several stories on the daily hazards of being a miner:

'... *they are special case ...because of their dirty, dangerous job ... and because for what they earn, they are productive workers.*' (Front page 27 January)

The *Daily Express*, by tradition, a Conservative paper, remarkably ran several sympathetic stories supporting the miners 'special case':

'*The cash must be found to fund the miners demand..... The crisis is utterly unnecessary.. everyone agrees miners deserve more money.*' (11 February 1972)

'*Your letters on the miners strike.... Yes they do deserve more money*' (12 February 1972)

On January 7, 1972, the *Financial Times* confidently argued that, 'it is extremely difficult to see what the miners hope to gain out of the national strike.' Four days later it went on to say: 'With the miners now seeming firmly involved in their first national strike since 1926 it now seems quite likely that the coalfields will remain closed for maybe as much as a month or more.' A month later the paper informed its readers: 'the Government ... has to decide what to do to end the coal strike...none of the parties involved have much if any idea where the compromise might lie.' On the same day the Government called the two sides in for talks at the Ministry of Employment. The next day, the paper commented: 'although everyone professes to be anxious for an early end to the strike... the two sides are still a long way apart.' The talks collapsed and a state of national emergency was declared. On 12 February, the paper declared that 'the seriousness of the situation created by the strike even began to be generally appreciated ... from the point of view of economy the upheaval which it now faces could hardly have come at a worse moment'. This reflected the mood of a government in retreat. The next issue insisted that 'the action of the miners shows the urgent need for the Government to redefine the permissible limits of picketing.'

Finally, after the first settlement, the *Financial Times* , in a long statement, examined the defeat of the Government, in contrast to its original prediction, and concluded: 'it will be some time before we shall be able to assess even the direct costs of the coal strike to the country.... But the immediate cost pales to insignificance compared to the potential long term damage done not merely to the economy but to the country as such. Most importantly....is that the authority of the Government has been damaged . In war, and that is what the miners' dispute turned out to be, the active support of the community as a whole is essential.

The Government failed to obtain it. That is why it lost'.

The *Financial Times* clearly referred to the way in which public sentiment, in general, was on the side of the miners. This may be partly due to the fact that the miners possessed a carefully documented brief which helped them win the support that the Government had assumed would flow to itself against the NUM.

The following extracts, emphasising the 'special case' issue, are further examples of the national press' editorials in the sample:

The Guardian Editorial: February 2, 1972
... *For the Government has decided to make its first serious attempt to conciliate in the miners dispute on the same day as the emergency regulations come into force....For if this conciliation fails the interval before the next attempt might take the strike into 6th or 7th week. ....The treatment of the miners' claim as special case still seems the best course, dangerous though it is.....Mr. Lever pledged the opposition to treat the miners as a special case and not to countenance leapfrogging by other unions. Mr Carr acknowledged that help but indicated that a nod, a wink, or a lead from the TUC....would be of even greater help. ...The miners ...are victims of that very reluctance of the TUC in the past as in the present, to commit itself to a communal attitude on anything....But they...must realize that the country expects a way out of this frightening and socially divisive dispute to be found this week.*

Daily Mail Editorial: February 11, 1972
This is the only way out-the court of inquiry-which the Daily Mail urged last week. But we are glad that Mr. Carr has at last ..recognised that the miners are a special case.... For most of us feel that miners of all grades are poorly paid for the grueling and dangerous work they do' "*Now let them go back to work.* p6

Daily Mirror Editorial: January 31, 1974
There isn't much time. The miners vote on their strike ballot today. If Britain is to escape the disaster of the coal strike, there must be fast movement. There is a lifeline. The Pay Board's proposals ...to examine the claim of any group of workers to be a special case, deserving of favourable treatment on pay. The miners could be case no1. But the Pay Board's plan is a lifeline that must be grasped quickly....Its immediate value is the opportunity it gives the government and the miners to pull back from a fatal confrontation.' Is this the lifeline? p2

The *Sun* Editorial: January 27, 1972: Stuff the norm! Get the miners back to work. pp1&2

...Today, The Sun puts forward its own plan for peace in the pits. The plan depends on universal recognition that the miners are a "special case". Of course they are. They are special because of the exceptional demands of their dirty, dangerous job. They are special because of their top-notch productivity record....The miners are special, so lets start treating them that way. Other unions say sympathetic words. What we need from them now is ACTION.

The SUN believes in an incomes policy which would recognize special cases. If the bosses of the big unions would accept that the miners are exactly that, it would be an important start...

They also know that public opinion is for a fair settlement with the miners and won't readily forgive anyone who stands in the way...

The *Times* Editorial: January 12, 1974, 'No good as it stands'- p13

...Ministers have said ...that the miners will not ... be permitted to be a special case beyond the commodious preferences which Phase 3 already grants them... The proposal is that no other union would cite the miners' "special case" in pursuance of its own claim....The knowledge that a special case has been authorized under duress would itself become an argument for applying duress.

The popularity of the 1970s miners' strikes can be related to the 'not so hostile' coverage of the strikes by the national press. The opinion polls published by Gallup in the 1970s externally validates this claim (Table 23).

Public opinion, as indicated above, shows a consistent support for the miners in the 1970s. Furthermore, this trend had been maintained even through the unstable political and social climate of early 1974 and the subsequent General Election.

Table 23 Q-Are your sympathies mainly with the employers or mainly with the miners in the dispute which has arisen in the coal industry?[26]

	Feb/1972	Dec 1973	Jan 1974
Employer	19	26	30
Miners	57	41	44
Neither	17	23	18
DK	7	10	8

(All figures in %)

Public support for the miners reached 57% by February 1972. This support for the miners' cause fell to 41% in December 1973, but increased slightly to 44% when the miners were in the crucial part of their negotiation with the government. The interesting point here is that at no point in the 1970s miners' disputes was public support for the employers higher than that for the miners.

Although the strike of 1974 was not being treated as a 'special case', there were signs of inconsistencies and 'ambivalence'

displayed by the papers in the sample. Some, the Sun for example, almost entirely avoided targeting individual miners leaders , whilst Mick McGahey and Scargill were the major targets for some others such as the *Daily Express*:

'Mick the Mouth'...... 'Scargill's Raiders' 30 January 1974

'Communists: the methods and menace' 1 February 1974[27]

'How McGahey, and other NUM officials, lived it up inBrussels.....they wined and dined by former transport house officials.' *Daily Mail* 11 February 1974

[26]Gallup Political Index – 1972-74
[27]My pilot research indicated that – up to 1974 general election- Gormley and Daly were hardly targeted by the press, in fact at times they were treated favourably: ' General Joe for short sharp battle', *The Sun*, 6 February 1974

'Labour and miners attack Mr. McGahey – Communist intervention in pay dispute condemned.' *The Times*, 31 January 1974

Remarkable as it may sound, a closer examination of the contents of selected national dailies indicates that the attack on McGahey and other NUM leaders was quite rare, with the exception of the *Daily Express*. In fact, it was Enoch Powell who was targeted more than any member of the NUM executive.[28]

Furthermore, although there were general supportive lines for the government, this support was at times contradictory, uneven and problematic. This is highlighted by a review of the *Daily Express*'s editorials.

'Make a deal with the miners', the *Daily Express* urged the Government on 2 February. The same paper, four days later, urged the Tories for a General Election, commenting that 'Heath should risk his future to do his duty for the country' (Page 10)

The very next day the government announced the day, February 28, for the General Election.

On 12 February, W. Terry, the *Daily Express*'s political editor finds no cosy, middle way out for Heath. Yet on February 14, the front page of the same paper gave '11% lead for the Tories and Heath surges in popularity too'. On February 20 the paper published a highly controversial story in which Ezra, Chairman of the NCB, gave his support to the miners' cause. The next day the *Daily Express* informed the nation that the chancellor, Mr Barber, may quit politics.

During this period, three highly detrimental issues, from the government's point of view, received universal attention; the Government's miscalculation of the miners' wages; Enoch Powell's support for Labour; and the CBI's Chairman,

---

[28] A sample of four tabloids, two broadsheets and a Sunday newspapers were chosen for this purpose. They were *Daily Express, Daily Mail, The Sun, Daily Mirror, The Times, Financial Times* and *The News of the World*.

Campbell Adamson's comment to 'scrap the Industrial Act'. On February 25, three days before the election, the *Daily Express* called the Labour leader 'Harold the Master' upstaging the Liberals (page 2).

Yet, despite all the political damages inflicted upon the government, some papers, such as the Sun believed that: 'In spite of the records, Ted's Tories look the better bet for Britain.- Get Britain out of the Red.' Indeed, if the Conservative papers became a source of discontent for the government, the miners also received 'bad press' from a Labour supporting paper:

Daily Mirror – Front page Editorial February 6, 1974
Today as Britain hangs on the cliff edge of industrial chaos,.... everybody, has gone mad. Yesterday the miner's executive called a national coal strike.... They said No to a last minute meeting with Mr. Whitelaw. Unless a miracle happens within the next four days, Britain will enter a long and ruinous conflict that could leave the country scarred and impoverished for years. The miners must certainly take their share of the blame.... they are demanding unconditional surrender from Mr. Heath.

The same paper, on two separate occasions, printed a full page Conservative Party advertisement supporting the government in the General Election.[29] Despite this contradictory and at times problematic editorials' by the press, public opinion remained sympathetic to the miners and their cause, as shown in Table 23. The attitude of the public, shown by the polls, is an important indicator to the way in which the press industry treated the miners' case. The national press, if not universally sympathetic, generally viewed the miners' as a 'special case'. Furthermore, the press seemed generally reluctant to use 'smearing, stigma or stereotype' tactics towards individual union leaders. It therefore seems that press reporting did not initiate public antagonism towards the miners.

To expand our analysis beyond the boundaries of the 1970s,

[29] *Daily Mirror*, February 5, 1974

we now turn to the theme of 'the enemy within' in the 1980s episode.

The Miners as 'The Enemy Within': 'The Standardization Process'

Films, radio, magazines [etc], make up a system which is uniform as a whole and in every part; Under monopoly capitalism all mass culture is identical' ... *'the achievement of standardization and mass production...'*[30]

In these passages, Adorno explains the roots of *standardization* in imitation and the increasingly concentrated ownership of cultural industries. Standardized cultural commodities, Adorno argued, are produced in conformity with the creative policies of the managers and owners of the culture industry. This section is an empirical examination of this concept in relation to the 1980s miners' strike.

It has long been established that the monumental strike of 1984-85 was the most important industrial dispute in Britain's postwar history. This dispute, unlike the strikes of the 1970s, produced the most potent blow against the miners, the NUM and the labour movement in general. The virulence of the denunciations of Scargill and the miners during the 1984-85 dispute went beyond the conventional boundaries of mainstream British politics. At its peak, in the summer of 1984, Mrs. Thatcher compared the dispute with the miners to the war against the Argentine junta over the Falkland islands in 1982:

We had to fight an enemy without in the Falklands, now the war had to be taken to the 'enemy within' which is much more dangerous to liberty.[31]

These remarks were accompanied with words like

---

[30]*Dialectic of Enlightenment*, op.cit
[31]Thatcher's speech at a gathering of Conservativ e backbench MPs. Quoted by S. Milne, op.cit, p 26

'conspiring' and 'subversive'. "This false prophet and his army of wild red guards should be treated as outlaws. They were enemies of the state and the people". By using these terms and 'the enemy within' Mrs. Thatcher was sending a calculated signal to all supporters of the government, including the press industry, that the gloves should come off in the war with the NUM.[32]

This section will demonstrate that far from being regarded as 'the special case', the national press, in accordance with Thatcher's notion of the miners as the 'enemy within', responded, with a *standardized sameness*, favourably towards the government and provided a treatment suitable for an 'enemy within'. The results of this research will be supported by external data produced by different public opinion agencies at the time.

The study outlines a sample of editorials from all the papers analysed in the research for their contribution to the Thatcherite notion of 'the enemy within'; most notably via the widespread usage of military and Nazi terminologies describing the picketing miners and their leaders as the 'red guards', 'disunited army', 'Scargill's Junta'.[33] This section will then proceed to individually analyse terms such as 'class war', 'against the elected government', and 'violence' to show the extent of their repetition across the national press. This section begins by presenting six editorials published by six national papers analysed in the sample:

The Daily Express **Editorial** *: July 12, 1984*
The Scargill's junta defied the law yesterday....They have shown from the start that they have no less contempt for the law of the land than they have for the rights of their members. The special delegates ... conference voted .... to establish kangaroo courts to 'try' those refusing to serve in King Arthur's revolutionary army.
The Daily Star **Editorial**: *August 9, 1984*

---

[32]Hugo Young, *'One of Us'*, op.cit. pp 371-2
[33]On May 15, 1984, the *Sun*'s front page reads: *Sun* Picture special: Mine Fuhrer showing Scargill giving a 'Hitler-style' salute

If the strikers hope to win their pay and jobs battle, they need the support of the British people. They are not getting it. Most people are being turned away from the NUM because of the various orchestrated thuggeries we saw yesterday ..... Britain hates bullies, our history is full of how the people have turned against and beaten those who would change our lives through intimidation.

The Daily Mirror Editorial: *January 28, 1985*
A. Scargill has lost the miner's strike. It is his defeat.. he has led the crack guards' regiment of the unions to disaster. A defeat for Scargill is also a defeat for the hard men of the left, the Benns – who dream of workers' triumph through the General strike. Their way has been tried and it has lost. There is no support for it.

The Sun Editorial: *March 30, 1984*
They went on strike in war.
It is cold, we are at war, Hitler's armies are just 20 odd miles across the channel. Production of coal is crucial to keep us warm and to help keep the Nazi machine at bay. But this seems to matter little to the miners of this tiny Kent Coalfield ... 1600 are on strike in a dispute about pay and conditions. ...They incense ...Churchill...eventually 3 pit leaders are jailed for 1-2 months with hard labour, each of the 1000 face workers fined £1 or £3. The dispute does not end there. They stay out on strike over their jailed comrades... settlement negotiated in jail with imprisoned mine leaders...Pit leaders released, colliery reopens, jailed leaders return as heroes and seen by the rest of the nations' miners as martyrs. A legend has been born about men who strike while others are fighting a war against fascism. They are still pigheaded....

Kent pits, March 1984
Since the dispute started Kent miners have been in the thick of it... When Arthur Scargill lost a strike ballot in 1982 Kent were firmly behind him. Perhaps they can afford it.. here face workers earn £175 per week. Yet all 3

pits lose money. It is estimated they lost £18m at the end of 1982. Not that it appears to worry Kent pitmen. Most believe strike action will solve the miners' problems ... it did in 1942.

The Guardian Editorial: February 1, 1985
Let us, for once, look at the pit strike from the point of view of the rational man in Whitehall or in Hobart House. Public opinion according to all polls, continues to run in favour of the government. The drift back to work continues, the NUM has broadened its negotiation team and offered to meet the Board without pre-condition.... Crudely the rational Conservative or our rational manager might argue, we owe Arthur slightly less than nothing...Mr Scargill asked for it and Mr. Scargill, eventually, got it... Let this be a lesson to all other putative proletarian enemies within.

The Times Editorial: July 20, 1984
There is a war on' '...For ministers, however, it is different now. There is a war on. There always has been such a war for the hearts and minds of the British people, at least since 1969 when Harold Wilson lost out to the trade union power. Mrs. Thatcher was elected in 1979 to reassert the power of Parliament and the law over the increasing challenges to them from trade unions. A combination of political neglect and gradualist legislation postponed any decisive confrontation in the first parliament. But it was always going to come and not necessarily in the guise of a general strike since the structure of the modern Trade Union movement makes that much less likely.

The majority of the papers analysed in the sample, including the *Guardian* and the *Daily Mirror*, were littered with editorials filled with 'standardized' military and Nazi analogies describing the striking miners and their leaders. The following section demonstrates the extent of the usage of certain terminologies by the national press during the strike. Certain relevant categories

Table 24 'War/ Battle' (all figures in percentages)

	1972-74	1984-85
The Sun	2 / 0	26 / 41
Daily Mail/ Daily Star	4 / 17	18 / 12
Daily Express	3 / 0	57 /15
Daily Mirror	0 / 2	29 / 9
Guardian	20 / 0	17 / 14
The Times	0 / 4	56 / 36

were isolated and searched for their repetition across the editorials of the newspapers in the sample. The findings were then compared with those of the 1970s. The results are shown in separate tables.

The first category in this selection was the obvious term 'war or battle', specifically when related to the picketing miners and their skirmishes with the police around the country. The table below shows the differential frequency of the terms 'War/Battle'[34].

Table 24 demonstrates a significant increase in frequency of the 'war/battle' categories during the 1980s dispute. It is important to note that this increase in frequency is apparent in all the newspapers analysed in the sample. However, further steps were required to capture the importance and the specificity of the conflict. The pilot study revealed the frequency of the term 'class war' in the 1980s was notably higher. It was then decided to search for comparative data on that specific category. Table 25 shows the frequency of this term in a comparative perspective.

As indicated, this category was hardly used by most of the papers in the 1970s, and its usage by *The Times* and the *Guardian* seems very minimal. In the 1980s, however, there is an

---

[34]The first figures represent the frequency of the term 'war': the second is for repetition of the term 'Battle'

Table 25 'Class war' (all figures in percentages)

	1972-74	1984-85
The Sun	0	20
Daily Mail/ Daily Star	0	8.7
Daily Express	0	19
Daily Mirror	0	14.6
Guardian	4	15
The Times	2	30

indication for a more common usage of the term. The *Times* represented the highest repetition and the *Daily Star* the lowest score. Another category that seemed useful to investigate in more depth was: *'Against the elected government'*. Prior to the selection of this phrase, it was noted that it did not occur so frequently in the beginning of the 1980s dispute. However, it become more frequent towards the middle to the end of the strike. Table 26 shows the percentages of its repetition in comparative perspective.

This category was an important selection for the purposes of this study. Its usage denoted that those opposed to the 'elected government' were opposing democracy and the people

Table 26 "Against the elected government" (all figures in percentages)

	1972-74	1984-85
The Sun	0	27.2
Daily Mail/ Daily Star	7.8	27.7
Daily Express	9.6	35.2
Daily Mirror	0	14.4
Guardian	0	0
The Times	3	40.8

Table 27 'The Red Guards' (all figures in percentages)

	1972-74	1984-85
The Sun	0	23.2
Daily Mail/ Daily Star	0	8.1
Daily Express	0	40.3
Daily Mirror	0	0
Guardian	0	1.5
The Times	0	8.7

who have elected the government. In the 1970s, three papers recorded zero frequency, and the highest scorer was the *Daily Express* with 9.6%, followed by the *Daily Mail* and *The Times*. In the 1980s, The *Times* had the highest frequency and the *Daily Mirror* the lowest. The *Guardian* sustained some consistency in this respect. Another category selected for analysis was the term 'Red Guards' to describe the picketing miners. This category was a favourite of the Conservative supporting papers, but it also occurred in other papers analysed in the sample (Table 27).

This category, entirely absent from our 1970s analysis, scored mostly with the very popular papers of the 1980s. The *Daily Express* had the highest score followed by The *Sun*, *The Times* and the *Daily Star* respectively.

Having outlined a selection of editorials and analysed the selected categories, it is necessary to assess the public opinion on these issues.

Public Opinion

The consumer is unwilling to recognize that he is totally dependent, and he likes to preserve the illusion of private initiative and free choice. Thus standardization... produces the veil of pseudo-individualism.[35]

[35] Adorno, 'A social Critique of Radio Music', *Kenyon Review*, Vol II, no.2, 1945, p.216

Table 28

Q. *Are your sympathies mainly with the employers or mainly with the miners in the dispute which has arisen in the coal industry?*

	July/1984	Sep/1984	Nov/1984	Dec/1984
Employer	40	43	52	51
Miners	33	32	26	26
Neither	19	18	17	18
DK	8	6	5	5

(All figures in %)

Having examined a selection of the editorials with specific reference to the issue of miners as the 'enemy within', this section will examine some data, produced by professional research bodies, in order to assess the degree of the public support, or lack of it, for the miners.

Table 28 represents Gallup's research over a seven month period in 1984.[36] The support for the employers (NCB) indicated a gradual rise reaching 52% in November 1984. Gallup's results can be compared with another public opinion poll conducted by the MORI polls for the *Sunday Times*.[37]

MORI polls also show a gradual rise in favour of the Coal Board. Comparatively, the results published by MORI and Gallup show a significant degree of similarity in the overall popularity of the employers (NCB) in the dispute.

Another important finding in the Gallup research is related directly to the way in which the miners chose to organize their pickets. As evident in this study, the national press were mostly hostile to the picketing tactics employed by the miners. In the course of presenting the qualitative dimension of our research, it will be shown that the picketing miners were depicted with

[36] Gallup Political Index, July-Dec. 1984
[37] British Public Opinion – Vol VI, no. 7, September 1984, pp 4-5

Table 29

Q. *On balance, who do you most support in the current dispute, the miners or the National Coal Board?*

	June 1984	August 1984
Miners	35%	30%
Coal Board	41%	46%
Neither / DK	23%	24%

Table 30 'Bully/Bullies' (all figures in percentages)

	1972-74	1984-85
The Sun	0	63
Daily Mail/ Daily Star	0.2	42
Daily Express	0.5	49
Daily Mirror	0	23
Guardian	0	30
The Times	1.2	46

'stereotypical' analogies such as 'bullies', 'thugs', 'mob', and 'troops'. Table 30 shows the usage of the term 'bully/bullies' by the papers analysed in the sample. Once again the results are compared to the 1972 and 1974 disputes.

The Sun was the highest scorer and the *Daily Mirror* the lowest in the sample. However once again, in a comparative analysis, all the paper in the sample frequently used the term during the 1980s strike.

In terms of measuring public opinion on the miners tactics in the 1980s dispute, Gallup produced the result shown in Table 31.

Table 31 clearly demonstrates the effect of the media's

Table 31

Q. *Do you think that the miners are using responsible or irresponsible methods in the dispute?*

	July 1984	Sep.1984	Nov 1984	Dec 1984
Responsible	12	11	10	4
Irresponsible	78	85	86	92
Don't Know	10	4	4	4

(All figures in %)

portrayal of the miners' dispute and the standardized reaction of the public in the 1980s. At its highest point, nine out of ten of the respondents felt that miners were irresponsible, and disapproved of their methods in the pursuit of their dispute. Also, three in four said that their impression of Scargill had deteriorated over his handling of the dispute.[38]

Comparatively speaking, Table 32 shows a more significant shift in public opinion away from the miners' tactics in conducting their picket line duties.

The result published by Gallup in both periods of the

Table 32

Do you approve or disapprove of the methods being used by the miners?

	Dec/1984	Jan/1974
Approve	7%	32%
Disapprove	88%	63%
Don't Know	5%	5%

[38]The Gallup Poll conducted exclusively for the *Daily Telegrpah*. Gallup Political Index, 12 December 1984, p.25

miners' disputes shows the significant change in public attitude at the height of the disputes. Whereas only 7% of the public approved of the miners' tactics in the 1984, 32% approved in 1974. Furthermore 88% of the public were dissatisfied in 1984, compared to 63% in 1974. To conclude, so far it was intended to demonstrate the differential coverage of the miners' strikes in a comparative analysis. In presentation and analysis of some of the evidence provided thus far, it seems more than a mere coincidence that during the 1980s the national press were more supportive of the NCB and the government and more hostile towards the miners. As argued before, during the early 1980s Thatcher was strongly supportive of the press management and proprietors in their preparation to relocate their newspapers to the East End of London. Chapter Three of this study analysed, in detail, several policies adopted by Thatcher which were more than helpful for this crucial transition.[39]

More crucially, however, two other government policies had a deeper and more immediate impact upon the process of relocation of the national press in favour of the proprietors. First, Thatcher's determination to reform the trade unions and reduce their power resulted in three separate trade union legislations; the 1980, 1982 and 1984 acts. These new legislations were firstly implemented on a large scale during the miners' strike. Secondly, in an unprecedented manner, Thatcher empowered the courts for sequestration of union assets should they refuse to observe the new acts. Once again, this policy was first used to confront the NUM in 1985. A year later in 1986, the combined forces of these legislations greatly weakened the print unions, SOGAT in particular, in their resistance to the proposed move. These policies were deemed by the press owners as more than helpful in their desire to move away from Fleet Street. In the following sections, these issues in the context of the *standardized* reaction by the national press will be considered in more detail. Accordingly, the following themes will receive detailed attention:

---

[39]*Business Week* (Europe), 22 August 1988, 'Murdoch adds a few mega tones to his arsenal'

- The miners dispute, the issue of 'law and order', and the press industry.
- The miners' dispute, the role of the Labour Movement, and the press.
- The miners' disputes, the wider context of the culture, and the press.

The Miners' Disputes, Law and Order, and the Press Industry: The Standardization Process

The struggle between the miners and successive Conservative governments has helped to shape the course of British politics over two decades. The problem of how to 'deal' with the miners and their 'militant' leadership became one of the obsessions of Conservative political life. Mrs. Thatcher seemed, more than any other Conservative leader, determined to reform the trade unions in general and to reduce the power of the NUM in particular.

The defeat of the miners in 1926 remained a heartache in the mining communities for a generation or more, so in recent times the shattering experience of the Conservatives caused by the two strikes of the 1970s laid the foundation for what became 'a twenty year vendetta against the miners; a deep desire to defeat the NUM and, if necessary, the bulk of the British coal industry'.[40]

Thatcher seemed more resolute than most Conservatives in the pursuit of defeating the NUM and the miners. She was one of only two Cabinet ministers during the 1974 coal strike to oppose Heath's decision to call a general election:

> *No name was scarred more deeply on the Conservative soul than that of the NUM. For Margaret Thatcher the miners were where she came in. If they hadn't humiliated the Heath government into fighting an election which it lost, she would not now be party leader and PM. But this*

[40]S. Milne, *'The Enemy within'*, op.cit.

mattered less than the memory of that bloody defeat itself, and the apprehension that it might always be capable of happening again.[41]

The 1984-85 miners' strike is an episode which demands a deeper and systematic reassessment. For Thatcher, the majority of the press industry, and the labour movement, the strike was treated as a regrettable episode of picket-line violence, undemocratic maneuvering, dogmatism and inevitable defeat. It was the tragic product of one man's political and personal ambitions. For those who actively took part and their supporters, it was a principled resistance to anti trade-union legislation in a way that no other organization in the country was prepared or able to do.

This section provides evidence from all the newspapers in the sample – including the Labour supporting *Daily Mirror* and the *Guardian* – of their active support of highly controversial laws to reduce the industrial power of the unions in general, and the NUM in particular. The NUM was enfeebled, not only by the exhaustion and the indebtedness of the miners, but by financial and legal problems on a monumental scale, and the threat posed by the government – backed Union of the Democratic Mineworkers. The NUM leadership was exhausted in their efforts to deal with litigation arising from the sequestration of the NUM's funds and the formal takeover of the union by an official receiver.[42] The *Daily Express* makes an explicit reference to this point:

> **The Daily Express Editorial:** *January 17, 1985*
> *The days of mass picket in the coal strike seems to be over. One reason is declining morale among the strikers, who know that the strike has failed. But the main reason is Scargill's cash crisis. Thanks to the law, the union funds he can use to send his 'red guards' around the country are running down.*

---

[41] Hugo Young, *One of Us*, op.cit
[42] P. Wilsher, D. MacIntyre, M. Jones, *Strike* (London: 1985), p.259

What follows below is an extraordinary chorus of approval, by the press, for the government's strategy to 'legally' weaken and defeat the miners. The important aspect of these editorials is the astonishing similarities and sameness in text and the words:

> **The Sun** Editorial: *August 1, 1984*
> *The £50,000 fine imposed on the NUM has nothing to do with the rights and wrongs of the coal dispute. It is not a decision against Arthur Scargill or in favour of MacGregor. The sole duty of the high court is to impose the law. .....The TUC bitterly oppose the Prior-Tebbit Acts... while they remain on the Statute Book, the Trade Unions must respect them as they respect our laws...*

Nearly two months later *The Times* and the *Guardian*, on the same day, put forward the same point made by the *Sun* :

> **The Guardian** Editorial: *October 11, 1984*
> *Scargill and the collective leadership of the NUM are not in conflict with the Tory judges and Thatcherite anti-union legislation, they are in conflict with long established civil law: specifically the law of contract which governs the rights of members of any organization... The TUC should be honest enough, and courageous enough to repudiate Scargill's vision of events and tell him publicly that what he is fighting is the long established and long accepted civil law of the land.*

> **The Times** Editorial: *October 10, 1984*
> *Mr Scargill and his union have not been fined for violating any of Mr.Prior's laws, or Mr.Tebbit's – but for disregarding sterling everyday laws- the common law of the land- established time out of mine, designed to protect members of any kind of association from abuse by its leaders contrary to natural justice.*

Two months later, with a striking similarity in tone and style, the *Daily Express* argues:

***Daily Express** Editorial: December 4, 1984*
The NUM SDC has endorsed the 'no surrender' cry of the Scargill junta. Only an optimist could have expected any other decision from this assembly of pithead militants.....Yet the law, despite Scargill's bluster will grind on, impartially and remorselessly. Not 'Thatcher's law, not 'Tebbit's law', not bosses law, but the common law of the England. The ancient law that has always been a defense against the power of the would be tyrants.

A day later, the *Guardian* returns to the same point which it had made earlier:

***The Guardian** Editorial: December 5, 1984*
...The action which has ended with the union in the hands of a receiver was brought by working miners under long standing civil law. They argued that the strike was unofficial because it had been called in violation of the union's own freely drafted rule book. The working miners won their case by default. Yet actions concerning the use and abuse of the union rule books are not unknown. Not so....set aside the obvious point- that ..Scargill is being under good old-fashioned civil law which applies as much to the company board, the county cricket club... as it does to the NUM.

Two days later the *Daily Mirror* joins the long-running debate:

***Daily Mirror** Editorial: December 6, 1984*
It would be lunacy for the miners...to continue to defy the courts. The miners can only lose by it, politically, financially and morally. It is not the Tebbit laws or the Prior laws or the Thatcher laws which the union is refusing to obey. It is the common law of the land. The Daily Mirror does not want to see the miners beaten...but if Scargill... not willing to comply with the law we are not willing to support them.

Having presented a selection of the editorials in the 1980s, it is necessary to compare these to three examples taken from the sample in the 1970s. The previous chapters outlined the historical events which took place at Saltley in 1972. That event was particularly violent and received unfavourable treatment by the media. The reader is reminded that the issue of 'law and order' was as topical in the 1970s as it was in the 1980s. However, the different tone of the press industry is quite notable. The following *Guardian* editorial was published shortly after the event of Saltley:

The Guardian **Editorial**: *February 11, 1972*
The law about picketing is little help in dealing with situations like that at Saltley. Indeed the law is no clearer when the relevant part of the Industrial Relations Act comes into force. When one has read through the legal inheritances from 19th century combination and conspiracy acts.....it is still not possible to be much more precise than Mr. Maudling was in the Commons on Wednesday: Peaceful picketing is lawful, intimidation is not.... But what is intimidation? One fact is clear: the law allows a lot of discretion to the policeman on the spot.... It is because Saltley is mass picketing that the police are finding it so difficult to handle.

The following two editorials, published by *The Times*, also attempt to deal with the important issue of the picketing law in 1974:

The Times **Editorial**: *March 23, 1974*
Victory in the coal strike was achieved less because the miners stopped digging than because their pickets succeeded in preventing the distribution of coal..... This end was brought about without the mass intimidation or clashes between strikers and the police that had been widely feared before-hand..... Such a triumph scarcely argues that the law gives pickets too little scope for effective action.

This section concludes with the inclusion of an editorial published by *The Times*, shortly before the General Election in 1974. It is important to note the way in which the paper invites the Conservative government, which it had always supported, for a rational approach to the miners' dispute:

> *The Times* Editorial: *January 1, 1974*
> ...*If the Government is seen to be forced to yield at this stage there really would be some basis for fashionable despair at our political institutions. Should the Government adopt the opposite political strategy: turn the heat on the miners, denounce the ulterior motivation of the communist and far-left elements in their leadership, and appeal for an electoral mandate to see the thing through to the bitter end? No, they should not. The class bitterness and political mayhem caused by an election entered into and conducted in that spirit would leave behind social wreckage that would take years to clear up – and that at a time when it has become stirringly obvious that the kind of economically complex and technically intricate society which the western industrial nations have created can only operate on the basis of acquiescence, collaboration, and toleration.*

This section presented evidence from all of the papers in the sample to show the standardized approval of the national press for Thatcher's trade union legislation and the power of judiciary for sequestration of NUM's assets. This seemingly universal approval was contrasted with a rather more 'less hostile' approach in the 1970s.

The next section will assess the extent of acquiescence to and toleration of the press industry for the miners and the labour movement, in particular, during the miners' disputes.

The Miners, the Labour Movement, and the Press: The 'Stereotype' Process

> *The stereotypes found in products of culture industry are*

.... cunningly calculated psychological models which aim to pattern people after mass production.[43]

This section deals specifically with yet another important theme which is closely connected to the miners' disputes, the involvement of the rest of the labour movement, and the national press' response to this involvement. This section will demonstrate the differential treatment by the industry over the three disputes. In the 1970s, some care was taken by the industry in its wordings and criticisms, but in the 1980s, a seemingly universal hostility prevailed amongst most of the national press. In this context, this section will also examine some of the stereotypical remarks used by the press in relation to the labour movement, the miners and other similar institutions.

This section begins with extracts of two editorials published by the same paper in two different miners' disputes:

The Times Editorial: February 12, 1974
...Undeniably there are now social tensions more acute than existed 10 years ago. There are tensions between classes and inside the classes.... In theory there is no reason why a hierarchical society such as Britain used to be should not be as stable or more stable than a more egalitarian one. In practice, however, people in Britain now want a society which they can regard as fair... A moderate Labour party is socially uniting. Such a Labour party believes in the work of everyone for society, even in the genuine importance of the business manager or the entrepreneur. Such a party believes in a society of greater equality, but wants a more equal society not least because it wants a more united one.

The Times Editorial: November 29, 1984
When is a communist not a communist? It is possible in this country to call somebody a fascist as a term of

---

[43] Adorno, 'Prolog Zum Fernsehen', *Gesammelte Schriften*, 10.2, (Frankfurt: Suhrkamp Verlag), p507, Translate by D. Cook

general abuse but it is less likely to call somebody a communist without running the risk of libel. Mr.Scargill is not now a member of the Communist Party though he was in his youth... He is a member of the Labour Party, but everything he says and does is consistent with a certain kind of communism and receives the full and open support from many close colleagues... One consequence of the coal strike is that Britain has woken up to the much wider involvement of formal and informal communists in industrial and political life than most people realized. The reds are not under the bed. They are on the TV screen or the radio. They share Labour platforms. They patronize the TUC. They intimidate Kinnock. They are feted at rallies. They are cheered as they abuse the police. Their parliamentary allies endorse their defiance of the law. Does this suggest that they have become respectable? Emphatically not. We have been warned.'

Throughout this study it has been noted that the 1980s dispute had far reaching consequences not only for the miners but for the Labour Party and the TUC. The stereotypical depiction of miners' leaders, and the ethos of 'Scargill bashing', adopted by the majority of the national press went beyond the parameter of the coal dispute, and reached the heart of the British labour movement as a whole. Throughout the strike, the labour movement underwent the most systematic barrage of journalistic attack which, even today, bears many irreversible consequences.

Astonishingly, while the Labour and TUC leadership seized the opportunity to politically distance themselves from the miners' defeat by turning their fire on the left, the press industry were turning the heat on the labour movement in general. This theme can only be developed in a more coherent and empirical manner by a comparative look at the 1970s, and the press industry's view of the wider involvement of Labour.

Two editorials from all of the papers in the sample will be

outlined. One was published in the 1970s and the other in the 1980s.

The Daily Mail Editorial: December 14, 1973
A time to stand together – p6

So how can they[miners] be persuaded to settle? May be the 'misery and unemployment they will cause among their brother trade unionists will move them before Britain grinds to a halt. If there are leaders who by their speeches can influence them, then those leaders are most likely to come from the heart of Britain's Labour movement. As the lights dim an anxious nation looks for some sign of statesmanship from the opposition or from the TUC. We are threatened by inflation and recession... That is all you have to admit Mr. Wilson. That is all You have to concede Mr.Murray.

The Daily Star Editorial: March 4, 1985

Even Scargill's hard men scorn him as the strike is called off.....One miner screamed at him, 'blood will flow for this, you have sold us down the river.

The Daily Star*'s message to Britain's miners today.... 'You deserve a better man than this...He has misled them, humiliated them, tricked them and almost demolished their industry'. The Star says: 'Go Now Scargill' ... Scargill haplessly underestimated the determination of Mrs. Thatcher and her government to prove that Union power no longer rules in this country. ...Scargill overestimated the support of the TUC and the Labour Movement...he failed to get the support of rank and file members of other unions because they know that only economic industries can survive in Britain today. Industrial relations throughout Britain should improve as union leaders have been made to face the harsh reality that strikes no longer win more money, more jobs, or better industry. ...Scargill should realize that the British people will only change government at the ballot box.*

The Sun, during the 1972 strike, outlines the position of the paper in relation to the miners' cause:

***The Sun* Editorial: February 15, 1972**
A Time for Good will" – p1
The Sun *is on the side of the miners still. We believe they have an unarguable case for a substantial increase... We were first in calling for an inquiry. We were quick to give the NUM's General Secretary L. Daly front page space to explain the miners case. It is because we are on the side of the miners that we feel entitled to speak frankly to them. Today The Sun says to its friends:*

IT IS TIME TO BEND A LITTLE.

......The biggest asset the miners have is public sympathy. This sympathy would evaporate overnight once people had cause to suspect that miners were staying out for political rather than industrial purposes. If the Board and Union make good will moves now, we will have a settlement.

In the 1980s, The *Sun* argued:

***The Sun* Editorial: January 26, 1985**
"Don't shed tears Mr Scargill"
The pit strike is all over bar the shouting. The CB, the government, the miners have worked on, and the entire country are on course for a famous victory. Yet suddenly...voices are being raised: We should not:

  -insist on surrender from NUM
  -turn Arthur Scargill into a martyr
  -upset the TUC

  To all the bleeding hearts the SUN addresses just one word: BUNKUM.. Scargill set out to humble the Coal Board and the Government.
  The nation should rejoice in his failure... are tempted to try the same kind of bullying blackmail.... Once again in our hour of trial Maggie Thatcher has shown the total

resolution that has become her hallmark. Would any other politician have shown such resolve?....How lucky we are to have her..'

The *Daily Express* also resembles the same format. In 1974 the paper argues:

***Daily Express* Editorial: January 15,1974 "One way out" – p8**
They talked and talked – and they got nowhere in the end...the likeliest conclusion to be drawn ....is that the people will be called upon to decide the country's future course at a General Election.
Mr. Whitelaw made it plain that he does not doubt the TUC's sincerity. Nor does any reasonable person. The good faith of the men who represent British Labour is not in question.
What is at issue at this moment is the TUC's ability to deliver what it promises. One way to break that deadlock without an immediate Election is for the miners to accept what is offered and get themselves-and Britain-going again.

In the 1980s, the 'good faith of the men who represent British Labour' had been reduced to 'stooges':

***The Daily Express* Editorial: October 26,1984**
The three stooges
The TUC's attempt to thwart settlement of the needless dispute between the CB and the NACODS shows to which extent the body has lost its way. The so called '3 wise men'-TUC General Secretary N. Willis, Train Drivers' leader R.Buckton and municipal workers leader D.Basnett- tried to make the NACODS executive keep the strike threat in play.... How typical, the TUC leaders behave as though they are scared stiff of A.S. but they do not hesitate to strong-arm the leaders of a more mod union... The 3 wise men ? the 3 stooges more like.

So far, I have presented examples of the 'Conservative supporting newspapers in the sample. The *Guardian* and the *Daily Mirror* were firmly on the side of the labour movement during the 1970s strikes:

> *The Guardian* Editorial: January 30, 1974
> **The Brink next week**
> *Put yourself in Mr. Heath's shoes and quake, even if he does not. In 10 days time the miners are due to start their strike and his options are closing fast....Put yourself in Mr. Wilson's shoes and quake just as much. Or in Mr. Gormley's ...everyone has a lot to lose.....*
>
> *Failing that- and the miners show little readiness to compromise an election, its [the government] remaining option. Who knows where that will lead? The Labour Party with blinding insight, has just seen some of the perils of fighting an election in the mining context and hurriedly repudiated Mr.M. McGahey.... For the Conservatives there are many perils , among them , the equally sudden realization that the business vote may not go its way, for who ,after all led the country into the mess and calamity that the miners' strike will bring? An election now will be as bitter and unpredictable as this country has ever seen. The road to conciliation is still vastly preferable.*

The Labour's blinding insight in 1974, had turned to a support for the 'blinding insight' of Thatcherism:

> *The Guardian* Editorial*: May 31, 1984*
> *Thatcherism means an end to riotous mass picketing, the introduction of secret ballots before the strikes, the abolition of closed shops...On its own terms it is hard to argue yet that the Government's industrial relations Legislation is a flop, misplaced...politically motivated... Ask Mr. Eddie Shah or the executive of the NGA. Ask the Post Office Engineering Union which saw its anti-privatisation strikes declared unlawful.*

Later on the *Guardian* argues:

September 29, 1984
Yesterday MORI poll showed support for the Labour Party has slipped back since its post-election boom and support for the Government has revived... the extra ingredient looks like the miners dispute...as the weeks and the months drag on Labour has become increasingly identified with Scargill's crusade.....And so this debilitating dispute drags on...debilitating to the social fabric and to the putative economic recovery. But above all debilitating to a new Labour who could have hoped for a better hand to play, and now drifts unhappily on the high tide of events.

The *Daily Mirror*, in the 1970s miners' disputes, maintained its support for the miners' cause even throughout the critical period prior to the General Election in 1974. In the following editorial the paper seems careful in its attempt to put its position forward.

The Daily Mirror Editorial: *February 6, 1974*
Then so be it, Mr. Heath
Today Britain hangs on the cliff edge of industrial chaos. Yesterday the miners' Executive called a national coal strike ...Unless a miracle happens... Britain will have entered a long and ruinous conflict that could leave the country scared and impoverished for years.

And yet, this is not a political confrontation, but a dispute about miners' pay. What now really separates Mr. Heath and the miners? It is the difference between cash on the table, demanded by the miners, and the virtual offer from the Government of a post-dated cheque guaranteed not to bounce.

In terms of incomes policy this is a tiny gap. So how can either side say that this is a sane reason for putting Britain's future in pawn?..... If a confrontation election is to be the outcome of nearly 4 years of Tory rule, so be it.

Better an election than the nation left at the mercy of a divided Government presiding over a 2 day week...with massive unemployment, growing shortages and a tottering Pound.

In the 1980s dispute, however, the *Daily Mirror*, along with the rest of the industry, expressed doubts about the purpose or the efficacy of the miners' strike. The following sequence of editorials present the paper's stance on the nature of trade union solidarity for the miners' dispute:

> *The Daily Mirror* Editorial: *August 27, 1984*
> Strike without reason
> *Do they (dockers) believe, along with Mr. Ron Todd, newly elected General Secretary of the Transport Workers that a 'big-bang' of strikes will bring victory to the miners? If they do, they are deeply, expensively, ruinously wrong. A national strike won't help anyone-steel men, miners, Dockers of Britain. And not every docker will support it.*

Three days later the paper continues its conviction on the futility of other workers supporting the miners:

> *The Daily Mirror* Editorial: *August 27, 1984*
> Politics in the dock
> *A political strike like this (dockers) can never succeed. There can be no solution to a political strike. The dockers know that. Political extremists will blame (everyone). But the truth is there is no one to blame but themselves.*

Four days later, the paper went one step further:

> *The Daily Mirror:* **August 31, 1984**
> Strike that is dying of shame
> *Just 4 days ago, it was clear that the strike might harm unions even more than the miners dispute. Now it threatens to disgrace them. The fraud and confusion at*

Tilbury was a blot on the good name of trade unionism. That will strengthen Thatcher's stand against the miners and her new law to ban strikes until a ballot has been held. Workers will not be lend into politically motivated, unwinnable strikes.

By November, the *Daily Mirror* demonstrates its 'unfavourable' stance:

The *Daily Mirror* Editorial*: November 1, 1984*
The miners dispute has reached the end of the road. There is a deep yearning for peace among all but the most pig-headed of the combatants.....Scargill wants total victory that is unattainable. No Government, not even a Labour one, would concede that.

The editorials presented above seem to capture *Daily Mirror's* 'unfavourable attitude' towards the 1980s miners' strike. Indeed in an extraordinary documentary screened on national television, nearly twelve years after the 1984-85 miners' strike, the editor of the paper at the time of the strike, Mike Molloy, publicly apologized to the miners and their leaders for the paper's unfavourable treatment of the strike.[44]

To sum up, this section aimed to demonstrate the press industry's shifting strategy in dealing with the wider body of the labour movement through the miners' strikes. The editorials presented above, collectively, seem to suggest that the miners and their strike were not the 'only' target of the national press. The evidence from all the newspapers in the sample, including the Labour supporting *Daily Mirror* and the *Guardian*, seem to suggest a 'general' support for Thatcher's 'highly controversial' legislation to weaken the industrial power of the unions, particularly the NUM. The analysis of these editorials insinuates that whereas there was a certain amount of restraint in the 1970s, even before and throughout the 1974 General Election, but the

---

[44]Network First: 'Breaking the Mirror' (Carlton Television) on February 18, 1997, at 22:40

Table 33

Q. Which party do you think has the best policies to deal with – Strikes and industrial disputes?[45]

	April/84	May/84	Oct/84	Dec/84	Feb/85
Conservatives	43	41	39	41	37
Labour	33	33	33	31	31
SDP/ Lib Alliance	7	7	9	8	14
Other	0	0	0	0	1
Don't Know	16	20	20	21	17

All figures in %

1980s witnessed widespread hostility by the press against the labour movement in general. As argued above, by adopting a non-supporting attitude for the miners, the industry in fact undermined the popularity of the Labour party during the dispute. In the light of this claim, Table 33 examines the attitude of the public.

Table 33 demonstrates the results of Gallup's research on the issue of industrial relations in the 1984-85 period. Clearly the Conservatives received a continuous support throughout the dispute for their policy on industrial relations. By December 1984 the conservatives achieved a ten point lead for their policy.

The next section will consider the depiction of the miners by the national press with a special reference to the press and social representations. This issue will be assessed by considering the role of the press industry in the gradual demoralization of the striking miners in the 1980s.

---

[45] Gallup Political Index: collected throughout the dispute to survey the public opinion with specific reference to the miners' strike

The Miners' Dispute, the Press and the Defeatist Culture: The Schematization Process

The culture industry's prime service to the consumer is to do his schematizing for him.[46]

In Adorno's usage of the term, schematization refers to the culture industry's own patterning or pre-forming of the audience's experience. It also refers to what Adorno calls the 'collapse of distinctions between culture and practical life'. The processes of schematization and stereotypes, Adorno argued, promotes conformity to prevailing behaviourial norms, they facilitate standardized reaction ensuring that recipients do not exceed the limits of what is socially acceptable.

In this context, this section will empirically examine the way in which the national press depicted the miners and the impact of this process upon the demoralization of the miners and their eventual defeat in the 1984-85 dispute.

Moreover, this section will assess the processes whereby the press industry performed its role in nurturing the 'Thatcherite multifaceted populism' .

As mentioned in the introduction to this chapter, this section will presents six editorials, one from each one of the papers in the sample, regarding the hostile attitude of the national press even *before* the strike was officially due to begin. These editorials can be seen as substantiating the claim that the press hostility in the 1980s was a foregone conclusion. In reading the following passages it is necessary to remind the reader that the strike officially began on 11 March 1984.

The Sun **Editorial:** *March 6, 1984, p6* (Almost a week before the beginning of the strike)
The *Sun* says: SHUT IT DOWN
Mob rule spreading among miners:
1. Ian MacGregor is knocked down outside a Northumberland pit

---

[46]Adorno and Horkheimer, *Dialectic of Enlightenement*, p.124

2. Pickets hurl bricks and stones at management trying to maintain safety precautions at Yorkshire Main.
3. They ought to close it altogether
4. Thugs, whether they are miners or soccer fans, must learn the lesson that VIOLENCE never pays.

The *Daily Express* Editorial: March 7, 1984, p8
MacGregor must win

....*Miners' leader Arthur Scargill wants us to believe that what is good for the NUM is good for Britain. It is not! What is good for Britain is coal as cheap as we can possibly get it. Preferably our own- but if that proves too expensive then someone else's.... The best coal industry for Britain- This is what the current battle between Arthur Scargill and Ian MacGregor is about. For the sake of the nation Mr. MacGregor must win.*

The *Daily Mirror* Editorial: March 8, 1984, p2
Suicide Strike

Britain's miners – fearing pit closures and angry about their wages – are sliding into an all out struggle with the Government which they cannot win. A national strike would only lead to humiliating defeat. Everything is stacked against the miners. Fighting to save jobs may be the right battle. But it comes at the wrong time. The miners would be doing what the Government wants them to do. The miners may ask: what else can we do? It is a fair question. But if a strike leaves them and their industry substantially weaker, then a strike is not the answer for it.

The *Times* Editorial: March 13, 1984, p13
Cutting the cost of coal

...It does not take a ruthless capitalist to work out what Mr. Ian MacGregor and the Coal Board should be doing. The 1974 Plan for Coal, the shocking Monopolies Commission report, the House of Lords select committee report on European Community coal policy, successive Commons select committees, ministers and Coal Board

managers have all concluded that the Board should invest in new low cost pits and close old uneconomic ones.... In his heart, even the most socialist-minded miner must see Mr.Scargill's insistence that there are no uneconomic pits as no more than Stalinist newspeak.

The Guardian Editorial: March 14,1984, p12
The Challenge of the Pickets
As the pit strike enters its 3rd day the NUM is in a predicted state of chaos and confrontation. Flying pickets from areas like Yorkshire, which are on official strike, without the luxury of ballot, are descending on neighbouring areas like Nottinghamshire where a ballot is to be held later this week. Traditionally miners are unhappy about crossing even symbolic lines and the pickets are exploiting this emotion in a quite disgraceful manner. Disgraceful because the policy of NUM is to leave each area to take an autonomous decision about whether to support the stoppage. That policy is being deliberately flouted by militants who intend to spread the stoppage domino fashion. They hope to bounce unwitting men from moderate areas into a national strike without the constitutional necessity of democratic constitution.

All the papers analysed in the sample viewed the miners strike as 'futile', 'senseless' and 'unnecessary', hence increasingly undermining the solidarity of the miners and cementing their eventual defeat. What follows are extracts of several editorials published by two pro-Conservative and two Labour supporting papers in the sample in order to substantiate the first hypothesis of this research outlined in the introduction to this chapter. The editorials of the *Daily Star* and the *Sun* will be presented first, followed by those of the *Daily Mirror* and the *Guardian*. The *Daily Star* tirelessly attempted to set the agenda on the issue of the miners solidarity:

Daily Star Editorial: *May 8, 1984*
A question the miners must ask: 'Where the hell is the

strike going? what chance has it of success? Am I sacrificing my future? ....In other words the miners strike is going nowhere. It is still not unanimous and until a national ballot is held it is unlikely to be so.... The miners will find it very hard to convince the nation that it should pay even more in subsidies... The time will come in the months ahead when that dedicated miner will have to ask himself 'is it worth it?

A few months into the dispute the paper reiterates its demand of the miners:

Daily Star Editorial: *August 1, 1984*
Daily Star says: 'The world doesn't owe Britain a living. And Britain doesn't owe the miners a living.' Every striking coal worker in Britain has a duty today. A duty to himself, his family, his job, and his country. And that duty is to stop and think very long about where the miners strike is taking him, his family, his job and his country. ....Look at the following facts:

1. Brother is fighting brother. Father opposes son, mother is against daughter. Families are split forever. Villages and towns are divided by hatred.
2. Miners trying to work are threatened, their homes damaged, their wives and daughters threatened with rape... AND IT CAN ONLY GET WORSE, for what?

To bring down the Government? Surely every sensible miner knows that cannot and will not happen.

With a remarkable similarity in style and message the paper, by late September 1984, returns to these themes by attempting to appeal to the 'common sense' of its readers:

Daily Star: September 20, 1984
Today the Daily Star *presents the truth about the miners*

strike....The dispute is about our way of life. Do we subsidies industries to keep people in work? Or do we force industries to pay their own way regardless of the loss of jobs? Do we keep paying out money on those inefficient industries again to preserve jobs?

The WE in these questions is not the same mythical government agency. It is us – the British people or more accurately the British tax-payer. Let's take the case of a miner and his neighbour a plumber. The miner feels that the government must guarantee him a job...now and in the future. The plumber goes to work every day without any government guarantee, but earns a living all on his own. What the miner is really asking for is for the plumber to contribute to his pay. We said before that the world does not owe Britain a living and Britain does not owe the miners a living either.

The strongest supporter of the government in the Thatcher years, amongst the national press, was The *Sun*. The following sequence of editorials demonstrates the extent of the commitment of the paper to the 'Thatcherite' ethos in the government's determination to defeat the miners. In its attempt to justify the 'new realism' in the sphere of industrial relations in Britain, the *Sun* launched a relentless attack upon the striking miners and their leaders almost immediately after the strike was officially begun. What follows is an extract of several editorials throughout the strike to demonstrate the paper's commitment to the Thatcherite agenda. The *Sun* began its campaign right from the start of the dispute:

The Sun **Editorial: March 8, 1984**
The biggest union wrecker in Britain today is not Mrs. Thatcher, Howe or Tebbit. It is Arthur Scargill. Look at what he is doing to the miners. When he took over as president, miners were a respectful force winning every battle with Tory and Labour Governments. Today he is bent on leading them to disunity and destruction..... Scargill says he is willing to stand for re-election as

president. Why do not the miners take him at his word? Either way he will finish on the scrap heap or they will.

By May 1984, the *Sun* had established itself as the front runner as the Government's ideological representative

The Sun: **May 3, 1984**
Someone has to say it: the miners' strike did not live up to expectations. [We] blame McGahey and the way his reds are sinking the workers. What is so odd about the pit strike... it is not hurting where it ought to be i.e. you, me and the Government. With his woolly class war rhetoric and communist double talk McGahey has tried to convince them that industrial suicide is the price of solidarity with the miners... But the tragedy of 1974 is likely to become the farce of 1984. He will fail to conquer the government and may help to annihilate part of an industry in his own beloved Scotland.

By November 1984, nine months into the dispute, The *Sun* reaffirms its long standing conviction that the miners' strike was a 'senseless strike' by connecting the dispute to the IRA, the most hated organization in Britain throughout the 1980s, arousing a sense of patriotism in the rank and file miners hoping to speed up the failure of the strike:

The Sun: **November 12, 1984**
Plain daft to stay out
The return to work last week of more than 2000 miners was the best news since the strike began. But the next 7 days would be even better and signal the end of Arthur Scargill's mad plan to bring industrial Britain to its knees. There are several good reasons why the 135000 striking miners must now accept it is senseless to stay out any longer... The IRA link .... Sinn Fein...are reported to have advised miners on how to combat police on picket lines.... One member of the NUM, Steve Green, is said to have hold a meeting in Dublin organised by Sinn Fein...

Towards the end of January 1985, the strike began to show signs of exhaustion by both the miners and their union. The *Sun* showed its utter jubilation:

> *The Sun:* **January 22, 1985, p6**
> **Scargill takes it to the bunker**
> *Scargill declares that he would rather go down fighting than surrender pits and jobs......Scargill's disappearance from the industrial scene would be a day of wine and roses for the entire country......This is Hitler in the bunker again. The Fuhrer destroying himself and willing to destroy all Germany......Are they [miners] really willing to follow Scargill and jump? or will they at last discover their courage and their guts and seek the settlement they could have had 10 long months ago?*

By mid-February 1985, nearly a year into the strike, the *Sun* was clearly applauding the Nottinghamshire miners, and their breakaway Union of Democratic Mineworkers, for their non-striking policy throughout the dispute.

> **The Sun:** *February 25, 1985*
> *Well done: 'The* Sun *congratulates the miners of Notts... Not only have they worked during the Scargill's strike. They are now going to defy his overtime ban too.. Lets hope they inspire 1000s who are on the brink of returning to their pits this morning.*

Finally, on the day of the miners' organised return to work, The *Sun* sums up its year long campaign to facilitate Thatcher's victory over the 'enemy within'.

> *The Sun:* **March 4, 1985**
> *The* Sun *Says: What about a ballot now?: 'The miners suffered the most shattering defeat in their history. There is no more room for any doubt over this ....All the privation, all the bitterness...have achieved precisely nothing for the strikers.... Predictably even now one man does not recognize the reality*

of defeat. A. Scargill demands a thugs charter and the reinstatement of the sacked men......After all that has happened in the past 12 months, we cannot believe that this will be the wish of the miners themselves....King Arthur has been cut down to size. It is now for the miners to demonstrate that Scargillism is just as dead in the mining industry as in all other industries where wreckers used to flourish.

The previous sections strived to demonstrate that, as far as the miners' dispute was concerned, there was a fine line separating the pro-Conservative papers and the pro-Labour newspapers in the sample. It was argued that, in relation to the 1980s miners' strike, it was rather difficult indeed to sustain such false distinction amongst the national papers.

The following section will produce evidence to demonstrate that the pro- Labour papers in our sample, the *Daily Mirror* and the *Guardian*, were as active in undermining the spirit of resistance by the miners in their conflict with the government.

The *Daily Mirror* perceived the strike as ill-conceived right from the start of the miners' campaign:

Daily Mirror: **March 8,1984**
Britain's miners, fearing pit closures and angry about their wages are sliding into an all out struggle with the government which they cannot win.

Soon after the paper repeats its conviction that:

Daily Mirror: **March 16,1984-'Mining disaster'**
The miners strike is drifting towards disaster. One man has died and others are hurt. Pitmen are fighting each other as well as the Coal. Board.This is a strike the miners cannot win.

A few months later the paper returns to its favourite issue:

Daily Mirror: **July 31, 1984**
Only the TUC can get the miners back
The miners have been offered nearly all that they have

demanded, there is not much more to win. But if they continue with their strike they head inevitably towards defeat. Murray knows how much the CB have conceded to what miners have demanded. He knows the union will not get much better.

Towards the end of July, the paper goes on to brand the miners as 'mad' to think that victory was conceivable:

Daily Mirror: **July 31, 1984**
Equally the miners are mad to think the government will be defeated.' It cannot be. Victory is a mirage...

By September, the paper had published several strictly anti-strike editorials, one of which claimed:

Daily Mirror: **September 10, 1984**
The weakness of the miners strike was always that the union never held a national ballot to find out if its membership as a whole supported it. As a result : a 1/3 of the miners stayed at work, the union suffered its worst split in 50 years, there was picket line violence which disfigured the respect in which the miners were always held.

By November, clearly frustrated with its advice falling on deaf ears, the *Daily Mirror* argues that the miners' leader is:

Daily Mirror: **November 6, 1984**
Scargill: Three times loser
...the pit strike goes on. And so will the hardship, the misery, the futility of it all. ..800 miners went back yesterday. Scargill says the miners are fighting for jobs. But if workers were frozen into the same jobs for ever more, we would still have 3m domestic servants and men lighting gas lamps in the street.

By December, the paper had no doubt that the strike had

gone on for too long:

Daily Mirror: **December 12, 1984**
The strike has dragged on for almost 10 months. It is doing grave political, social and industrial damage.

Upon considering the reasons for the defeat of the miners, the *Daily Mirror* had adopted a tone which was indistinguishable from the pro-Conservative papers:

Daily Mirror: **January 28, 1984**
Arthur Scargill has lost the miners' strike. It is his defeat....he has led the crack guards' regiment of the unions to disaster. A defeat for Scargill is also a defeat for the hard men of the left, the Benns who dream of workers' triumph through the General Strike. Their way has been tried and it has lost. There is no support for it.

Towards the end of the strike, the paper brought the message of defeat home to the miners:

Daily Mirror: **February 7, 1985**
The stoppage is no longer just crumbling at the edges. It is collapsing at the heart. Even the most militant areas...know the strike is lost...

The *Guardian*'s approach, although somewhat different from the rest of the industry, still contained a similar hostility. On the crucial issue of the industrial relations laws, the Labour supporting papers, including the *Guardian*, favoured the government's approach. Also, it was shown that these papers were as crude as the rest of the industry when writing about the NUM leadership or the question of ballot and picket-line violence.

The following section, will outline several editorials with which the *Guardian* repeatedly repudiated the strike, its motives, its leaders and, above all, 'the hard men of the left' within the rank and file of the Labour Party. As early as the third day of the dispute, the *Guardian* showed its position on the fundamental issues of the strike. The paper heavily emphasised the 'democracy and the right to work' of the 'moderate' miners of Nottinghamshire, who were clearly in the minority at the beginning of the dispute.

The Guardian: March 14, 1984
...But the moderate miners of Notts and elsewhere have every reason to expect that they will be jostled, punched and spat upon if they decide democratically to brave the picket line which should not be there.

Two months into the strike, the *Guardian*, having highlighted the issue of ballot and democracy, regarded the NUM's request for solidarity and the stepping up of the stoppage as 'bullying':

The Guardian: May 24, 1984
...But the 20% of miners who are not on strike are equally solid, they will neither be moralised or bullied out against their own democratic area decisions.... In much the same spirit, it is not easy to collect funds for striking miners when their own union, one of the richest in the country with assets of more than £32m, elects not to give one single penny in strike pay.

By September 1984, the paper was clearly convinced that the miners were on the road to defeat, and prepared its readers to abandon support for the striking miners:

The Guardian: September 5, 1984
The more Scargill insists upon absolute victory and not, to use Len Murray's carefully chosen words 'a fair and satisfactory solution', the harder it will be to maintain support for the miners.

Ten days later, the *Guardian* perceived the idea of a defeat of Thatcher by the striking miners as 'nonsense':

The Guardian: **September 15, 1984**
...Equally, the initial militant nonsense about 'smashing Maggie' rings pretty hollow these days...The Government, in theory, stands aloof from what is, in practice, a deeply politicised dispute.

By December 1984, the *Guardian* showed as much a trait of 'tabloidism' in its style and convictions as the Sun. Having branded the NUM president with the then well-established stereotypical phrase 'King Arthur', an analogy which was maintained for the latter part of the dispute, the paper repeatedly outlined its pessimistic outlook:

The Guardian: **December 7, 1984**
...Deep down [Scargill] may be shallow...he may be cynical, opportunistic, ...and he may be leading his members to a monumental a defeat as that suffered by the miners in 1926 and under the equally charismatic leadership of ARTHUR COOK. He is without a doubt a man whose judgment was deeply flawed. After all it takes a perverse sort of pride to call a pit strike in the spring with 24m tons of coal stockpiled on the surface.....Yet Scargill survives and it would be a bold man who suggested that the ultimate unconditional destruction of Scargill's strike... would mean the destruction of Scargill.

By January 1985, the *Guardian* was not only supporting a breakaway, government backed UDM, but it displayed a certain anxiety for its collapse by the lack of initiative from the leaders of the Nottinghamshire miners:

The Guardian: **January 15, 1985**
A certain confusion....is inevitable when a major national institution starts to break down...If the 32,000 men of Notts are to be driven out...it would be to their distinct advantage if their leaders had some faith in the exercise. It is far from clear how many Notts men want to take their constitutional and democratic defiance of the Scargill

Table 34 "Senseless strike" (all figures in percentage)

	1972-74	1984-85
The Sun	0	9.1
Daily Mail/ Daily Star	0.3	5.6
Daily Express	1.9	23.3
Daily Mirror	0	11.5
Guardian	0	9.2
The Times	2	17

Table 35 "A dispute miners cannot win" (all figures in percentage)

	1972-74	1984-85
The Sun	0	17
Daily Mail/ Daily Star	2	21
Daily Express	3.8	20
Daily Mirror	0	6
Guardian	0	4
The Times	1.5	9.5

machine to the point of a long march. Now there are rumbles that some Notts men would rather accept NUM membership, king Arthur star chamber and all, rather than split 'their' union.

Having outlined these editorials, the reader is invited to consider Tables 34 and 35. As part of the theoretical hypothesis of this section two categories were selected to measure the frequency of each in two periods of the miners' disputes. The first is the sentence senseless strike', and the other is 'a dispute miners cannot win'. Table 34 deals with the percentage frequency of the sentence 'senseless strike'.

Table 34 shows the comparative analysis of the term

'senseless strike'. In the 1970s the frequency of the term was almost negligible, but in the 1980s it increased significantly. In the 1970s three national papers shared zero-frequency and three others scored no more than 2%. During the 1980s dispute, however, all the papers in the sample had a frequency of more than 5%. The most significant increases are in the cases of the *Guardian* and the *Daily Mirror*; from zero-frequency in the 1970s to more than 9% for the *Guardian*, and the *Daily Mirror* scoring 11.5%.

Let's now consider the next selected category which may enhance the analysis offered above. Once again, Table 35 demonstrates a significant increase in the usage of the term during the 1980s dispute. In the 1970s, the *Daily Express* scored the highest frequency, but once more, three national papers recorded zero-frequency. Significantly, in the 1980s, *all papers* showed significant increase in the usage of the category.

There are two important conclusions to be drawn out of this particular aspect of the research. Firstly, in the introduction to this section, it was argued that the press industry was instrumental in the growth of the 'Thatcherite multi-faceted populism' in general, and against the miners in particular, during the 1980s dispute. This section provides a glimpse of the industry's role in 'schematizing' a mood of pessimism for the strike's outcome. As demonstrated above, the consensus amongst the national press was one of an expectation of a 'monumental' defeat for the miners. This, in turn, we believe, not only affected public opinion, but also had an impact on the miners' aspirations and sense of solidarity. Tables 34 and 35 show the industry's conviction that the 1980s dispute was indeed a 'doomed' exercise. As shown above, some papers announced this conviction as early as the second day of the dispute.

Secondly, when a more detailed consideration of the 'consensus' of the national press and the miners' lack of hope for a victory in their campaign are combined, the results are even more controversial. The combination of the categories of 'senseless strike' with that of 'a dispute miners cannot win', shows every national paper in the sample would have a score of more than 13% devoted to these discouraging messages.[47]

In the 1970s, however, the highest combined score was less than 5%, and three national papers did not mention either terms.[48]

The wider consequences of the erosion of the miners' hope and solidarity was reflected in the way other unions responded to the solidarity calls by the NUM leadership. It is well-documented that these calls went unheeded.

The Trade Unionists' Opinion

In order to get a better sense of what other trade unionists felt about the strike, MORI polls directly aimed to measure the solidarity of union members with the miners in their strike (Table 36).

We can note that a staggering 50% of the trade unionists believed that they should not support the miners in their campaign. Only 2% of the respondents pledged full support for the miners, and 34% were in favour of very minimal support for the pitmen.

Similarly, in an interesting research project, published by

---

[47]The combined per centages of the frequency of the categories 'senseless strike' and ' A dispute miners cannot win' for the 1980s are as follows:

    The Sun: 26.1%
    Daily Star: 26.6%
    Daily Express: 43.03%
    Daily Mirror: 17.5%
    The Guardian: 13.2%
    The Times: 27%

[48]The combined per centages of the frequency of the categories 'senseless strike' and ' A dispute miners cannot win' for the 1970s are as follows:

    The Sun: 0
    Daily Star: 2.3 %
    Daily Express: 4.7%
    Daily Mirror: 0%
    The Guardian: 0%
    The Times: 3.5%

Table 36 MORI polls on the miners' dispute[49]

Q. [To union members only] In which of these ways, if any, do you think your union should support the miners strike?

Agreeing not to cross NUM picket lines	20%
Joining a national one day 'strike'	14%
Taking part in industrial action in support of the miners	7%
Joining in an extended national strike	2%
I do not believe my union should support the miners' strike	50%
Don't know	13%

Broadcasting Research Unit, Guy Cumberbatch *et al.* show that the majority of the public claimed that their respect for the miners had gone down during the strike. Broken down by social class the figures are: ABC1 60 per cent; C2 56 per cent; DE 53 per cent, and 46 per cent of trade union members said their respect had gone down against 60 per cent of non-members. In terms of newspaper readership Cumberbatch shows that 60 per cent of *Daily Express* readers reporting a decline in respect compared with 46 per cent of *Daily Mirror* readers. The most interesting aspect of Cumberbatch research is in terms of voting behaviour, with 35 per cent of Labour supporters reporting a decline in respect compared with 74 per cent of Conservatives.[50]

Table 37 shows MORI poll results on public opinion in general.

The most notable issue emerging out of Table 37 is the high unpopularity of Scargill as opposed to the high approval given by the public to the police and their handling of the strike. This table confirms the industry's success in establishing two

[49] As part of its survey of public opinion for the *Sunday Times* at the end of August 1984, MORI used 54 sampling points throughout the country among a representative quota sample of 1,021 electors
[50] G. Cumberbatch *et al*, *Television and the Miners' Strike* (London: Broadcasting Research Unit), 1986. For an interesting debate between the authors of this research and Colin Sparks see: *Media, Culture and Society*, Vol. 9, no.3, July 1987, pp 369-84

Table 37

Q. On balance do you think:
  a) Mr. MacGregor has handled the dispute well or badly...?
  b) Mr. Scargill has handled the dispute well or badly...?
  c) The police have handled the dispute well or badly?

	Well	Badly	No Opinion
A) MacGregor			
June '84	35%	49%	16%
August '84	37%	47%	16%
B) Scargill			
June '84	17%	76%	7%
August '84	14%	79%	7%
C) Police			
June '84	77%	16%	8%
August '84	71%	18%	11%

important issues. Firstly, Scargill as the epitome of 'the enemy within' and secondly, the firmness of the police in dealing with the internal threat.

Conclusion

This chapter aimed to assess the utility of three hypotheses. The first hypothesis proposed that *all newspapers* in the sample tended to provide a more favourable coverage of the government's handling of the miners' dispute in the 1984-85 period. The quantitative and the qualitative dimensions provided substantial evidence for the national press' favourable support for the government's handling of the dispute. The most important result emerging from this study is that all the chosen newspapers in the sample maintained their hostility towards the miners throughout the dispute.

The second hypothesis proposed that *most* newspapers in the sample were supportive of the miners in the 1970s period. This hypothesis was also substantiated through empirical evidence. It must be noted, however, that while the first miners' strike of 1972 received universal recognition by the industry the second miners' strike of 1974 was treated somewhat less favourably. A combined analysis of both strikes in the 1970s proved that there was far less editorial hostility than in the 1980s.

The third hypothesis suggested that the coverage of the miners' disputes by the major national press in each period influenced sufficient numbers of their readers to affect the popularity or unpopularity of the miners strikes.

By proposing these hypotheses this study is not suggesting that the press coverage had a direct effect on the popularity or unpopularity of the miners' strikes. The empirical data, however, suggests a correlation between press coverage and popularity through an aggregate level of public dissatisfaction/ satisfaction with the miners' strikes. The public image of the 1980s strike was also heavily influenced by the television coverage of the picket-line violence and other media input. Elsewhere in the book, however, it was argued that it is the national press industry that sets the news agenda for television and other forms of media communications.

Finally, the most important finding of this study is that, in terms of 'supporting the miners during the 1984-85 miners' strike, there was no such distinction between the 'Conservative-supporting' and 'Labour-supporting' papers. This , it distinction, it was claimed, was barely noticeable in the 1970s. As far as the 1980s strike was concerned, this study aimed to empirically support the notion that the Labour supporting papers, the *Guardian* and the *Daily Mirror*, were as 'unsympathetic' as the rest of the papers in the sample. This aspect of the research was theoretically supported by Adorno's concepts of standardization, schematization and stereotype to argue that the modern press industry in Britain can be seen as an integral part of the culture industry which is connected both to corporate capitalism and the political system most useful to encourage and nurture that state of affairs.

In this context, and by using the historical events of the miners' disputes, it has been empirically demonstrated that at least in the domains of political and social communication, the magnitude of the persuasive effect of the press media is significant.

EPILOGUE

This study set out in search of a better understanding of the function, and organisation, of the contemporary British press industry. This task began by establishing a sociological concepts and indicators model of analysis. Working within a theoretical parameter influenced by the Frankfurt School's theory of 'culture industry', it was argued that the modern institution of press in Britain can be seen as an integral component of culture industry which functions in a simultaneous connection with the international corporate capital on the one hand and the political system on the other. Within this theoretical context, it was argued that, at a general level of analysis, the theory of culture industry examines the ways in which the structure and processes of the public sphere are determined by capitalist commodity production. At a specific level, Adorno, more than any other critical thinker, was concerned by the impact of the larger socio-economic context upon the individual psyche which is weakened by reification and the loss of economic autonomy.

Through a re-examination of Adorno's works after the *Dialectic of Enlightenment*, it was maintained that Adorno's analysis of contemporary capitalism, the culture industry and commodity consumption goes beyond Marx by arguing that the commodity form had permeated and transformed areas of life outside of the economic sphere. Chapter One argued that the theory of culture industry, revised and reconsidered by Adorno over two decades after its original conceptualization, remains important by posing questions against a conventional political economic approach to culture. The culture industry is nurtured, and strengthened, by the profit-making ethos of the modern system. In this respect both the culture industry and individual psychology have become social facts. The culture industry continues its relentless endeavour to mass produce standardized materials for distribution and exchange on the market. The focal point of the theory is, therefore, an assessment of the processes of 'commodification of cultural outputs' rather than giving primacy to economic determinism. In the final analysis, the theory examines the ways in which 'certain crucial schemas are manufactured' in modern, socio-politically advanced societies. Indeed, this process is greatly encouraged by the institution of media, particularly the television and to a lesser extent, the mass circulating newspaper industry.

In order to more closely examine these climes, the methodological axis of this research began by re-evaluating the institution of the national press in Britain, particularly during the Thatcher epoch. In order to study the contemporary institution of mass media within the model of culture industry two important theoretical considerations were proposed. Firstly, the model would have to be able to account for significant societal and cultural transformations of recent decades and an implicit, and extensive, consideration had to be given to the importance of 'agency'. Essentially, this study proposed that, in spite of a seemingly unchallenged consensus within the academic circles, the theory of culture industry and individual agency do not necessarily oppose one another. Chapter One attempted to demonstrate that not only individuals in the advanced capitalist societies were seen by Adorno as the beneficiaries of the Enlightenment, but he also progressively, over a period of twenty years, paid more attention to the value of agency in complex social contexts. This claim was documented with two examples. In his 'Stars Down to Earth' Adorno demonstrates his expectation for the active participation of the readers of astrology columns. In this particular study, Adorno shows that the processes of reception and consumption mediate, but do not necessarily undermine, the power of mass mediatic messages. Acknowledging that audiences are 'active recipients' does not mean that the media are ineffectual. Recognizing the role of 'active interpretation' by the readers of astrology columns does not invalidate the process of influence of their messages. Moreover, through an empirical analysis of the wedding of Princess Beatrix of Holland, outlined in his *'Free Time'*, Adorno viewed individuals in modern societies as 'deceiving themselves' about the products of the culture industry and the established order reproduced by it.

Against this background, and to ensure an adequate inclusion of the role of agency, it was argued that the 'relative autonomy' of modern culture could be incorporated by emphasizing the significance of the roles of individuals and groups of actors in different spheres of society, their vested interests and their interaction with each other, in their struggle for upholding a societal arrangement favourable to themselves. Accordingly, the concept of 'macro agency' together with a distinction between 'mega and collective actors', was introduced and analysed to capture the significance of the role of agency in a complexly hierarchical society, such as Britain. Indeed, by using the example of contemporary press industry, this study aimed to demonstrate that this institution is a site of contest and conflict. It involves struggle over media ownership, state intervention, advertising and media presentation. It also covers discussion about the use of media technologies, interpretation and public understandings.

Secondly, as argued in the course of Chapter Two, this book indicated that the theory of culture industry could be employed to generate new conceptual paradigms in order to provide an analysis for the expansion of popular political projects such as Thatcherism. The concept of 'multi-faceted populism' was proposed, in an attempt to adequately capture the complex, and at times, reciprocal relationship between the mega actors in the political, economic and cultural spheres. A specific example of this notion was scrutinized in some detail during the course of Chapters Three and Four with a particular reference to the reciprocal liaison between Mrs. Thatcher and Rupert Murdoch,- mega actors in the political sphere and those in the domain of the media.

Through an empirical analysis of the role of Murdoch's newspapers in three general elections involving Thatcher, Chapter Three argued that the special relationship between Thatcher and Murdoch had a deeper impact not only upon the press industry but British society as a whole. The utility of the concept of 'multi-faceted populism', it was maintained, can be an indication of contemporary relevance of the theory of culture industry as an important sociological paradigm in assessing the complex relationship between the modern media and an authoritarian, yet simultaneously popular political project such as Thatcherism.

In an attempt to carry out an effective research project based on this theoretical proposals, this study outlined a set of methodological indicators. Within this 'concepts-indicators' model, two implicit issues were addressed by this book. First, it aimed to argue that the messages produced by mass media do have important consequences for individuals, society and culture. This notion was examined by using two examples; the events at Wapping, an example from the internal sphere of the press industry, and the miners' strikes in two separate occasions, an example used from the external sphere. Within the industry, the Wapping episode highlighted an intensification of the 'formal rationality', the underlying rationale of the culture industry. The press, in the post-Wapping age were expected to adhere to the basic principles of global business, they were projected to create investor dividends like any other business. Moreover, Wapping was a defeat for the principle of 'collective bargaining' and represented a major shift in power and resources away from print unions and the labour force in support of owners and executive management. Wapping, highlighted the industry's escalating desire to generate greater profit margins and further accumulation of capital through increasingly efficient production system. It also transformed traditional distribution practices, wholesaling arrangements, and the structure of the labour negotiation process across the industry.

In the external sphere, the relevance of the culture industry theory was examined in relation to the miners and their strikes of the 1970s and 1980s. The position, and the perceived impact, of the press industry on the strikes and its consequences for individual miners, their leaders, their union, the formation of the UDM, and the coal industry as a whole was subjected to an empirical investigation.

According to this methodological principle, this study devised a research plan which included a 'qualitative' and 'quantitative' content analysis of a 'randomly selected' sample of the national press which was outlined, and assessed, in a comparative manner. The result of the research, outlined extensively in Chapters Three and Four, raises some interesting and perhaps controversial points. Primarily, the most conclusive finding of the research, as shown by Chapter Four, is the confirmation of a distinct correlation between the editorial contents of the national press and public opinion for both the periods of the miners' strikes in 1970s and the 1980s. It is firmly the belief of this study that this correlation, no doubt, is imperfect. It would be naïve not to admit this, nevertheless some imprecision is unavoidable. Directly measuring a media product's influence on public opinion would confront intractable problems, not least is establishing causation.

However, and perhaps more reassuringly, there are other findings which may be regarded as sociologically important. A major finding of this research project is that, as far as the 1984-85 miners' strike was concerned, there was no qualitative difference between the 'standardized' editorials of the 'Conservative supporting' and the 'Centre-Left' newspapers in their approach to the miners and their strike. Whereas this distinction was only just evident in the 1970s. The section entitled 'the miners dispute, the press industry and the defeatist culture: the schematization process', attempted to demonstrate that the *Guardian* and the *Daily Mirror* were rather unsympathetic towards the NUM, and its president Arthur Scargill and increasingly pro UDM as the rest of the national press examined in this sample. Additionally, this section provides an indication of the industry's role in 'schematizing' a mood of pessimism for the strike's outcome. By outlining a series of editorials and front page articles from all the papers in the sample, it was argued that we can safely deduce that, the consensus amongst the national press was one of an expectation of a 'catastrophic' defeat for the miners. This, in turn, not only affected the opinion of the readers but also affected the miners' aspirations and sense of solidarity.

Having gathered and analyed all the relevant data, this study maintained that, at least in the domain of political and social communications, mass media have important consequences for individual citizens, society and culture. Although it is impossible to establish a causal connection or make reliable predictions about the future does not nullify this conclusion.

Moreover, in terms of the power of mass media, it was argued that those who own and control them regard this form of communication as a valued property to seek greater economic and social power. Multiple ownership of newspapers gives mega actors in the internal sphere of the press, immense power vis-à-vis the mega actors in the political sphere. Mega actors in the political sphere, on the other hand, depend on 'friendly' press owners for positive publicity.

Extensive media impact is indeed somewhat difficult to see. But this should not be seen as a reason to discredit the theoretical validity of this book. Rigorous assessment may, nonetheless, be achieved by the isolation of important historical events in the context of an appropriate theoretical framework.

Finally, by admitting to the limitations and shortcomings, this study may serve as an opportunity for further research in the domains of popular culture, political and social stability and the methods of consciousness control in modern, technologically advanced societies.

APPENDIX 1

Content Analysis of the Categories for the 1984–85 Sample

The Times 1984-85 (110 Editorials)

Word/s	Frequency	Percentage
Militant	71	64
Undemocratic	86	78
Law/Order	77	70
Dispute	106	96
Moderate	66	60
Nation	59	53
Britain	51	46
Scargill	153	139
MacGregor	106	96
Mob	63	57
Rule	71	64
Violence	99	89
Picket/s	129	117
Class	58	53
War	62	56
Ballot	112	101
Troops	43	39
Scargillism	28	25
Thatcherism	4	4
Thatcher	91	82
Political	89	81
Strike	136	112
Bullies/Bully	51	46
Police	109	102
NUM	113	102
TUC	64	58

Selected sentences as categories

Word/s	Frequency	Percentage
Cannon fodder	17	15
Rebel miners (Notts miners)	24	21
Uneconomic pits	65	59
A dispute miners cannot win	10	9.5
Against the elected government	45	40.9
General Scargill	0	0
King Arthur	12	10
Senseless strike	19	17
The red guards	9	8.9

APPENDIX

The *Guardian* 1984-85 (135 Editorials)

Word/s	Frequency	Percentage
Militant	81	60
Undemocratic	74	54
Law/Order	104	77
Dispute	124	91
Moderate	86	63
Nation	60	44
Britain/British	23 / 12	17 / 8
Scargill	178	132
MacGregor	117	8
Mob	39	29
Rule	57	42
Violence	92	66
Picket/s	112	82
Class war	21	15
War	24	17
Ballot	87	64
Troops	9	7
Scargillism	6	4
Thatcherism	9	6
Thatcher	76	47
Political	82	54
Strike	126	93
Bullies/Bully	40	31
Police	78	57
NUM	118	87
TUC	80	59

Selected sentences as categories

Word/s	Frequency	Percentage
Cannon fodder	0	0
Rebel miners (Notts miners)	63	46
Uneconomic pits	77	57
A dispute miners cannot win	5	4
Against the elected government	0	0
General Scargill	0	0
King Arthur	19	14
Senseless strike	13	9.2
New realism	15	11

The *Daily Express*- 1984-85 (155 Editorials)

Word/s	Frequency	Percentage
Militant	111	71
Undemocratic	104	67
Law/Order	125	81
Dispute	131	84
Moderate	97	64
Nation	81	52
Britain/British	54 / 41	35 / 26
Scargill	171	110
MacGregor	126	81
Mob	88	57
Rule	78	51
Violence	110	71
Picket/s	131	84
Class	30	19
War	89	57
Ballot	112	72
Troops	61	39
Scargillism	31	20
Thatcherism	12	8
Thatcher	81	51
Political	86	55
Strike	98	63
Bullies/Bully	91	58
Police	76	51
NUM	104	67
TUC	32	21

Selected sentences as categories

Word/s	Frequency	Percentage
Cannon fodder	18	11
Rebel miners	61	39
Uneconomic pits	128	82
A dispute miners cannot win	31	20
Against the elected government	55	35
General Scargill	11	7
King Arthur	23	15
Senseless strike	36	23
The red guards	62	40

The *Daily Mirror* – 1984-85 (130 Editorials)

Word/s	Frequency	Percentage
Militant	47	36
Undemocratic	58	44
Law/Order	91	70
Dispute	109	83
Moderate	68	52
Nation	59	45
Britain/ British	69 / 38	53 / 29
Scargill	110	84
MacGregor	88	67
Mob	55	42
Rule	16	12
Violence	98	75
Picket/s	59	45
Class war	19	14.6
War	38	29
Ballot	81	62
Troops	25	19
Scargillism	0	0
Thatcherism	2	1.5
Thatcher	79	61
Political	69	53
Strike	92	70
Bullies/Bully	31	23
Police	73	56
NUM	84	64
TUC	72	55

Selected sentences as categories

Word/s	Frequency	Percentage
Cannon fodder	0	0
Rebel miners	9	6
Uneconomic pits	29	22
A dispute miners cannot win	5	3.6
Against the elected government	19	14.4
General Scargill	2	1.5
King Arthur	12	9.2
Senseless strike	15	11.5
The red guards	0	0

The Sun 1984-85 (115 Editorials)

Word/s	Frequency	Percentage
Militant	88	84
Undemocratic	79	75
Law/Order	71	67
Dispute	82	78
Moderate	73	69
Nation	49	47
Britain/ British	65 / 53	61 / 51
Scargill	124	119
MacGregor (Big Mac)	93 (16)	88
Mob	77	73
Rule	68	65
Violence	82	78
Picket/s	110	104
Class war	21	20
War	28	26
Ballot	93	88
Troops	49	46
Scargillism	3	2.8
Thatcherism	0	0
Thatcher	79	75
Political	65	62
Strike	87	82
Bullies/Bully	66	63
Police	83	79
NUM	73	70
TUC	55	52
Wrecker*	31	29

Selected sentences as categories

Word/s	Frequency	Percentage
Cannon fodder	3	3.2
Rebel miners	64	61
Uneconomic pits	43	41
A dispute miners cannot win	18	17
Against the elected government	29	27.2
General Scargill	5	4.7
King Arthur	31	30
Senseless strike	7	9.1
The red guards	24	23

* This term was used by the Sun with a specific reference to A. Scargill

APPENDIX

The *Daily Star* 1984-85 (148 Editorials)

Word/s	Frequency	Percentage
Militant	78	53
Undemocratic	85	57
Law/Order	116	78
Dispute	39	26
Moderate	69	47
Nation	97	75
Britain/ British	98 / 81	66 / 55
Scargill	177	119
MacGregor	110	74
Mob	68	46
Rule	72	49
Violence	119	80
Picket/s	104	70
Class war	13	8.7
War	27	18
Ballot	112	75
Troops	11	7.4
Scargillism	0	0
Thatcherism	0	0
Thatcher	76	51
Political	88	59
Strike	94	63
Bullies/Bully	62	42
Police	79	53
NUM	56	38
TUC	44	29

Selected sentences as categories

Word/s	Frequency	Percentage
Cannon fodder	0	0
Rebel miners	66	44
Uneconomic pits	58	39
A dispute miners cannot win	31	21
Against the elected government	41	27.7
General Scargill	22	14.8
King Arthur	14	9.4
Senseless strike	7	5.6
The red guards	12	8.1

APPENDIX 2

Content Analysis of the Categories for the 1972–74 Miners' strikes

The *Times* 1972-74 (49 Editorials)

Word/s	Frequency	Percentage
Militant	11	22
Extremists	8	16
Undemocratic	9	18
Law/ order	24	49
Moderate	15	30
Violence	35	71
NUM	39	79
TUC	56	114
NCB	10	20
Community	15	30
Nation	21	42
Britain	29	59
Gormley	32	65
Heath	63	128
Ballot	12	24
War	0	0
Class War	1	2
Political	7	14
Strike	42	85

Selected sentences as categories

Word/s	Frequency	Percentage
Income policy	28	57
Stage Three	21	42
Uneconomic pits	5	10
Pay Board	12	24

APPENDIX

The *Guardian* 1972-7 (48 Editorials)

Word/s	Frequency	Percentage
Militant	13	27
Extremists	0	0
Undemocratic	9	18
Law/ order	4	8.3
Moderate	0	0
Violence	31	64
NUM	41	85
TUC	62	129
NCB	10	20
Community	14	29
Nation	29	60
Britain	8	16
Gormley	54	112
Heath	62	129
Ballot	18	37
War	10	20
Class War	11	23
Political	9	18
Strike	46	95

Selected sentences as categories

Word/s	Frequency	Percentage
Against the elected government	0	0
A dispute miners cannot win	0	0
Senseless strike	0	0
Miners as special case	23	48
Labour relations	5	10.4
Income policy	8	16
Stage Three	11	22
Uneconomic pits	3	6.2
Pay Board	17	35

The *Daily Express* 1972-74 (52 Editorials)

Word/s	Frequency	Percentage
Militant	9	17
Extremists	4	7.6
Undemocratic	2	3.8
Law/ order	7	13
Moderate	0	0
Violence	32	61
NUM	51	98
TUC	57	109
NCB	13	25
Community	10	19
Nation	31	56
Britain	27	52
Gormley	49	94
Heath	62	119
Ballot	6	11.5
War	0	0
Class War	0	0
Political	6	11.5
Strike	32	61

Sentences as categories

Word/s	Frequency	Percentage
Against the elected government	5	9
A dispute miners cannot win	2	4
Senseless strike	1	2
Labour relations	5	9.6
Miners as special case	11	39
Income policy	4	7.6
Stage Three	17	32
Uneconomic pits	8	15
Pay Board	4	7.6

APPENDIX

The *Daily Mirror* 1972-74 (49 Editorials)

Word/s	Frequency	Percentage
Militant	3	6.1
Extremists	0	0
Undemocratic	2	4
Law/ order	3	6.1
Moderate	5	10.2
Violence	12	24
NUM	47	95
TUC	51	104
NCB	10	20
Community	9	18
Nation	38	77
Britain	32	65
Gormley	41	83
Heath	53	108
Ballot	9	18
War	0	0
Class War	0	0
Political	6	12
Strike	29	59

Sentences as categories

Word/s	Frequency	Percentage
Against the elected government	0	0
A dispute miners cannot win	0	0
Senseless strike	0	0
Miners as special case	15	30
Labour relations	8	16
Income policy	11	22
Stage Three	21	42
Uneconomic pits	3	6.1
Pay Board	9	18

The *Sun* – 1972-74 (49 Editorials)

Word/s	Frequency	Percentage
Militant	2	4.8
Extremists	0	0
Undemocratic	3	6.1
Law/ order	10	20
Moderate	3	6.1
Violence	8	16
NUM	38	77
TUC	41	83
NCB	10	20
Community	4	8.1
Nation	28	57
Britain	35	71
Gormley	41	83
Heath	58	118
Ballot	4	8.1
War	1	2
Class War	0	0
Political	4	81
Strike	41	83

Sentences as categories

Word/s	Frequency	Percentage
Against the elected government	0	0
A dispute miners cannot win	0	0
Senseless strike	0	0
Labour relations	4	8.1
Miners as special case	19	39
Income policy	6	12
Stage Three	10	20
Uneconomic pits	3	6.1
Pay Board	4	8.1

APPENDIX

The *Daily Mail* 1972-74 (51 Editorials)

Word/s	Frequency	Percentage
Militant	21	41
Extremists	3	5.8
Undemocratic	3	5.8
Law/ order	9	17
Moderate	15	29
Violence	6	11
NUM	41	80
TUC	28	54
NCB	12	23
Community	11	21
Nation	35	68
Britain	47	92
Gormley	38	74
Heath	54	105
Ballot	12	23
War	2	4
Class War	0	0
Political	3	5.8
Strike	41	80

Sentences as categories

Word/s	Frequency	Percentage
Against the elected government	4	7.8
A dispute miners cannot win	2	3
Senseless strike	2	3
Labour relations	5	9.8
Miners as special case	16	31
Income policy	9	17
Stage Three	18	35
Uneconomic pits	2	4
Pay Board	15	29

MANUFACTURED SCHEMA

The *Sun*

	1972-74			1984-85	
Word/s	Frequency	%		Frequency	%
Militant	2	4.8	Militant	88	84
Extremists	0	0	-	-	-
Undemocratic	3	6.1	Undemocratic	79	75
Law/order	10	20	Law/Order	71	67
-	-	-	Dispute	82	78
Moderate	3	6.1	Moderate	73	69
Violence	8	16	Violence	82	78
Nation	28	57	Nation	49	47
Britain	35	71	Britain/British	65 / 53	61/51
NUM	38	77	NUM	73	70
TUC	41	83	TUC	55	52
Ballot	4	8.1	Ballot	93	88
Political	4	81	Political	65	62
Strike	41	83	Strike	87	82
War	1	2	War	28	26
Class War	0	0	Class war	21	20
Gormley	41	83	Scargill	124	119
NCB	10	20	MacGregor	93 (16)	88
Community	4	8.1	-	-	-
- - -	Mob	77		73	
Heath	58	118	Thatcher	79	75
-	-	-	Rule	68	65
-	-	-	Picket/s	110	104
-	-	-	Troops	49	46
-	-	-	Scargillism	3	2.8
-	-	-	Thatcherism	0	0
-	-	-	Police	83	79
-	-	-	Wrecker*	31	29
Labour relations	4	8.1	Bullies/Bully	66	63
Against the elected government	0	0	Against the elected government	29	27.2
A dispute miners cannot win	0	0	A dispute miners cannot win	18	17
Senseless strike	0	0	Senseless strike	7	9.1
Miners as special case	19	39	Miners as special case	0	0
Uneconomic pits	3	6.1	Uneconomic pits	43	41
Income policy	6	12	Cannon fodder	3	3.2

APPENDIX

	1972-74		1984-85		
Word/s	Frequency	%		Frequency	%
Stage Three	10	20	Rebel miners	64	61
Pay Board	4	8.1	-	-	-
-	-	-	The red guards	24	23
-	-	-	General Scargill	5	4.7
-	-	-	King Arthur	31	30

* This term was used by the Sun with a specific reference to Scargill

The table provides a comparative study of various categories (word and sentences) for the *Sun*'s editorial approach to the miners' strikes in 1970s and 1980s. There are a number of rather interesting points to observe. First, generally the *Sun* seems a great deal more involved in the 1980s than in 1970s. The words such as 'militant', 'law and order', 'violence', 'ballot', 'political', 'police', and 'war' had much higher frequency in the 1980s than in the 1970s. However the most notable difference in the *Sun*'s approach appears in a schematic comparison of the 'selected sentences' for both periods. Sentences such as 'against the elected government', ' a dispute miners cannot win', 'senseless strike', 'uneconomic pits' and 'miners as special case' show a 'significant' differential in frequencies.

The reader is invited to examine the remainder of the data for the rest of the national newspapers in the sample. The reader is also reminded that the '*Daily Star*' and the *Daily Mail* are excluded from this comparative assessment because the *Daily Star* which was randomly selected was not being published in the 1970s and, therefore, the *Daily Mail* was included for the 1970s period only.

MANUFACTURED SCHEMA

The *Guardian*

	1972-74			1984-85	
Word/s	Frequency	%		Frequency	%
Militant	13	27	Militant	81	60
Extremists	0	0	-	-	-
Undemocratic	9	18	Undemocratic	74	54
Law/ order	4	8.3	Law/ order	104	77
-	-	-	Dispute	124	91
Moderate	0	0	Moderate	86	63
Violence	31	64	Violence	92	66
Nation	29	60	Nation	60	44
NUM	41	85	NUM	118	87
Britain	8	16	Britain/British	23 / 12	17 / 8
TUC	62	129	TUC	80	59
NCB	10	20	MacGregor	117	86
Community	14	29	Community	4	1.5
Political	9	18	Political	82	59
Strike	46	95	Strike	126	93
-	-	-	Mob	39	29
-	-	-	Rule	57	42
Gormley	54	112	Scargill	178	132
Heath	62	129	Thatcher	76	47
			Picket/s	112	82
War	20	31	War	26	17
Class War	3	4	Class war	28	15
Ballot	18	37	Ballot	87	64
-	-	-	Troops	9	7
-	-	-	Scargillism	6	4
-	-	-	Thatcherism	9	6
-	-	-	Bullies/Bully	40	31
-	-	-	Police	78	57
Against the elected government	0	0	Against the elected government	0	0
A dispute miners cannot win	0	0	A dispute miners cannot win	12	4
Senseless strike	0	0	Senseless strike	15	9.2
Miners as special case	5	10.4	Miners as special case	1	0.7
Income policy	8	16	-	-	-
Stage Three	11	22	Rebel miners	77	46
Uneconomic pits	3	6.2	Uneconomic pits	77	57

APPENDIX

The *Daily Express*

	1972-74			1984-85	
Word/s	Frequency	%		Frequency	%
Militant	9	17	Militant	111	71
Extremists	4	7.6	-	-	-
Undemocratic	2	3.8	Undemocratic	104	67
Law/order	7	13	Law/Order	125	81
-	-	-	Dispute	131	84
Moderate	0	0	Moderate	97	62
Violence	32	61	Violence	110	71
Nation	31	56	Nation	81	52
Britain	27	52	Britain/British	54 / 41	35 / 26
NUM	51	98	NUM	104	67
TUC	57	109	TUC	32	21
Gormley	49	94	Scargill	171	110
Heath	62	119	Thatcher	81	51
NCB	13	25	MacGregor	126	81
Ballot	6	11.5	Ballot	112	72
-	-	-	Mob	88	57
-	-	-	Rule	78	51
Community	10	19	Community	1	0.7
-	-	-	Picket/s	131	84
Class War	0	0	Class war	30	19
War	2	3	War	89	57
Political	6	11.5	Political	86	55
Strike	32	61	Strike	98	63
			Troops	61	39
			Scargillism	31	20
			Thatcherism	12	8
Bullies/Bully	1	0.5	Bullies/Bully	62	49
			Police	76	51
Against the elected government	5	9	Against the elected government	31	35.2
A dispute miners cannot win	2	4	A dispute miners cannot win	31	20
Senseless strike	1	2	Senseless strike	36	23
Labour relations	5	9.6			
Miners as special case	11	39	Miners as special case	0	0
Income policy	4	7.6	Cannon fodder	61	39
Stage Three	17	32	Rebel miners	61	39

The *Daily Mirror*

Word/s	1972-74 Frequency	%		1984-85 Frequency	%
Militant	3	6.1	Militant	47	36
Extremists	0	0			
Undemocratic	2	4	Undemocratic	58	44
Law/order	3	6.1	Law/Order	91	70
Nation	38	77	Nation	59	45
-	-	-	Dispute	109	83
Violence	12	24	Violence	98	75
Moderate	5	10.2	Moderate	68	52
Britain	32	65	Britain/British	69	53
Community	9	18	Community	0	0
NUM	47	95	NUM	84	64
TUC	51	104	TUC	72	55
Gormley	41	83	Scargill	110	84
NCB	10	20	MacGregor	88	67
Heath	53	108	Thatcher	79	61
Political	6	12	Political	69	53
Ballot	9	18	Ballot	81	62
War	0	0	War	38	29
Class War	0	0	Class war	19	14.6
Strike	29	59	Strike	92	70
-	-	-	Mob	55	42
-	-	-	Rule	16	12
-	-	-	Picket/s	59	45
-	-	-	Troops	25	19
-	-	-	Scargillism	0	0
-	-	-	Thatcherism	2	1.5
-	-	-	Police	73	56
-	-	-	Bullies/Bully	31	23
Against the elected government	0	0	Against the elected government	15	14.4
A dispute miners cannot win	0	0	A dispute miners cannot win	8	6
Senseless strike	0	0	Senseless strike	14	11.5
Miners as special case	15	30	Miners as special case	0	0
Uneconomic pits	3	6.1	Uneconomic pits	29	22
Labour relations	8	16	-	-	-
Income policy	11	22	-	-	-

APPENDIX

The *Times*

	1972-74			1984-85	
Word/s	Frequency	%		Frequency	%
Militant	11	22	Militant	71	64
Extremists	8	16	Extremists	43	39
Undemocratic	9	18	Undemocratic	86	78
Law/ order	24	49	Law/Order	77	70
Moderate	15	30	Moderate	66	60
Nation	21	42	Nation	59	53
Britain	29	59	Britain	51	49
Community	13	29	Community	2	0.9
Violence	35	71	Violence	99	89
NUM	39	79	NUM	113	102
Gormley	32	65	Scargill	153	139
Heath	63	128	Thatcher	91	82
Ballot	12	24	Ballot	112	101
NCB	10	20	MacGregor	106	96
TUC	56	114	TUC	64	58
-	-	-	Dispute	106	96
War	0	0	War	62	56
Class War	1	2	Class War	38	30.5
Political	7	14	Political	89	81
Strike	42	85	Strike	136	112
-	-	-	Mob	63	57
-	-	-	Rule	71	64
Pickets	33	67	Picket/s	129	117
Troops	0	0	Troops	43	39
-	-	-	Police	88	80
-	-	-	Scargillism	28	25
-	-	-	Thatcherism	4	4
Bullies/Bully	1	1.5	Bullies/Bully	51	46
Against the elected government	2	3	Against the elected government	45	40.8
A dispute miners cannot win	1	1.5	A dispute miners cannot win	10	9.5
Senseless strike	3	2	Senseless strike	21	17
Miners as special case	17	35	Miners as special case	0	0
Uneconomic pits	5	10	Uneconomic pits	65	59
Income policy	28	57	-		
Stage Three	21	42	-		

Bibliography

Report of the Committee on the Official Secrets Act – 1972
Royal Commission on the Press 1947-9 Report – 1949
Royal Commission on the Press 1961-2 Report – 1962
Royal Commission on the Press Interim Report – 1976
Royal Commission on the Press 1974-7 Final Report
Royal Commission on the Press Final Report Appendices – 1977
Royal Commission on the Press, 'Analysis of Newspaper Content: A report by Professor Denis McQuail', Research Series 4, July 1977
The Thompson Organisation Limited, Reports And Accounts – 1975
Survey Of The National Newspaper Industry, (London: Economist Intelligence Unit), 1965
TUC Annual Report – 1974
TUC: 'Working for Your Future', (TUC: London), 1993
Trades Union Congress, 'Bargaining in Privatised Companies', (London: TUC), 1987
Private Management Inquiry, Commissioned by newspaper publishers, 1966
National Council And News National Dispute: NGA Print, March 1987
News International In The Docklands, News International Promotional Material
Political And Economic Planning (1938) Report On The British Press
JICNARS, January – December 1975
National Coal Board, 'Plan For Coal', London, 1974
J. & R. Winterton, Memorandum No. 60, House Of Commons Select Committee On Energy, The Coal Industry, HC 165 – I, London, 1980
Gallup Political Index, 1972-74
Gallup Political Index, July – December 1984
British Public Opinion, Vol. VI, No. 7, September 1984
N. Hartley & P. Gudgeon and R. Crafts, 'Concentration of Ownership in Provisional Press'
Central Society of Education Publications, III, 1839
Cabinet War Papers – 66/12 – 4 October 1940
The Sun Maid Plan 1929-1930 – J. Walter Thompson Ltd Records
Champers Encyclopedia, vi, (London: W. & R. Champers), 1890
Willings Press Guide, (London: Reed International Services), 1980
Industrial Relations Journals
Northcliffe Papers, British Library
The Press Council's *Annual Reports*, (London: The Press Council), 1966
The Press Council's *Annual Reports*, 1974
   Who Owns Whom, 1987
Daily Herald reader interest surveys recommendations, (London, Odham Ltd

Records), 1955
Rajani Palme Dutt: 'The Rise and Fall of the Daily Herald' (Pamphlet: 1964)
Business Week (Europe), 22 August 1988
National Council for Civil Liberties: ' No way in Wapping: the effect of the policing of the News International dispute on Wapping residents', London 1986

TELEVISION DOCUMENTARIES

Inside Story: 'Tiny Rowland: The Rebel Tycoon', BBC1 transmission, February 15, 1993
Dispatches: 'Spy in the Camp', Channel 4 transmission, November 23, 1994
Panorama: 'Crisis at the Coalface', BBC1 transmission, March 2, 1992
Panorama: 'The Great Pit Disaster', BBC1 transmission, January 11, 1993
Public eye: 'Poll tax – Community charge: the missing millions, BBC2 transmission, March 6, 1992
Henessy, Peter: 'What has become of us?', Channel 4, November 27, 1994
Cockrell, Michael: 'Class rule: the class factor from 1945-1991', BBC2, December 1992
Dispatches: 'Democracy in danger', Channel 4, March 22, 1992, presented by Hugo Young
Network First: 'Breaking the Mirror', ITV (Carlton) transmission, February 18, 1997
Tebbit, Norman: Norman Tebbit: A loner in politics', BBC2, March 2, 1993
Blakeway, D.: 'Thatcher: the Downing Street years'. BBC1, October, 21, 28, November, 3, 10, 1993

BOOKS AND JOURNALS

Abercrombie, N., Longhurst, B., *'Audiences: A Sociological Theory of Performance and Imagination'*, (London: Thousand Oaks), 1998
Abrams, M., *'Social Surveys and Social Action'*, (London: Heinemann), 1951
Acton, H., Seldon, A., *'Agenda for a Free Society'*, (London: Hutchinson), 1961
Adeney & Lloyd, *'The Miners' Strike 1984-85: Loss Without a Limit'*, (London: Routledge & Kegan), 1986
Adorno and Hokheimer, *'The Dialectic of Enlightenment'*, Translate by j. Cumming, (London: Allen Lane), 1973
Adorno and Hokheimer, *'The Schema of Mass Culture'* in Berstein, J. M., *'The Culture Industry: Selected Essays on Mass Culture'*, (London: Routledge), 1991
Adorno, 'How to look at Television' in Bernstein, J. M., op.cit
Adorno, 'Freudian Theory and the Pattern of Fascist Propaganda', in Arato and Gebhardt (Eds), ' The Essential Frankfurt School Reader', (New York; Continuum), 1982
Adorno, 'Erpresste Versohnung', Noten Zur Literatur, (Frankfurt: Suhrkamp), 1961
Adorno, 'Negative Dialectics', Trans: E. B. Ashton, (New York: Seabury), 1973

Adorno, 'Prisms', (Cambridge: MIT Press) 1981
Adorno, 'Sociology and psychology', New Left Review, 46, 1967, Trans: Wolfharth. I
Adorno, 'The Stars Down to Earth', Telos, No. 19, Spring 1947
Adorno, 'Television and The Patterns of Mass Culture', in T. W. Adorno, 'Frezeit' in Stichwort: Kritische Modelle 2, (Frankfurt: Surhrkamp), 1969
Adorno, 'Aesthetic Theory', (London: Routledge & Kegan), Trans: C. Lenhardt, 1987
Adorno: 'Minima Moralia: Reflections from Damaged Life', Trans: E. F. N. Jephcott, (London: New Left Books), 1974
Adorno et.al. 'The Positivist Dispute in German Sociology', (London: Heinemann), 1976. Translated by Adney, G., Frisby, D.
Adorno, 'Thesis Against Occultism', in S. Crook (ed), 'Stras Down to Earth and other essays on the International Culture', (London: Routledge), 1994
Adorno, 'The Psychological Technique Of Martin Luther Thomas's Radio Addresses', Gesammelte Schriften, (9.1), (Frankfurt: Suhrkamp), 1975
Adorno, 'Kann das Publikum Wollen?', Gesammelte Schriften, (20.1), (Frankfurt: Suhrkamp), Trans: D. Cook
Adorno, 'scientific Experiences Of A European Scholar in America', Trans: D. Flemings et.al, in: D. Flemings, B. Bailyn (eds), 'Intelectual Migration: Europe and America 1930-1960', (Cambridge, Mas: Harvard University Press)
Adorno, 'Erpresste Verohnung', Noten Zur Literatur II, (Frankfurt: Suhrkamp), 1961
Adorno, 'Prolog Zum Fernsehen' Gesammelte Schriften, (102), (Frankfurt: Suhrkamp), 1975
Adorno, 'The Culture Industry Revisited', New German Critique, No. 6, 1975
Adorno, 'Reflexionen zur klassentheorie', 'Sociologiche Schriften, (Frankfurt: Suhrkamp), 1972
Adorno, 'Society', Trans: F. Jameson, Salmagundi III, No. 10-11, 1969-70
Adorno, 'On Popular Music', Studies in Philosophy and Popular Research, IX, 1941
Adorno, 'A Social Critique of Radio Music', Keynon Review, Vol. II, No. 2, 1945
Adorno, 'Theory of Pseudo – Culture', Telos 95, Spring 1993, Trans: D. Cook
Adorno, 'Late Capitalism or Industial Society', in V. Meja, D. Misgeld, N. Stehr (eds), 'Modern German Sociology', (New York: Columbia University Press), 1987
Anderson, P., 'The Antimonies of Antonio Gramsci', New Left Review, No. 100, 1976
Anstey, J. (eds), 'The Observer Observed', (London: Barrie & Jenkins), 1991
Archer, M. S., 'Culture and Agency', (London: Cambridge University Press), 1988
Arnold, M., 'Culture and Anarchy', (London: Smith and Elder), 1989
Ashton, T., 'Economic And Social Investigations In Manchester, 1833-1933',

(Hassocks: Harvester Press), 1977
Badgikian, B., *'Media Monopoly'*, (Boston: Beacon Press), 1992
Baistow, T., *'Fourth-Rate Estate: An Anatomy of Fleet Street'*, (London: Comedia), 1985
Ball, S., and Seldon, A. (eds), *'The Health Government 1970-1974: A Reappraisal'*, (London: Longman), 1996
Barton, A., and Lazarsfeld, P., 'Some Functions of Qualitatatiive Analysis in Social Research', *Sociologica*, 1, pp 321-61, 1955
Barnett, 'Iron Britannia', *New Left Review*, No. 134
Barnouw, E., *'Tube of Plenty: The Evolution of American Television'*, (London: Oxford University Press), 1977
Basset, P., *'Strike Free'*, (London: Macmillan), 1989
Baxter, D., *'The Common People'*, (London: Cole and Postgate), 1938
Baudrillard, J., *'Simularca and Simulations'*, in his Selected Writings, (Cambridge: Polity Press), 1988
Beales, A., *'Education: A Framework for Choice'*, (London: I. E. A.), 1967
Beaumont, P., *'The Decline of Trade Union Organisation'*, (London: Croom helm), 1987
Beesley, M. E., (ed), *'Markets and the Media: Competition, Regulation and the interest of the Consumers'*, (London: The Institute of Economic Affairs), 1996
Behrens, R., *'The Conservative Party from Heath to Thatcher'*, (London: Saxon House), 1980
Belfield, R., Hird, C. and Kelly, S., *'Murdoch: The Fall an Empire'*, (London: MacDonald), 1991
Bell, D., *'Cultural Contradiction Of Capitalism'*, (London, Heinemann Educational), 1979
Bell, D., *'The Coming of Post-Industrial Society: A Venture in Social Forcasting'*, (New York: Basic Books), 1973
Benjamin, W., *'Illuminations'*, Ed and intro. Hennah Arendt, tran: Harry Zohn, (New York: Schocken Books), 1969
Benjamin, W., *'Understaniding Brecht'*, Translated by Anna Bostock (London: NLB), 1977
Bennett, T., Martin, G., *'Culture, Ideology and Social Process'*, (London: Open University Press), 1981
Berger, D., *'Media Research Techniques'*, (London: Sage Publications), 1991
Berridge, V., *'Newspaper History'* – in G. Boyce et al, (London: Constable), 1978
Berridge, V., *'Popular Journalism And Working Class Attitudes'*, 1854-86, (London: University of London, Unpublished PH.d. thesis), 1976
Beynon, J., 'Ten Years of Thatcherism', *Social Studies Review*, Vol. 4, No. 5, pp 170-78
Beynon, H. (ed), *'Digging Deeper'*, (London: Verso), 1985
Bhaduri & Steindl, *'The Rise of Monetarism as a Social Doctrine'*, (London:

Thames Working Papers in Political Economy), 1983
Billington, R., *'Culture and Society'*, (London: Macmillan), 1995
Blumer, H., 'Public Opinion Polls and Public Opinion Polling', *American Sociological Review*, 13, pp. 342-9, 1948
Blumer, M. (ed), *'Sociological Research Methods: An Introduction'*, (London: Macmillan), 1977
Blumer, M., *'Social Survey Research and Postgraduate Training in Sociological Method'*, Sociology, 6, pp. 267-74, 1972,
Bocock, R., *'Hegemony'*, Key Ideas Series, (London: Open University), 1986
Bottomore, T., *'The Frankfurt School'*, (Chichester: Horwood), 1984
Bourdieu, P., *'The Field of Cultural Production'*, (Cambtidge: Polity), 1993
Bourdieu, P., *'Distinction'*, (Cambridge: Routledge & Kegan), 1984
Bourne,R., *'Lords of the Fleet Street'*, (London: Uniwin & Hyman), 1990
Bower, T., *'Maxwell: The Final Verdict'*, (London: Harper Collins), 1995
Boyce et al. (eds), *'Newspaper History'*, (London: Constable), 1978
Brantlinger, P, *'Crusoe's Footsteps: Cultural Studies in Britain'*, (London: Routledge), 1990
Brantlinger, P, *'Bread and Circuses: Theories of Mass Culture as Social Dacay'*, (London: Cornell University Press), 1983
Brendon, P., *'Life and Death of Press Barons'*, (London: Secker & Warburg), 1982
Briggs, A., Colbey, P., *'The Media: An Introduction'*, (Edinburgh: Longman), 1998
Brown, L., *'Victorian News and Newspapers'*, (Oxford: Clarendon), 1985
Brown, M., *'Murdoch sales figures sought by ad agencies'*, (London: The Guardian), February, 6, 1986
Burns, A. et.al., *'The Miners And The New Technology'*, Industrial Relations Journal, 1983, 14, 4
Butler & Kavanagh, *'The British General Election Of February 1974'*, (London: Macmillan), 1974
Callinicos, A. & Simon, A., *'The Great Strike'*, (London: 1985)
Cantelon, H. & Gruneau, R. (eds), *'Sport Culture And Modern State'*, (Toronto: University Of Toronto Press), 1982
Caplan, M., 'Theories Of Fascism', *History Workshop*, No. 3, 1977
Carley, K., *'Coding choices for textual analysis: A Comparison of content analysis and map analysis'*, Sociological Methogology, Vol. 23, 1993
Chippindale, P., Horrie, C., *'Disaster! The Rise and Fall of News on Sunday: Anatomy of a business failure'* (London: Sphere Books Ltd), 1988
Chippindale, P., Horrie, C., *'Stick It Up Your Partner!: The rise and fall of the Sun'*, (London: Heinemann), 1990
Channon, M., *'The Strategy And Structure Of British Enterprise'*, (London: Macmillan), 1976
Chester, L., Fenby, J., *'The Fall of the House of Beaverbrook'*, (London: Andrew Deutsch), 1979

Chisholm, A., Davis, M., *'Beaverbrook: A Life'*, (London: Hutchinson), 1992
Christian, H. (ed), 'The Sociology of Journalism and the Press', *The Sociological Review Monograph*, October 1980
Cleverley, G., *'The Fleet Street Disaster: British National Newspapers as a Case Study in Mismanagement'*, (London: Constable), 1976
Cicourel, A., *'Methods and Measurement in Sociology'*, (New York: Free Press), 1964
Clarke, S., *'Capitalist Crisis and the Rise of Monetarism'*, Socialist Register, 1987
Clarke, T., *'Nothcliffe in History'*, (London: Hutchinson), 1950
Coates, D., *'The Crisis of Labour'*, (Oxford: Philip Allan), 1989
Cockburn, C., *'Brothers'*, (London: Pluto Press), 1983
Cockrell, M., Henessy, P. and Walker, D., *'Sources Close to the Prime Minister: Iniside the hidden World of News Manipulators'*, (London: Macmillan), 1985
Cockett, R., *'David Astor and Observer'*, (London: Andrew Deutsch), 1991
Collet, C., *'History Of The Taxes On Knowledge'*, (London: Fisher Uniwin), 1899
Connerton, P., *'The Tragedy of Enlightenment'*, (Cambridge: Cambridge University Press), 1980
Cranfield, G., *'The Press and Society'*, (London: Longman), 1978
Crewe, I., Harrop, M., (eds), *'Political Communications: The General Election Campaign of 1983'*, (Cambridge: Cambridge University Press), 1986
Crouch, C., 'Conservative Industrial Relations Policy: Towards Labour Exclusion', in O. Jacobi (et. al), *'Economic Crisis, Trade Union and the State'*, (London: Croom Helm), 1986
Cumberbatch, G. et.al., *'Television and the Miners' Strike'*, (London: Broadcasting Research Unit), 1986
Curran, J., *'Mass Communication as a Social Force in History'*, Unit 2, Open University course, (Milton Keynes: Open University Press), 1977
Curran, J. & Sparks, C., 'Press and Popular Culture', *Media, Culture and Society*, 1991, Vol. 13, 2
Curran, J. & Seaton, J., *'Power without responsibility'*, (London: Routledge), 1986
Curran, J., *'The British Press: A Manifesto'*, (London: Macmillan), 1978
Curran, J., Gurevitch, M., 'Political Effects Of The Mass Media: A Retrospective', in: *'The Audience'*, (Milton Keynes: Open University Press), 1977
Clutterbuck, R., *'Britain in Agony'*, (London: Faber & Faber), 1978
Coulter, J., Miller, S., Walker, M., *'State of Siege: Politics and Policing of the Coalfields'*, (London: Canary Press), 1984
Dahlgren, P. (ed), *'Journalism and Popular Culture'*, (London: Sage), 1992
Dahrendorf, R., 'Changing Social Values Under Mrs. Thatcher', in R. Skidelsky (ed), *'Thatcherism'*, (London: Chatto and Windus),1988
Davies, I., *'Cultural Studies and Beyond'*, (London: Routledge), 1993

Denzin, N., *'The Research Act'*, (London: Butterworths), 1970
During, S. (ed), *'The Cultural Studies Reader'*, (London: Routledge), 1993
Dunleavy, P., Husbands, C., *'British Democracy At The Crossroads'*, (London: George Allen, and Unwid), 1985
Edelman, M., *'The Mirror: A Political History'*, (London: Hamish Hamilton), 1966
Edgell S., Duke, V., *'A Measure of Thatcherism: A Sociology of Britain'*, (London: Unwin Hyman), 1991
Eldridge, J., *'Getting the Message: News Truth and Power'*, (London: Routledge), 1993
Engel.M, *'Tickle the Public: One Hundred Years of the Popular Press'*, (London: Gollancz), 1996
Escott. T.S, *'Social Transformation of the Victorian Age: A Survey of Court and Country'*, (Publisher Unknown), 1897
Evans.E.J, *'Thatcher and Thatcherism'*, (London: Routledge), 1997
Evans.H, *'Good Times, Bad Times'*, (London: Coronet), 1984
Feenberg.A, *'Lukacs, Marx and the Sources of Critical Theory'*, (Oxford University press), 1986
Fienburgh.W, *'25 Momentous Years: a 25 Anniversary of the Daily Herald'*, (London: Oldhams Press), 1995
Fine & Millar (Eds.), *'Policing the Miners Strike'*, (London: Lawrence and Wishart), 1995
Fiske,J, *'Understanding Popular Culture'*, (London: Unwin Hyman), 1989
Fiske,J, 'Television: Polysemy and Popularity', Critical Studies in Mass Communication, 3, (4), 1986
Fiske,J, *'Television Culture'*, (London: Methuen), 1987
Fiske,J, *'Reading the Popular'* (London: Unwin Hyman), 1990
Fiske,J & Hartley, *'Reading Television'*, (London: Methuen), 1987
Francis, H, 'Mining: The Popular Front', Marxism Today, February 1985
Frankfurt Institute, *'Ideology'*, in 'Aspects of Sociology', (London: Heinemann), 1979
Forman, F, *'Mastering British Politics'*, (London: Macmillan), 1991
Fromme, E, *'The Sane Society'*, (New York: Holt & Rinehart & Winston), 1976
Gamble, A, *'The Free Economy and the Strong State'*, (London: Macmillan), 1994
Gamble, A, *'The Conservative Nation'*, (London: Routledge and Kegan), 1974
Gamble, A, 'The Strike the Tories Wanted', New Socialist, April 1985
Gans, H, *'Popular Culture and High Culture'*, (New York: Basics Books), 1974
Galtung and Rue, 'The Structure of Foreign News: The Presentation of the Congo, Cuba and Cyprus Crises in Four Foreign Newspapers', *Journal of International Peace Research*, 1, 1965
Granham, N, 'Impact of New Information and Communication Technologies on Information Diversity in North America and Western Europe', in C.

Sparks (Ed.): *'New Communication Technologies: A Challenge for Press Freedom'*, Unesco Publications, No.106
Granham,N, 'Contribution to a Political Economy of Mass Communication', *Media, Culture and Society,* I , 1971, pp 123-46
Greetz, C, *'The Interpretation of Culture'*, (New York: Basic Books), 1973
Gendron, B, 'Theodore Adorno Meets the Cadillacs', in T. Modelski (Ed.), *'Studies in Entertainment: Critical Approaches to Mass Culture'*, (Indianapolis: Indiana University Press), 1986
Gennard, J, *'A History of The National Graphical Association'*, (London: Unwin Hyman), 1990
Gerbner, G, *'Journey Into Media Violence: A Happy Land of Power, Politics and Publicity and Maybe Profit'*, mimeograph, 1991
Giles, P, *'Sunday Times'*, (London: Murray), 1986
Gibbon, P, 'Analysing The British Miners' Strikes of 1984-85', *Economy and Society,* May 1988, Vol.17, no. 2, pp139-94
Giddens, A, *'The Class Structure of Advanced Societies'*, (London: Hutchinson), 1981
Giddens, A, *'The Rules of Sociological Methods'*, (London: Hutchinson), 1977
Giner, S, *'Mass Society'*, (London: Martin Robertson), 1976
Gilmour, I, *'Dancing with Dogma'*, (London: Simon& Schuster), 1992
Golding, P, 'Rethinking Common Sense About Social Policy', in Bull. D and Wilding. P (Eds.), *'Thatcherism and the Poor'*, (London: Child Poverty Action Group), 1983
Goodman, G, *'The Miners Strike'*, (London: Pluto), 1985
Gramsci, A, *'The Prison Notebooks'*, (London: Lawrence and Wishart), 1971
Gray, T, *' Fleet Street Remembered'*, (London: Heinemann), 1990
Greensdale, R, *'Maxwell's Fall'*, (London: Simon and Schuster), 1992
Griffiths, D (Ed), *' The Encyclopedia of the British Press: 1422-1992'*, (London: Macmillan), 1992
Griffiths, D, *'Plant Here The Standard'*, (London: Macmillan), 1996
Grossberg, L, 'Strategies of Marxist Cultural Interpretations', *Critical Studies in Mass Communications*, 1, 1984
Hall, S, 'The Great Moving Right Show', in Hall and Jacques (Eds), *'The Politics of Thatcherism'*, (London: Lawrence and Wishart), 1983
Halsey, A (Ed), *'Trends in British Society Since 1990)*, (London: Macmillan), 1972
Hansen, M, 'Mass Culture as Hieroglyphic Writing: Adorno, Derrida, Kracauer', *New German Critique*, 56, Spring-Summer 1992, pp 43-73
Hargreaves, J, 'Sport and Hegemony: Some Theoretical Problems', in Harris, D, *'From Class Struggle to the Politics of Pleasure'* (New York: Routledge), 1992
Harris, R, Seldon, A, *'Advertising in a Free Society'*, (London: I.E.A), 1956
Harris, R, *'Good and Faithful Servant'*, (London: Faber & Faber), 1990
Harrison, R, *'Before The Socialists'*, (London: Routledge & Kegan), 1955
Hart-Davis, D, *'The House the Berrys Built: Inside the Telegraph'*, (London:

Coronet), 1991
Lord Hartwell, *'William Camrose: Giant of Fleet Street'*, (London: Weidenfeld & Nicolson), 1992
Heath, E, *'The Course of My Life'*, (London: Hodder & Stoughton), 1998
Heath, A, Jowell, R, Curtice, J, *'How Britain Votes'*, (Oxford: Pergamon), 1988
Held. D, *'Introduction to Critical Theory'*, (Los Angeles: UCLA Press), 1980
Hennessy. P, *'Whitehall'*, (London: Seeker and Warburg), 1989
Hennessy. P, Seldon. A, *'Ruling Performance: British Governments From Atlee to Thatcher'*, (London: University Press), 1987
Hirsch. F and Gordon. D, *'Newspaper Money'*, (London: Hutchinson), 1975
Hobson. J, *'The Selection of Advertising Media'*, (London: Business Publications), 1955
Hoch. P, *'The Newspaper Game: The Political Sociology of the Press'*, (London: Calder&Boyars), 1974
Hoggart. R, *'The Uses of Literacy: Aspects of Working Class Life, With Special References to Publications and Entertainments'*, (London: Chatto & Windus and Harmondsworth, Penguin), 1957
Holms. M, *'The First Thatcher Government, 1979-1983: Contemporary Conservatism and Economic Change,* (Brighton: Wheatsheaf), 1985
Horkheimer. M, *'The Eclipse of Reason'*, (New York: Oxford University Press), 1947
Horkheimer. M, 'The Authoritarian State', *Telos*, no.15, Spring, 1973
Horkheimer. M, 'Art and Mass Culture', in *'Critical Theory: Selected Essays'*, (New York: Herder & Herder), Translated by M.J. O'Connell, 1973
Horkheimer. M, 'Authority And The Family', *'Critical Theory: Selected Essays'*, (New York: Herder & Herder), Translated by M.J. O'Connell, 1973
Honneth. A, *'The Critique of Power: Reflective Stages in an Critical Social Theory'*, (Cambridge: Mass: The MIT Press), 1991, Translated by Bayness.K
Hoffman. J.D., *'The Conservative Party in Opposition'* (London: MacGibbon & Kee), 1964
Howard. P, *'Beaverbrook: A Study of Max the Unknown'*, (London: Hutchinson), 1964
Howell. D, *'The Politics of NUM: A Lancashire View'*, (Manchester University Press), 1989
Hoy. M, 'Decline in Docklands', *The Times*, 24 September, 1990
Hughes. J and Moore. R, *'A Special Case? Social Justice and the Miners*, (London: Penguin), 1976
Huyssen. A, 'Introduction to Adorno', *New German Critique*, 6, Fall 1976
Huyssen. A, *'After the Great Divide: Modernism, Mass Culture and Postmodernism'*, (Indianapolis: Indiana University Press), 1986
Illich. I, *'Deschooling Society'*, (London: Harper Collins), 1991
Ingham. B, *'Kill the Messenger'*, (London: Harper Collins), 1991
Jameson. D, *'The Last of the Hot Metal Men'*, (London: Ebury Press), 1990

Jay. M, *'Dialectical Imagination'*, (Boston: Little Brown), 1973
Jessop. B et.al., *'A Tale of Two Nations'* (Oxford: Polity Press), 1988
Jenkins. S, *'Newspapers: The Power and the Money'*, (London: Faber & Faber), 1979
Johnstone. R, *'A Nation Divided'*, (London: Longman), 1988
Jones. A, *'Powers of the Press: Newspapers, Power and the Public in Nineteenth-Century England'*, (Aldershot: Scolar Press), 1996
Jones. N, *'Soundbites and Spin Doctors: How Politicians Manipulate the Media- and Vice Versa'*, (London: Cassell), 1996
Jones.N, *'Strikes and the Media'*, (Oxford: Basil Blackwell), 1986
Jouet.J and Coudray.S, *'New Communication Technologies: Research Trends'*, UNESCO, 1990, 105
Kando.T, *'Leisure and Popular Culture in Transition'*, (Toronto: The C.V. Mosby Company), 1980
Kavanagh. D, *'Thatcherism and British Politics'*, (Oxford: University Press), 1987
Keegan.W, *'Mrs Thatcher's Economic Experiment'*, (Harmondsworth: Penguin), 1984
Kidder. L, Smith. D, Judd. C, *'Research Methods in Social Relations'*, (New York: CBS College), 1986
Kingston. J, *'No Such Thing as Society? Individualism, Collectivism and Citizenship'*, (Buckingham: Open University Press), 1992
Klingender. F.D. and Legg. S, *'Money Behind the Screen'*, (London: Lawrence and Wishart), 1973
Krieger. J, *'Regan, Thatcher and the Politics of Decline'*, (Cambridge: Polity Press), 1986
Kross. S, *'The Rise and Fall of the Political Press in Britain'*, (London: Hamish Hamilton), 1981
Kraus, S, and Davis. D, *'The Effects of Mass Communication on Political Behaviour'*, (Pennsylvania Press), 1976
Laclau. E and Mouffe.C, *'Hegemony and Socialist Strategy'*, Translated by Moore. W and Cammack, 1985, (London: Verso Press), 1985
Laclau. E, *'Politics and Ideology in Marxist Theory'*, (London: New Left Books), 1977
Lamb. L, *'Sunrise'*, (London: Macmillan), 1989
Lawrence. J and Barber. L, *'The Price of Truth: The Story of the Reuters Millions'*, (London: Sphere Books), 1986
Lawson. N, *'The View From No. 11: Memoirs of a Tory Radical'*, (London: Corgi Books), 1993
Layder. D, *'Understanding Social Theory'*, (London: Sage), 1994
Leapman. M, *'Barefaced Cheek: Rupert Murdoch'*, (London: Coronet), 1983
Lee. A, *'The Origins of the Popular Press, 1844-1914'*, (London: Croom Helm), 1976
Leiss. W, et.al., 'Marcuse Bibliography', in Kurt and Barrington Moore (Eds), *'The Critical Spirit: Essays in Honor of Herbert Marcuse'*, (Boston:

Beacon), 1967

Leiss. W, *'The Limits to Satisfaction: An Essay on the Problems of Needs and Commodities'*, (Montreal: McGill University Press), 1988

Leman.S and Winterton. J, 'New Technologies and the Restructuring of Pit Level Industrial Relations in the British Coal Industry', *New Technology, Work and Employment*, 1991, 6, pp54-64

Letwin. S. R, *'The Anatomy of Thatcherism'*, (London: Fontana), 1992

Levy. P, 'Thatcherism', *Social Alternatives*, no 1-2, Spring 1992

Littelton. S, *'The Wapping Dispute'*, (London: Avebury), 1992

Lloyd.J, *'Understanding the Miners' Strike'*, Fabian Society Pamphlet, 1985

Lovell. T, *'Pictures of Reality: Aesthetics, Politics and Pleasure'*, (London: BFI), 1980

Lowenthal. L, 'The Triumph of Mass Idols', in *'Literature, Popular Culture and Society'*, (Englewood Cliffs, N.J: Prentice-Hall), 1961

Lukacs, G, *'The Old Culture and the New Culture'*, Translated by P. Breines and S. Weber, Telos, 5, 1970

Lukacs. G, *'History and Class Consciousness: Studies in Marxist Dialectics'*, Translated by Livingstone. R, (London: Merlin Press), 1977

MacArthur. B, *'Eddy Shah, Today and the Newspaper Revolution'*, (Newton Abbot: David and Charles), 1988

Macdonald. D, 'A Theory of Popular Culture', *Politics*, 1, February, 1994

MacIness. J, *'Thatcherism at Work'*, (Milton Keynes: Open University Press), 1987

MacGrgor. I, Taylor. R, *'The Enemies Within: the Story of the Miners' Strikes, 1984-85*, (London: Collins), 1986

McCarthy, *'The Critical Theory of Habermas'*, (Cambridge: MIT Press), 1978

McIlrory. J, *'Trade Unions in Britain Today'*, (Manchester: Manchester University Press), 1987

McKenzie and Silverstone, *'Angels in Marble'*, (London: Heinemann), 1963

McLuhan. M, *'Understanding Media'*, (New York: McGraw & Hill), 1955

McNair. B, *'News and Journalism in the UK'*, (London: Routledge), 1994

McQuail. D (Ed.), *'The Sociology of Mass Communication: Selected Readings'*, (Harmondsworth: Penguin), 1972

Mann. M, 'Consciousness and Action', *American Sociological Review*, Vol. 35

Marcuse. H, *'Eros and Civilization'*, (New York: Vintage), 1962

Marcuse. H, *'The Aesthetic Dimension'*, (Boston: Beacon), 1978

Marcuse. H, *'Five Lectures'*, (Boston: Shapiro & Webber), 1970

Marcuse. H, *'Counterrevolution and Revolt'*, (Boston: Boston Press), 1972

Marliere. P, 'The Rules of the Journalistic Field: Pierre Bourdieu's Contribution to the Sociology of the Media', *European Journal of Communication*, Vol 13, no 2, 1988

Marsh. D, 'Public Opinion, Trade Unions and Mrs. Thatcher', *British Journal of Industrial Relations'*, Vol 28, 1990

Marsh. D, *'The New Politics of British Trade unionism'*, (London: Macmillan), 1992

Marsh. D, Rhodes. R, 'Implementing Thatcherism: A Policy Perspective', *Essex Papers in Politics and Government*, 62, 1989

Marx. K, *'Capital: A Critical Analysis of Capitalist Production'*, (London: 1887)

Mattelart. A, *'Advertising International: The Privatisation of Public Space'*, (London: Comedia), 1984

Mattelart. A, Mattelart. M, Delacourt. X, *'International Image Markets'*, (London: Comedia), 1984

Mattelart. A, Mattelart. M, *'Rethinking Media Theory'*, (Minneapolis: University of Minnesota Press), 1992

Melver. L, *'The End of the Street'*, (London: Methuen), 1986

Milne.S, *'The Enemy Within'*, (London: Verso), 1994

Miller. W, Clarke. H, Harrop. D, LeDuc. L, Whiteley, *'How the Voters Change'*, (Oxford: Clarendon Press), 1990

Miller. M, *'Media and the Voters: The Attitude, Content, and Influence of Press and Television at the 1987 General Election'*, (Oxford: Clarendon Press), 1991

Middlemas. K, 'The Supremacy of Party', *New Statesman*, June 10, 1983

Minouge. K, Biddis. M, *'Thatcherism, Personality and Politics'*, (London: Macmillan), 1987

Morgan. W, 'Adorno on Spot: the Case of Fractured Dialectic', *Theory and Society*, No.17, 1988

Morgan. W. J, 'The Nottinghamshire coalfield and the British miners' strike 1984-85', *Occasional Paper*, (University of Nottingham, Department of Adult Education), 1990

Morss, *'The Origins of Negative Dialectics'*, (Hassocks, Sussex: Harvester), 1978

Mouffe. C, 'Hegemony and Ideology in Gramsci', in Bennett. T, et.al, *'Culture, Ideology and Social Process'*, (Oxford: University Press), 1981

Mouzelis. N, *'Back to Sociological Theory: Constitution of Social Order'*, (London: Macmillan), 1991

Munster. G, *'Rupert Murdoch: A Paper Prince'*, (Ringwood: Viking), 1985

Murdoch. G, Open University course, DE 353: *Mass Communication and Society*, Unit 10: 'Patterns of Ownership; Question of Control', (OU Press), 1977

Murdoch. G, 'Class, Power and the Press: Problems of Conceptualisation and Evidence', in Christian. H (Ed.), *'The Sociology of Journalism and the Press'*, (Keel: University of Keel), 1980

Murdoch. G, Golding. P, 'For a Political Economy of Mass Communication', *'Socialist Register,* 1973

Mutz. D, Sniderman. P, Brody. R (Eds), *'Political Persuasion and Attitude Change'*, (Michigan: University Press), 1996

Narin. T, *'The Break Up of Britain'*, (London: Verso), 1981

Newton. K, 'Do People Read Everything They Believe in the Papers?', in Crewe. I, Norris. P (Eds.) *'Newspapers and Voters in the 1983 and 1987 Elections'*, British Parties and Election Yearbook, (London: Simon &

Schuster), 1991
Neumann. F, *'Behemoth: The Structure and Practice of National Socialism'*, (London: Gollancz), 1944
Ortega. J, *'The Revolt of the Masses'*, (New York: Norton), 1957
O'Shea. A, 'Trusting the People: How Does Thatcherism Work?', in *'Formation of Nation and People'*, (London: Routledge & Kegan), 1984
Ottey. R, *'The Insiders's Story'*, (London: Sidgwick & Jackson), 1986
Parkin. F, *'Class Inequality and Political Order: Social Stratification in Capitalist and Communist Societies'*, (London: MacGibbon & Keen), 1971
Penniman. H (Ed.), *'Britain at the Polls'*, (Washington D.C: American Enterprise Institute), 1981
Plant. M, *'The English Book Trade: An Economic History of the Making and Sale of Books'*, (London: Allen and Unwin), 1974
Phillips. J, 'The Growth of Journalism' , in Waller. A (Eds.), *'Cambridge History of English Literature'*, (Cambridge: University Press), 1953
Pollock. F, 'State Capitalism', SPSS, Vol.9, 1941
Pounds. R, Harmsworth. G (Eds.), *'Northcliffe'*, (London: Cassell), 1959
Powell. E, *'Saving in a Free Society'*, (London: Hutchinson), 1960
Pryce. S, *'Presidentializing the Premiership'*, (Basingstoke: Macmillan), 1987
Ralph. S, Bloomfield.B, Boanas.G, *'The Enemy Within: Pit Villages and the Miners' Strike of 1984-85'*, (London: Routledge & Kegan), 1986
Ranelagh. J, *'Thatcher's People: An Insider's Account of the Politics, the Power and the Personalities'*, (London: Harper Collins), 1991
Ransome. P, *'Antonio Gramsci'*, (New York: Harvester Wheatsheaf), 1992
Lord Robens, *'Ten Year Stint'*, National Coal Board Publication, 1972
Regan. S, *'Rupert Murdoch: A Business Biography'*, (London: Angus & Robertson), 1976
Rees. L, *'Selling Politics'*, (London: BBC Books), 1992
Rees. G, 'Class, Community and the Miners: The 1984-85 Miners' Strike and its Aftermath', *Sociology*, Vol. 27, Part 2, pp 307-12
Richards. H, *'The Bloody Circus: The Daily Herald and the Left'*, (London: Pluto Press), 1997
Richards. A, *'Miners' Strike: Class Solidarity and Division in Britain'*, (Oxford: Berg), 1996
Ritzer. G, *'Sociological Theory'*, (London: McGraw & Hill), 1992
Rose, G, *'The Melancholy Science: An Introduction to the Thoughts of Theodore. W. Adorno*, (London: Macmillan), 1978
Rosenberg. B, Manning White. D (Eds.) *'Mass Culture: The Popular Art in America'*, (New York: Free Press), 1957
Ross. J, (Ed.), *'What is Cultural Studies'*, (London: Arnold), 1996
Ryan. B, *'Making Capital From Culture: The Corporate Form of Capitalist Cultural Production'*, (New York: W. DeGruyter), 1991
Sanders. D, Marsh. D, Ward. H, 'The Electoral Impact of Press Coverage of the British Economy, 1979-1987', *British Journal of Political Science*, 1993, Vol. 23, April

Sasson. A.S, *'Gramsci's Politics'*, (London: Hutchinson), 1987
Saville. J, *'Ernest Jones'*, (London: Lawrence & Wishart), 1952
Schiller. H, *'Mass Communications and the American Empire'*, (Boston: Beacon), 1971, 1992
Schiller. H, 'Not Yet the Post-Imperialist Era', in Roch.C (Ed.), *'Communication and Culture in War and Peace'*, (California: Newbury Park), 1993
Schiller. H, *'Information and Crisis Economy'*, (New Jersey: Ablex), 1984
Schumacher. E, *'Coal: The Next Fifty Years'*, NUM Study Conference, Britain's Coal, London, 1960
Seaman. W, 'Active Audience Theory: Pointless Populism', *Media, Culture and Society*, 14, 2, 1992
Seymour-Ure. C, *'The British Press and Broadcasting Since 1945'*, (Oxford: Blackwell), 1991
Seymour-Ure. C, *'The Political Impact of Mass Media'*, (London: Constable), 1974
Seymour-Ure. C, *'The Press, Politics and the Public: An Essay on the Role of the National Press in the British Political System'*, (London: Methuen), 1968
Shawcross. W, *'Rupert Murdoch: Ringmaster of Information Circus'*, (London: Chatto & Windus), 1992
Shills. E, *'The Intellectuals and the Powers and Other Essays'*, (Chicago: University of Chicago Press), 1972
Smith. A, *'The Wealth of the Nation: An inquiry into the nature and causes of the wealth of the nations'*, (London: Everyman's Library), 1991
Smith. A (Ed.), *'Newspapers and Democracy'*, (Cambridge MA: MIT Press), 1980
Snoddy. R, *'The Good, The Bad, and the Unacceptable'*, (London: Faber and Faber), 1992
Spark. C (Ed.), 'New Communication Technologies: A Challenge for Press Freedom', Unesco Publications, no. 106
Spark. C, 'Popular Journalism: Theories and Practice', in Dahlgren. P (Ed.), *'Journalism and Popular Culture'*, (London: Sage), 1992
Spark. C, 'The Popular Press and Political Democracy', *Media, Culture and Society*, Vol. 10, 1988
Swingewood. A, *'The Myth of Mass Culture'*, (London: Macmillan), 1977
Swingewood. A, *'Marx and Modern Social Theory'* , (London: Macmillan), 1975
Stempel. G, Westley. B, *'Research Methods in Mass Communication'*, (New Jersey: Prentice & Hall), 1989
Tan. A, *'Mass Communication: Theories and Research'*, (New York: J. Wiley and Sons), 1981
Taylor. A, *'Beaverbrook'*, (Harmondsworth: Penguin), 1974
Taylor. S, *'Shock! Horror! The Tabloids in Action'*, (London: Bantam Press), 1991

Taylor. S, *'The Great Outsider: Northcliffe, Rothermere and the Daily Mail'*, (London: Weidenfeld & Nicolson), 1996
Tebbit.N, *'Upwardly Mobile'*, (London: Weidenfeld & Nicolson), 1988
Thompson. J, *'Ideology and Modern Culture'*, (Cambridge: Polity), 1990
Thompson. E.P., *'The Making of the English Working Class'*, (Harmondsworth: Penguin), 1968
Tetztaff. D, 'Divide and Conquer: Popular Culture and Social Control in Late Capitalism', *Media, Culture and Society*, 13, 1, 1991
Thatcher. M, *'The Downing Street Years'*, (London: Harper and Collins), 1995
Thompson. J, Engleman. R, *'The Industrial Relations Act: A Review and Analysis'* (London: Martin Robertson), 1975
Tunstall. J, *'The Westminster Lobby Correspondents'*, (London: Routledge & Kegan), 1970
Tunstall. J, *'The Journalists at Work'*, (London: Constable), 1971
Tunstall. J,, *'The Newspaper Power: The New National Press in Britain'*, (Oxford: Clarendon Press), 1996
Tunstall. J, Palmer. M, *'Liberating Communications: Policy-Making in France and Britain'*, (Oxford: Blackwell), 1990
Tunstall. J, Palmer. M, *'Media Moguls'*, (London: Routledge), 1991
Trice. J, *'Methods of and Attitudes to Picketing'*, Criminal Law Review, May, 1975
Trist. E, Bamforth. W, Some Social and Psychological Consequences of the Longwall Method of Coal Getting, *Human Relations*, 1951, 4
Turner. J, *'The Shocking History of Advertising'*, (London: M. Joseph), 1952
Veljanovski. M, *'The Media in Britain Today'*, News International Today, London, 1990
Waller. R, *'The Dukeries Transformed'*, (Oxford: Clarendon), 1983
Walters. A, *'Economists and the British Society'*, Occasional Papers, IEA, 54, 1978
Webb. R, *'The British Working Class Readers'*, (London: Allen & Unwin), 1955
Weber. R, *'Basic Content Analysis'*, (London: Sage), 1990
Weber. W, *'The Methodology of Social Sciences'*, (Glencoe, Free Press), 1949
Webster. F, Robbins. K, *'Information Technology: a Luddite Analysis'*, (New Jersey: Ablex), 1986
Weeks. B et.al., *'Industrial Relations and the Limits of the Law'*, (Oxford: Blackwell), 1975
Williams. F, *'Dangerous Estate'*, (London: Longmans Green), 1976
Williams. R, *'Culture and Society'*, (New York: Harper and Row), 1966
Williams. R, 'Base and Superstructure', *New Left Review*, no.82, 1973
Williams. R, 'The Problem of the Coming Period', *New Left Review*, no.140, 1983
Williams. R, 'The Press and Popular Culture', in Boyce et.al., *'Newspaper History'*, (London: Constable), 1978
Williams. R, 'Radical and Respectable', in Boston. R, *'The Press We Deserve'*,

(London: Routledge & Kegan), 1970

Williams. R, *'Television: Technology and Cultural Form'*, (London: Fontana), 1974

Willis. R, *'Learning to Labour'*, (Franborough: Saxon House), 1977

Willis. P, *'Common Culture'*, (Milton Keynes: Open University Press), 1990

Wilenskey. H, *'Organisational Intelligence'* (New York: Basic Books), 1967

Wilsher. P, et.al., *'Strike'*, (London: Pluto), 1985

Wintour. C, *'The Rise and Fall of the Fleet Street'*, (London: Hutchinson), 1989

Williamson. J, Karp. D, *'The Research Craft: An Introduction to Social Science Methods'*, (Boston: Little-Brown), 1977

Wigham. E, *'Strikes and the Government 1893-1974'*, (London: Macmillan), 1976

Winterton. J, 'The 1984-85 Miners' Strike and Technological Change', *British Journal of History of Science*, 1993, 26

Winterton. J, 'The Miners' Strike: lessons from the literature', *Industrial Tutor*, Vol. 4, 4/5, 1987

Winterton. J, Winterton. R, *'Coal, Crisis and Conflict'*, (Manchester University Press), 1989

Woods. O, Bishop. J, *'The Story of The Times'*, (London: Hutchison), 1955

Young and Soloman, *'The Thatcher Phenomenon'*, (London: BBC Books), 1986

Young. H, *'One of Us'*, (London: Macmillan), 1989

Lord Young, *'Enterprise Years'*, (London: Headline), 1990

Zuidervaart. L, *'Adorno's Aesthetic Theory: The Redemption of Illusion'*, (Cambridge: Mass, MIT Press), 1991